The Globalization of Sexuality

JON BINNIE

SAGE Publications
London • Thousand Oaks • New Delhi

First published 2004

SAGE Publications Ltd
1 Oliver's Yard
55 City Road
London EC1Y 1SP

SAGE Publications Inc
2455 Teller Road
Thousand Oaks, California 91320

SAGE Publications India Pvt Ltd
B-42, Panchsheel Enclave
Post Box 4109
New Delhi 110 017

British Library Cataloguing in Publication data

A catalogue record for this book is available
from the British Library

ISBN 0 7619 5935 1
ISBN 0 7619 5936 x (pbk)

Library of Congress Control Number 2003109256

Typeset by C&M Digitals (P) Ltd., Chennai, India
Printed and bound in Great Britain by Athenaeum Press, Gateshead

Contents

Acknowledgements

I would like to thank David Bell for reading through and commenting on earlier drafts of chapters in this book. I would also like to thank Robert Rojek, Chris Rojek, Kay Bridger and Ian Antcliff at Sage for their help and guidance throughout this project. I would also like to thank my supportive colleagues at MMU, particularly Julian Holloway, Dave Lambrick and Liz Price. I am also indebted to the friendship and support of Steve Calvert, Michael Darbyshire, John Fitzgerald, Ruth Holliday, Mark Jayne and Bev Skeggs.

1

Sexuality and Social Theory

The Challenge of Queer Globalization

This book critically examines the relationship between sexuality, the nation and globalization. The mass of literature on the subject of globalization attests to its centrality within social theory and to the growth of critical interest in the politics of space. However, despite the volume of work produced on globalization, relatively little attention has been paid to theorizing the links between globalization, nationalism and sexuality in any sustained manner. Where sexuality does appear it often does so in a homophobic sense, for example within discourses on sex tourism that pathologize western gay men as predatory paedophiles. It is my aim in this book to critique the heteronormativity of writing on globalization and to provide a queer perspective on the subject. Why should globalization matter to students of sexuality? It should matter because of the impasse within work on sexuality. As Michael Warner argues, the transnational has often been neglected in discussions about sexual politics:

> In the middle ground between the localism of discourse and the generality of 'the subject' is the problem of international – or otherwise translocal – sexual politics. As gay activists from non-western contexts become more and more involved in setting political agendas, and as the rights discourse of internationalism is extended to more and more cultural contexts, Anglo-American queer theorists will have to be more alert to the globalizing – and localizing – tendencies of our theoretical languages. (1993: xii)

Specifically, globalization is deeply implicated within three major tendencies within current scholarship on sexuality. The first is the turn towards acknowledging the social and material components of sexualities; one problem identified with theorizing on sexuality in the early 1990s (when queer theory took off) was the lack of a wider social and economic perspective. This criticism is not unique to queer theory and has been made of the 'cultural turn' more generally within social theory. The second is the increasing focus on the intersections of race and nation and impacts on sexual politics and vice versa. See for instance the racialized nature of debates on assimilation and transgression within claims for sexual citizenship and Philip Brian Harper's (1997) critique of Andrew Sullivan's writing on AIDS. Questions and concepts associated with postcolonial scholarship such as the transnational politics of movement, migration and diaspora have come to the fore within scholarship on sexualities. The third tendency has been a growth of interest in the state, which has crystallized around questions of sexual citizenship. The state has until recently not been terribly well-theorized in writing on queer theory and lesbian and gay studies (though see Duggan, 1995a; Smith, 1994). However, the burgeoning literature on sexual citizenship (e.g. Bell and Binnie, 2000; Brown, 1997; Evans, 1993; Phelan, 2001; Rahman, 2000; Richardson, 1998, 2000; Weeks, 1999) has been significant in re-focusing critical attention on the state. This redresses the imbalance from the earlier hegemony within queer theory in which questions of redistribution, the market and the state were at best overlooked in an emphasis on textual analysis.

Globalizing Discourses on Sexuality

The attempt here is not to produce a definitive, or authoritative last word on globalization, nationalism and sexuality – what I would term a globalized discursive truth about sexuality – but rather to examine what links can be teased out and articulated between globalization, the nation-state and sexuality. What commonalities and points of difference can be ascertained by comparing and contrasting different formations of nation and sexualities and local experiences of global processes? In *Outside Belongings*, Elspeth Probyn (1996) argues against the adding on of sexuality to a pre-given or pre-determined political subject. Accordingly my aim here is not to 'add on' sexuality to studies of the national and globalization, but rather to examine how these are produced through sexuality. However, there are real dangers in theorizing the relationships between sexuality, nationalism and globalization. For example, there is the accusation of ethnocentricity and metropolitanism. In attempting to theorize these relations across and between national borders there are concerns about the desirability of disembedding concepts and material situated in specific historical and geographical contexts. By making the nation visible there is the danger of reifying it: one risks being accused of affirming and celebrating it. Then there is the question of whose nation – whose sense and construction of nationhood? Is it possible to generalize about what we mean by the nation and nationalism?

As Parker et al. (1992: 3) argue in their introduction to *Nationalisms and Sexualities*: 'there is no privileged narrative of the nation, no "nationalism in general" such that any single model could prove adequate to its myriad and contradictory historical forms'. Moreover, there are dangers in not attempting to create a more substantial and sustained understanding of the relationships between nationalism, globalization and sexuality. In *Legislators and Interpreters*, Zygmunt Bauman (1987) argues that the job of the intellectual in postmodern society is to act as interpreter. Any claims for knowledge advanced by this book are therefore only partial and tentative.

Work on sexuality, like any other is commonly produced within specialist knowledge communities (e.g. Hispanic/Latin American Studies, Asian-Pacific Studies, European Studies) and is not always debated elsewhere. Research on sexuality clearly is far from immune to disciplinary mechanisms that regulate and control the production of knowledge. I hope this book will have something meaningful to say that will address readers across the humanities and social sciences. There is a real need to bring together the insights of political geography and international relations – work from a political economic perspective has tended to marginalize sexual politics, cultures and communities – with other approaches rooted in cultural studies, the humanities and cultural geography.

In the invitation I received to submit the proposal for this book, the two major concerns of Robert Rojek, my commissioning editor at Sage, were that it 'must be written for an interdisciplinary market', and that it must appeal to an English-speaking global audience – that is, the book 'must mean something to people in Milwaukee, Manchester, Melbourne and all points in between'. Obviously the English language is itself a key factor in globalization, and this book reproduces this linguistic hegemony. The book does not set out to be a definitive statement about the transnational basis of sexual cultures, communities and politics. While seeking to articulate the sexualized nature of global/local links, I cannot claim to be authoritative about sexual cultures globally. I am not claiming to be an expert or authority on Melanesia, nor Macedonia, Cuba, Vancouver or Moscow. In this sense, this book is trying to resist a globalizing discourse of sexuality and the claims to truth and knowledge advanced on the basis of a class-based cosmopolitan (moral) authority – a problem that taints much of the current literature on sexuality and globalization. In the preface to their edited volume on sexualities in the Asia-Pacific, Manderson and Jolly argue:

> As researchers and theorists of sexuality, we often not only occupy the site of the West but take it as our point of view as the normative measure of sameness and difference. We thereby presume our global centrality and deny our global connections. (1997: 22)

This statement should be considered alongside Aihwa Ong's (1999) discussion of the cultural politics and economics of transnational communities. In *Flexible Citizenship*, Ong states that it is dangerous to over-state or over-simplify the nature of transnational connections. Specifically she asks: where are the centres and the margins in contemporary global society? She is critical of the hegemonic status of postcolonial writing on transnational flows, which obscures the complexity of the power relationships in transnational communities more generally. Questions of authority and reflexivity routinely come into play in discussions of sexuality and globalization. Skeggs (2002) points towards the class basis of the concept of self-reflexivity. Self-reflexivity is important in the project of deconstructing the anthropological self and creating a space for work informed by queer perspectives. Some writers, however, argue that a lack of reflexivity characterizes much gay anthropology. For instance in his essay 'Arrested Development or the Queerness of Savages', Neville Hoad (2000: 149) takes to task some gay anthropologists, arguing that: 'a wealth of gay studies anthropology fails to consider what may be at stake in its related figuration of certain acts as homosexual'. In *Global Sex*, Dennis Altman (2001) demonstrates a certain modesty about his limitations in not knowing everything about sexual cultures all over the globe – but then proceeds to reel off a long list of places he has been privileged enough to visit. In the introduction to the book, he notes that:

> One of the striking aspects of the burgeoning literature on globalization [...] is the extent to which authors draw upon serendipity as much as scholarship for their examples. The very nature of writing of the 'global' means we must appear at home everywhere, yet at the same time none of us can know more than a small fragment of the world. (2001: xi)

This ability to feel (or at least appear to be) at home everywhere is a pretty good definition of the cosmopolitan critic taken to task in Timothy Brennan's *At Home in the World*. We cannot all be cosmopolitan, as being cosmopolitan means that others are excluded from that identity. Those excluded from a cosmopolitan identity lack the requisite cultural (and other) capital to be a cosmopolite. According to Slavoj Žižek (1997) the other of the cosmopolitan is nationalist and fascist. The Others created by Altman are the passive gay men who are represented in his work as cultural dupes – victims of their own false consciousness and enslaved to the hedonistic desires promoted by global gay consumer culture. These are not the only set of Others created by cosmopolitan discourses, of course. Certain axes of difference are easier to commodify than others.

The queer cosmopolitan is routinely located within the major urban centres of gay consumer culture (Binnie, 2000). The other to this cosmopolitan is therefore rural and provincial, pointing towards the neglect of the provincial and rural within work on queer globalization. Commentaries on queer consumer culture commonly imagine that the world ends at the boundaries of the metropolis. This point is astutely made by Vincent Quinn (2000) in his essay on sexual politics in Northern Ireland in which he rails against the metropolitanism of writers such as Mark Simpson, who generalize about gay life based on their own metropolitan London experience. As Phillips and Watt (2000: 15–16), introducing Quinn's essay, state 'consumerism and globalization are not equally pervasive in all Western countries and regions – even within the United Kingdom very different patterns emerge'.

Globalizing processes operate unevenly and have differential impacts upon individual nation-states (as well as within them). It is imperative that any geographical or other analysis of queer globalization respects both national differences and differences within national boundaries. In prefaces and introductions to books and papers on globalization it is customary to state one's relationship to the subject – to come clean about how one is personally situated or located (as in a feminist politics of location). For instance take Robert Holton's *Globalization and the Nation-State*. In the introduction to his book, Holton (1998: 20) puts down much of his interest in the subject to his own experience of migration from Britain to Australia: 'migration has done something to unsettle a Eurocentric Northern Hemispheric vision of global order'.

When it comes to sexuality it is even clearer that questions of authority and autobiography come into play. Gilbert Herdt also constitutes himself as cosmopolitan critic. On the dust jacket for his *Same Sex, Different Cultures*, we learn that Gilbert Herdt 'resides in Chicago and Amsterdam', as if to add weight to his authority as scholar of global gay culture. In terms of my own engagement with globalization and nationalism, my interest in the subject and need to write about stems from my simultaneous decision to 'come out' and to study abroad in Denmark as an exchange student, where I found the distance and space to 'come out' as a gay man and explore my sexuality in the leather bars of Copenhagen and Hamburg. Being an exchange student I was able to take advantage of programmes to promote student mobility within the European Community. I learnt many of the slang terms for homosex in Danish before I learned them in English. My estrangement from Englishness and Britishness and my Europhilia, then, marked my first degree. Simultaneously the experience of being constituted as 'Thatcher's child' by Danish students marked my Otherness, as did being patronized by Danish gays for coming from such a backward and under-developed society in terms of its sexual politics. Living in Copenhagen in the year that saw Section 28 of the Local Government Act (Smith, 1991, 1994) come into law at the same time as the Danish law on registered partnerships (Bech, 1992) made me realize how wide a gulf there appeared to be between Britain and Denmark in terms of sexual politics, culture and everyday life. It also sparked my continuing interest in theorizing the spatial politics of sexuality. In particular it helped to shape my concern with the transnational basis of sexual cultures and communities within Europe.

National Formations of Lesbian and Gay Studies

While there is a growing awareness of national differences in sexual cultures, it is important that we also recognize national differences in the way sexual cultures have been studied. In *Global Sex*, Dennis Altman's argument reproduces the view that globalization has led to an accelerated Americanization and homogenization of (gay) culture. The implication from reading Altman's work is that the globalized gay culture he critiques represents a false consciousness on the part of those who passively consume it. However, Altman's reductionism fails to scratch the surface of the reasons why this consumer culture is so appealing to so many. As Christopher Lane writes in his reply to Altman's earlier online essay:

> We cannot summarily dismiss the issue of queer globalization as simply a phenomenon North America has foisted egregiously on other cultures. Altman's points about 'exporting the American dream', though well taken, leave unanswered more difficult and pressing questions. What, for instance, is so compelling about the queer model of desire that numerous lesbians and gay men in different countries have received it with a kind of avidity Altman finds galling. (1996: 1)

While I wish to take issue with Altman's anti-Americanism and the way he rather simplistically equates globalization, homogenization and Americanization, I am acutely aware of the US dominance of lesbian and gay cultural life and of lesbian and gay studies. This dominance is recognized by some writers working within the field, such as Jarrod Hayes, who takes US queer activists to task for 'assuming the history of US lesbian, gay, bisexual, transgender, and/or queer resistance holds a monopoly on inspiration for a global queer politics' (Hayes, 2001: 94). Some authors, moreover, have sought to examine anti-American discourses within European debates on sexual politics. In his discussion of the development of the *Pacte Civil de Solidarité* (PACS) in France, for instance, Carl Stychin (2001) argues that opponents of the PACS articulated anti-Americanism suggested that the PACS represented an imposition of an alien American identity politics into French society and the national republican political tradition:

> republicanism frequently has deployed anti-Americanism in different forms. This 'displacement' of American within republicanism is central to the way in which the wider ideological implications of the PACS are characterized by both sides. (2001: 362)

Eric Fassin moreover, has questioned the extent to which what he terms the 'rhetoric of America' was invoked in French debates on the PACS. He claims that references to the Americanization of French society and culture declined sharply at the height of public debate on the PACS. In thinking through debates on gay marriage on both sides of the Atlantic, Fassin (2001: 218) argues that while the 'rhetoric of America' has been influential in contemporary French politics, the same cannot be said of the rhetoric of France within the American polity: 'there is no symmetry between the two sides of the transatlantic mirror: the 'rhetoric of France' clearly does not carry the same weight in the United States as its counterpart does in France'. In terms of academic knowledge production, US dominance is reflected by publishers insisting on using American examples to heighten the marketability of books (though this dominance could more accurately be termed an Anglo-American one). Scholars working outside of the US and the UK are now challenging this dominance, however. For instance, in a guest editorial of the leading geographical journal *Society and Space*, Larry Berg and Robin Kearns (1998: 128) bemoan the marginalization, which they claim affects 'almost all geographers working outside of Britain and America'. One solution towards rectifying the situation is more collaborative work between writers working in the centre and periphery. However it is also dangerous to make assumptions about what constitutes the centre and the margins, considering for instance the strength of feminist cultural geography 'down under' (Binnie, Longhurst and Peace, 2001). Conversely it is important to reflect upon whether anti-American sentiment lies behind criticism of queer theory in Britain and Europe, given the legacy of anti-Americanism within European academia and in the European Left. I also detected an anti-American tone at a conference on the direction of lesbian and gay studies in Europe in the mid-1990s. Queer theory was rubbished by some delegates and represented as something 'American' that we don't do over here in Europe. At the conference various 'authorities' representing different disciplines and European nations were asked to speak on the current state of lesbian and gay studies within their respective discipline and country. One delegate, Alibhe Smyth, presented a thoughtful paper that challenged the remit she had been given, arguing that if she was to present a paper on the state of lesbian and gay studies in Ireland, then she had to begin by examining the highly contested boundaries of the Irish state (Smyth, 1995).

I was minded at the conference of the general failure of lesbian and gay studies to adequately address questions of nationalism. The book that was produced out of the conference (Sandfort et al., 2000) ended up being organized around disciplines as opposed to nation-states. This suggests that it is perhaps easier for scholars in lesbian and gay studies to work across disciplinary boundaries then national ones. Perhaps we have less invested in maintaining disciplinary identities. It was also unfortunate that something of the complexity and richness of the different national approaches to lesbian and gay studies was lost in the final publication, and that the book is dominated by British and Dutch academics. Thus the perspectives of German, Finnish, Italian scholars and the discussion of the state of lesbian and gay studies in their countries became marginalized. This is significant because it reinforces Berg and Kearns' argument about the American and British dominance of academic production.

In this introduction I have cautioned against the paradoxical parochialism of current debates on the globalization of sexualities. The failure to acknowledge non-western perspectives on sexualities has been increasingly challenged by post-colonial and other writers. However, parochialism takes many forms. For instance what of the parochialism that fails to address the different configurations of the relationships between globalization, nationalism and sexualities in Eastern Europe (e.g. Essig, 1999; Long, 1999; Sieg, 1995, Stychin, 2002), Southern Europe (e.g. Nardi, 1998) and the Celtic periphery of Europe (e.g. Conrad, 2001; Flynn, 1997; Moore, 2000)? Lesbian and gay studies is an emerging field that has its own centres (literature, sociology, cultural studies) and its margins (geography, law, politics, international relations). Parochialism can also result from working within narrow disciplinary frameworks that can lead to the failure to recognize the value of work in other disciplines. This issue is particularly salient for globalization, which John Tomlinson suggests, constitutes a challenge to traditional academic boundaries: 'Globalizing phenomena are, of their essence, complex and multidimensional, putting pressure on the conceptual frameworks by which we have traditionally grasped the social world' (1999: 14). Writers in other disciplines have written about interdisciplinarity and the 'discipline question' in lesbian and gay studies. Lisa Duggan (1995b) has written about the particular marginalization of scholars working on sexuality within history and the neglect of historical perspectives within lesbian and gay studies. Given the US dominance of lesbian and gay studies, and the low status of geography within the academy in the United States, the marginalization of geographical perspectives within lesbian and gay studies is perhaps unsurprising. The growth of interest and excitement in all matters spatial that characterized social and cultural theory in the 1990s has not always been reflected in the enhanced status of the discipline. Duggan calls for greater recognition of work from disciplines other than English: 'Queer studies must recognize the importance of empirically grounded work in history, anthropology, and social and cultural theory' (1996: 188).

While rooted in human geography this book is committed to interdisciplinarity. In particular I am deeply committed to bringing the compartmentalization of phenomena into distinctive spheres of the cultural, political, economic and social. I also seek to challenge the dichotomy that has been set up by Nancy Fraser (1995) between the politics of redistribution and the politics of recognition; and which has been critiqued by Judith Butler (1997), Iris Marion Young (1997) and Majid Yar (2001). Key features of this book are the re-instatement of class and questions of redistribution into theories of globalization and sexuality. I shall now proceed to explain how the book is organized.

Structure of the Book

In the next chapter, 'The Nation and Sexual Dissidence', I examine the relationship between nationalism and sexuality. Drawing on literature from a wide range of geographical and historical contexts I argue that sexuality plays a crucial role in the symbolic enclosure of space in nationalism. Moreover, I explore how sexuality is key to the nation's survival and to the reproduction of the nation's population.

Chapter 3, 'Locating Queer Globalization', argues against the heteronormativity of the literature on globalization. Despite the vast amount of material on the subject, very few writers on globalization discuss sexuality at all. Feminist critiques of globalization have emerged, though these are still marginalized. In this chapter I discuss how globalization may be queered within the academy and everyday life. The chapter examines the literature on globalization and finds that some of the material is useful for conceptualizing the link between globalization and sexuality. This establishes the theoretical framework of the book.

Materialist feminists such as Rosemary Hennessy (2000) maintain that lesbian and gay men occupy a very particular relationship to global capitalism and that the global economic dimension is lacking from discussions of queer politics. In Chapter 4, 'The Economics of Queer Globalization', I examine the relationship between materiality, consumption and the global economy. Anxieties about the global economy are routinely displaced onto particular bodies. For instance, discourses about globalization stressing the need for competitiveness among cities for mobile capital are deployed to purify spaces within particular cities (e.g. New York) and in the UK, government arguments for welfare reform are couched in terms of the need to increase competitiveness within the global economic system (Haylett, 2001). While some writers argue that globalization has become a fetish, or banal, I argue that there remains much to do to tease out the relationships between sexuality and globalization, without lapsing into moralizing judgments on gay hedonism.

In Chapter 5, 'Queer Postcolonialism', I critique both the universalist tendencies within lesbian and gay politics and the heteronormativity of post-colonial criticism. The dangers of a universal gay rights discourse are discussed in the context of international campaigning groups such as the ILGA. Particularly dangerous is the ethnocentricity of the basic vocabulary of lesbian and gay studies. Is there an assertion of a global gay imaginary and queer consciousness within international lesbian and gay politics that parallels the declarations of 'global sisterhood'? How injurious is this to non-hegemonic queer sexualities?

While globalization champions the free movement of capital and goods, the free movement of persons is more problematic. In Chapter 6, 'Queer Mobility and the Politics of Migration and Tourism', I argue that for queers, free movement across global space is difficult given the biological basis of laws on acquiring citizenship. In states where same-sex relationships are recognized for the purposes of naturalization, there are restrictions – and the basis for migration is the unit of the (monogamous) couple. As the literature on gender and international migration reminds us, mobility is itself a highly gendered phenomenon. Here I examine the notion that tourism is a sexualized phenomenon. Literature on sexuality and tourist practices is dominated by discussions of sex tourism, which tends to pathologize gay men's tourism, depicting western gay men as paedophiles. This masks the fact that all tourism is sex tourism to the extent that tourist practices are sexualized and embody sexualized values (e.g. the notion of heterosexual romance). There are certain types of tourist experience, and certain tourist gazes (Urry, 1990) that are represented as 'normal' – the family (in the narrowest, straightest sense) package tour to the Mediterranean for example. Other tourist experiences such as global lesbian and gay events like the Gay Games are treated with bemusement.

In Chapter 7 'AIDS and Queer Globalization', I argue that the pandemic has been significant in accelerating awareness of a global sense of place. It has reinforced the awareness of the porosity of national boundaries, and the need for global policy responses. However I maintain that significant differences in policies reflect and reproduce national sexual and political cultures.

Chapter 8 'Queering Transnational Urbanism', examines cosmopolitanism and the nature of consumption practices within the global city, arguing that the distinction between cosmopolitanism and provincialism has been at the heart of queer narratives of self and queer consumption practices. I examine this through an analysis of strategies to promote cities and festivals as queer-friendly. I contrast the marketed visions of queer urbanism with emerging queer critiques of the commodification and gentrification of queer urban space.

In Chapter 9 I offer suggestions for future research in this area, and ponder how the sexual politics of globalization could and should be taken forward. Having outlined the structure and logic of the book, I now go on to discuss the relationship between sexuality and the nation as this is a key theoretical underpinning to the book.

2

The Nation and Sexual Dissidence

The relationship between nationalism and sexuality remains relatively under-theorized. Sam Pryke argues that 'theoretically, there is very little in the most influential accounts of nationalism or sexuality to help in discerning a relationship between them' (1998: 530). The under-theorization of the relationship between nationalism and sexuality is especially problematic as the exact nature and condition of the interrelationships between the nation-state, nationalism and globalization remains subject to considerable disagreement. The question of whether globalization threatens the nation-state, or leads to the promotion of nationalism has been at the forefront of debates on the subject. Some argue that globalization means the inevitable decline in significance and power of the nation-state; others suggest that nationalism appears to be far from finished. Robert Holton (1998) claims there is in fact a symbiotic relationship between globalization and the nation-state. His *Globalization and the Nation-State* provides a clear discussion of the extent to which the nation-state's power is being challenged by globalizing processes. In the discussion of what he terms 'some problems with globe-talk', Holton considers questions of identity alongside political economic approaches. Extreme caution when discussing some of the bolder claims of the proponents in the debate has characterized many recent accounts and studies of globalization. Holton points towards the resurgence of nationalism as one of the major counter-trends towards the globalization of everyday life. He argues that 'globe talk' stresses conflict between globalization and the nation-state, whereas he writes that: 'the "national" and the "global" are in many ways complementary rather than necessarily conflicting social forces' (1998: 7). Moreover, he argues that much global rhetoric tends to underplay the historical dimension to globalization, and to over-state the uniqueness of contemporary globalizing processes.

Unfortunately the complexity of debates on the relationship between globalization and the nation-state is not always reflected in the literature on queer globalization. Work on the globalization of sexual cultures and economies often presumes the declining power of the state. Among writers who have produced more nuanced theoretical work on nationalism and sexuality, Jarrod Hayes argues: 'the globalization of capital has coincided not with a withering away of nationalisms, but with their intensification. While capital is certainly transnational, therefore, in many ways identity is still rooted in the Nation' (2000: 10). Hayes' argument about identity residing in the nation is itself problematic, as others such as Michael Peter Smith (2001) stress that identity as well as capital is becoming increasingly transnational. Hayes recognizes that globalization has led to the proliferation of nationalisms and the deepening of nationalist sentiment. Rather than nationalism disappearing with the acceleration of globalizing processes, therefore, the opposite has in fact been the case. In this chapter I examine the relationship between sexuality and the nation, because this often gets overlooked in work on queer globalization. The cosmopolitan focus of this literature is understandable, but this should not blind us to the importance played by nationalism within contemporary lesbian and gay politics. I maintain that national differences in the regulation and control of sexualities do matter and reveal much about the specific constructions of national identity and sexual cultures. I proceed to examine the role of sexuality in nationalist conflicts, especially the role of rape and violence. Central to my thinking on nationalism and sexuality in this chapter is the role these play in the formation of class identities. A key question I address is why is it that control over sexualities is so crucial to nationalist projects?

The Nation Matters

In the introductory chapter I stressed the importance of national formations of lesbian and gay studies. Here we can see how imperative an awareness of the nation is, and see that national differences do matter when we come to the geographies of sexual citizenship. Significant differences still exist between nation-states in the control and regulation of sexuality. If we consider the legality of same-sex acts between men within European nation-states we see important and significant national differences, which tend to be overlooked. For instance, if we look at the example of the United Kingdom, same-sex acts between consenting men were decriminalized in England and Wales through the Sexual Offences Act in 1967. But they were only made legal in Scotland in 1980 under the Criminal Justice Scotland Act and were only made legal in Northern Ireland in 1982.

According to the International Lesbian and Gay Association's World Legal Survey (www.ilga.org), male and female same sex acts are illegal in countries such as Algeria, Bangladesh, Bardados, Iran, Morocco, Pakistan and Tunisia. In addition, same sex acts between men are illegal in others – Armenia, Burma, Jamaica, Kenya, Malaysia, Nigeria and Singapore. In some countries in Europe such as Cyprus and Bosnia-Herzegovina (excluding the Republika Srpska), same sex acts were only decriminalised in the late 1990s. Similarly in terms of recognition of same-sex relationships, there are considerable national differences. For instance Article 8 (4) of the Dutch Nationality Act 1985 affords recognition of same-sex relationships for the purpose of acquiring Dutch citizenship (Binnie, 1997a). There are correspondingly wide-ranging differences in the national formations of activism and politics around matters of sexuality. For instance, Jan Willem Duyvendak (1996: 421) draws attention to the different degree of radicalism within activist movements in the United States, France and the Netherlands: 'In contrast to the United States and France, which have seen a renewed radicalization of the gay movement, the Dutch gay identity proceeds on its course towards depoliticization'. While we need to be sensitive to national differences in the way gay identity is constructed and regulated, it is imperative that we recognize the differences between sexual dissidents. Lesbianism has routinely been figured as an abject Other within nationalist discourses. In the UK there have been significant differences in the way lesbianism has been represented within nationalist discourses compared to gay male sexuality. In her analysis of British parliamentary debates on Section 28 of the Local Government Act 1987–1988 which prohibited 'the promotion of homosexuality as a pretended family relationship' within local authorities, Anna Marie Smith (1994) argues that gender was deployed in constructions of 'good' and 'bad homosexuals'. She states that gay men were represented as the 'bad homosexuals' – hypersexual and promiscuous, a sexual threat and danger. Lesbians on the other hand were seen as 'good homosexuals', symbols of sexual restraint and responsibility. Thus the homophobia of 1980s British nationalism reinforced gendered norms. Lesbians as women should be asexual, chaste and pure. Gay men were seen as a particular danger as they were seen as hypersexual and predatory. Commenting on Anna Marie Smith's construction of the 'good' and 'bad homosexual' which framed New Right discourses on sexuality in the late 1980s in Britain, Stychin argues that there has been a transformation in the character of the 'good homosexual' during the 1990s with the development of New Labour discourses on sexuality. While gender difference framed the distinction between responsible, asexual lesbians and promiscuous, hypermasculine gay men in the 1980s, the New Labour good homosexual is characterized by the focus on stability, monogamous relationships and financial independence, which inevitably produces the good homosexual as affluent and middle-class (Stychin, 2000b: 619). 'The gendered differences in the symbolic inclusion of lesbians and gay men within 1980s British nationalist politics demonstrates that there is no simple relationship between nationalism and sexual dissidence'. It is clear that the nation matters more for some sexual dissidents than others. Many lesbians and gay men serve in the armed forces and feel fiercely patriotic and strongly identify with the nation they serve. For instance, if you are a young working-class lesbian from an economically disadvantaged region, the armed forces may offer a way to escape the constraints of family and local community. These factors should be taken into consideration in discussions of the exclusion of lesbians and gay men from the armed forces on the basis of their sexuality (Bell and Binnie, 2000). However for immigrant queers, such a strong sense of nationalist belonging and sentiments may seem alien, indeed alarming given the racism and xenophobia they may be exposed to.

Rethinking Nationalism and Sexuality

Before I go any further I feel it is necessary to consider what we mean by the terms 'sexuality' and 'nation'. How we conceive of sexuality has implications for the politics of nation and vice versa. Each definition of both 'nationalism' and 'sexuality' has implications for theorizing links between them, especially if we take on board Pryke's point about the lack of a common theoretical language to conceptualize nationalism and sexuality. It is necessary to examine both terms as they are so easily naturalized in the 'love of country' (Patton, 1999). Perhaps it is 'love' and 'country' that we also need to examine – because it is through these that identities and differences are naturalized. Sexuality can be defined as a private affair – belonging in the private sphere. Essentialist notions of sexuality see it as a biological question rooted in nature. Social constructionism views sexuality as socially constructed – subject to the structures of capitalist society. Nationalism is particularly pernicious, as it tends to remain invisible in mundane everyday life. Nationalism's power rests in its very ability to remain invisible as a category within politics. Unfortunately much of the literature on nationalism, even the feminist literature, fails to address sexuality and where it does sexuality tends to be elided with gender. While recognizing the gendered construction of nationalism, it is imperative that sexuality is not overlooked – for instance lesbianism. There is also a danger that feminist work on nationalism does not adequately address the relationship between masculinity and nationalism. Joanne Nagel (1998) argues that scholarship on the gendered nature of states and nations, while valuable in addressing women's experience of these institutions, must not ignore men and masculinity.

While scholars of nationalism need to pay attention to sexuality, researchers on sexuality need to acknowledge national differences in the regulation of sexual cultures and economies. Nationalism matters for sexual dissidents because of the focus within nationalism on fixity and a common culture. There are also fundamental differences between nation-states – in terms of the regulation of sexual dissidence. An accident of birth means you may enjoy certain rights and privileges of (sexual) citizenship in one state that you would not if you were born in another nation-state. Sexuality is seen to be a threat to the nation-state because it is something that it is difficult to control. Take for instance the Operation Spanner case (Bell, 1995a and b) and the criminalization of same-sex consenting sadomasochism in which the defendants were punished by the state for representing a challenge to the nation-state's monopoly of violence. Conrad writes that homosexuality constitutes a particular threat to the fixity of the category of the nation:

> Any identity category potentially troubles the national border, but homosexuality in particular threatens the stability of the narrative of Nation: the very instability and specific historical contingency of the definition of homosexuality makes the category more fluid than most, and thus brings into question the fixity and coherence of all identity categories. (2001: 125)

Conrad argues that homosexuality represents a very particular threat to the ordering and categorizing imperative of the modern nation-state. Of course the stability of categories of identity formation has been challenged within post-structuralist theory. It might therefore be useful to turn to post-structuralist and relational models of identity in helping to think through the relationship between homosexuality and nationalism. Anna Marie Smith uses Derrida's theory of supplementarity to help think through the place of sexuality within British nationalism in the late 1980s. Smith's use of Derrida draws attention to the use of space in the production of Self and Other. For instance, geographical boundaries are key to the process of distinction-making between Self and Other. Smith argues that sexuality is deeply implicated in the processes of boundary formation. However, while useful in bringing into focus the geographical basis of identity formation, the relational model of difference has also been criticised. What is problematic with this relational model of difference is that it reproduces the logic and subjectivity of the Same. A generic Other is produced, yet there are differences between the way identities, subjectivities and communities are othered, and the processes of Othering within them. This is especially true of black queers/queers of colour who are made doubly invisible within this particular mode of theorizing. Thus far I have argued that sexuality represents a particular challenge to the nation-state and plays a specific role within nationalism. Smith's examination of the policies of race and sexuality in *New Right Discourse* is a classic example of this. Her analysis of both race and sexuality is incisive, and her book makes an important contribution to thinking through the connections between the politics of race and sexuality. However, what does tend to get lost in her argument is the theorization of racism within lesbian and gay cultures and communities, and homophobia within black communities. One does not get much sense of sexual dissident agency and how many sexual dissidents invest in the discourses about identity formation that she so eloquently examines. Smith makes insightful observations about migration policy in Britain, but there is little explicit discussion of the British migration policies towards the immigration of lesbians and gay men. A post-structuralist view of nationalism puts the focus on the production of symbolic order, and the assertion of the nation as the prime basis of loyalty. Conrad, like Hull and Mosse, maintains that homosexuality represents a particular threat to the class identity of the middle class, which has invested in the nationalism and respectability based on the nuclear family: '…homosexuality does not fit neatly within the discourse of bourgeois nationalism, since it threatens the reproduction of the heterosexual familial narrative of the Nation/State' (2001: 215). The bourgeois respectability at the heart of British nationalism brings us to a discussion of the significance of class in thinking though the relationship between nationalism and sexuality.

The Significance of Class

George Mosse's *Nationalism and Sexuality* represents one of the most significant works on nationalism and sexuality. In this book he argues that middle-class respectability in modern Germany was produced through the simultaneous promotion of nationalism and the regulation of sexual morals (Mosse, 1985). Nationalism and sexuality were thus central to class formation, specifically to the formation of the bourgeoisie. Reflecting on Mosse's essay on 'nationalism and respectability' (the precursor to his book), Isabel Hull (1982) makes some interesting observations and provides a thoughtful and detailed critique of Mosse's work. She argues that class anxieties led to Victorian sexual repression. She discusses class-based notions of civility in which the working classes were seen as uncivilized, quoting from Richard Kraft-Ebing's work on the link between civilisation, social order and sexual restraint (1982: 251). Kraft-Ebing wrote that it was the mark of a civilized man: 'under all circumstances he must be able to master his sexual

urge as soon as it comes in conflict with the altruistic demands of society'
(Hull, 1982: 251). Sex was seen as the Other of civilization – a threat to
social order, modernity and the nation, a threat to progress. Queers were
produced as perverted, dangerous Other. While the relationship between
nationalism, regulation of sexuality and the production of the Victorian
middle-classes may be at least documented and studied, it is necessary that
a much broader examination of the relationship between class, nationalism
and sexuality be produced. Hull (1982: 265) calls for a much more sys-
tematic examination of the relationship between sexuality and class:

> The bourgeoisie and its discontents have run like a red thread through these
> reflections. The other classes, their sexual behaviour and sexual worldviews have
> been eclipsed. This imbalance must be redressed through research, because the
> intimate connection among sexual behaviour, mores and class makes clear that
> we cannot understand culture's sexual system without seeing how all its units
> interrelate.

While the relationship between class, nationalism and sexuality remains
under-theorized, there have been a number of studies examining the prurient interest of scholars in the sexual habits and mores of the working classes.
Peter Gurney's (1997) essay on the Mass Observation movement in England
demonstrates that the sexual mores of the English working-classes have
long provided a prurient anthropological interest for English upper-class
researchers. There is a danger that in answering Hull's call, some classes are
seen as more proper objects of study than others. Thus the sexual mores of
the establishment, the upper-classes and nowadays the transnationalist capitalist class are normalized and rendered invisible. In this regard Sklair's
study of what he terms 'the transnationalist capitalist class' is worthy of
note, as I suggest that something similar may be happening now at the start
of the new millennium as the production of a commodified western sexual
subjectivity is becoming universal.

In 'nationalism' and 'modernity', capital spread through the establishment of the bourgeoisie and the assertion of their power vis-à-vis the working class and the aristocracy. Desires that were a threat to the forging of this
new social order needed to be reined in through moral regulation – the
family was seen as a brake on irresponsibility and fecklessness among the
working classes. Desire was subject to the gaze of the state, and the gaze of
the mother and father within the panoptic family. Meanwhile, in late capitalism we see that global capital is promoting desire in a bid to promote
products, and the expansion of production (Lowe, 1995). In this way the
respectable, responsible gay or lesbian living in a so-called family of choice
is promoted as a responsible consumer, as opposed to the dangerous queer
whose desires cannot be so easily commodified.

17

Within an emerging discourse around the growth of English identity as opposed to British identity, it is very much the case that a New Labour promoted vision of contemporary British identity is becoming associated with multiculturalism and cosmopolitanism, whereas English nationalism is associated with the embarrassing working-classes whose chauvinism is a shameful excess and threatens the New Labour vision of a sophisticated, globalized, flexible economy. English nationalism is seen as something done by the working class. It is an unsophisticated discourse, the Other of a sophisticated cosmopolitanism. Just as some bodies are seen as being more marked and visible as being racialized, so I would argue some bodies are more marked as nationalist than others. Chris Haylett's work on social policy, class and poverty under New Labour and an emerging body of work on the new politics of class are drawing attention to how class has become central to theorizing on identity and difference.

In this section I have traced the connections between sexuality, class and nationalism. I readily acknowledge that while studies of these interconnections are underdeveloped, there are a myriad of ways in which they can be theorized, from different geographical and historical perspectives. For instance in Chapter 7 I will go on to discuss the class basis of AIDS activism in New York City in the 1990s. We can see that the formation of groups such as Act-Up and Queer Nation were classed, as well as gendered and racialized. Thus the production and celebration of a queer nationalism must be tempered with this insight. Having outlined the relationship between nationalism, class and sexuality I proceed to consider how violence fits into the equation between nationalism and sexuality.

War, Sexuality and Violence

In *Bananas, Beaches and Bases*, Cynthia Enloe (1990) posits a relationship between militarism and the global subordination of women. Thus for any global or transnational perspective on gender, the military is a key area of concern. The gendered nature of the nation has been studied, for instance by Nagel (1998), who argues that in traditional models of nationalism, woman is equated with passivity and needs to be protected and safeguarded by men. The male soldier fights to protect the honour of the nation embodied as woman. The woman's role is to maintain the moral guardians of the nation. Thus the defiling of the enemy's women is the defilement of the enemy nation and thereby a potent weapon. The control of women's sexuality is necessary for the successful completion of a war campaign. Thus the woman's role is as reproducer of the nation and breeding warriors. This gender ideology of nationalism helps underpin the homophobic constructions of the 'good' and 'bad homosexual' discussed by Anna Marie Smith. Lesbians are expected to uphold the values of purity and chastity. It should also be noted that in extreme nationalist politics such as national socialism lesbians incarcerated in concentration camps were used for the sexual gratification of guards (Schoppmann, 1995). The use of rape in war has been well documented, for instance in the essay by Ruth Harris (1993). While the rape of women in war and nationalist struggles is more documented and studied, work is now emerging on the rape of men. Sasho Lambevski's work on male rape and nationalism in Macedonia demonstrates the extent to which male rape is deployed as a weapon in nationalism, and used to punish those who transgress national sexual norms. Lambevski (1999) argues that discourses about male rape in Macedonia construct Albanian men as the savage, violent 'Other'.

The discussion of the use of rape as a weapon in war demonstrates the importance of the violent control of sex and sexuality. Thus the control over non-reproductive desire and sex has been fundamental to nationalist struggles. This is particularly the case when the nation is seen to be under threat, as Carl Stychin argues:

> ... it does seem clear that when the nation state perceives a threat to its existence, that danger is frequently translated into sexualized terms. Same sex sexuality is deployed as the alien other, linked to conspiracy, recruitment, opposition to the nation, and ultimately a threat to civilization. (1998: 9)

However, how is this version of traditional gender roles being challenged and transformed by the ever-greater presence of gay men, lesbians and other women in the military? We also need to consider the role often afforded World War Two in accounts of the growth of urban sexual communities in the US. Militarism and modern western gay culture are closely intertwined. This is not to equate queer sexual cultures with militarism, but merely to recognize that the military provides same-sex spaces that offer opportunities for same-sex sexual bonds and relations away from the constraints of family life. Studies of post-World War Two queer communities in the United States point to the congregations of demobbed men and women in naval cities in the US such as San Francisco and San Diego as key factors in the development of queer communities. While World War Two meant liberation for some, the post-World War Two period witnessed the state's repression of homosexuality. This culminated in the height of the Cold War with, for instance, the homophobic basis of McCarthyism in 1950s political and popular culture. This was of course not limited to the US and took on different forms in specific national polities and sexual cultures (for instance, see Katrin Sieg's [1995] work on cold-war sexualities in West and East Germany).

I do have a number of problems with the whole 'gays and the military debate'. Sonia Otalvaro-Hormillosa (1999) argues that many Asian Pacific Queers within the US have been unable or unwilling to identify with the struggle for inclusion of gays in the US Military. They associate US Armed Forces with the US military bases located within South East Asia, most notably the Phillippines, where such bases have been the focus of considerable opposition. It is hard to identify with an institution which is seen as a reflection or symbolic of US imperialism. However, I also acknowledge the complexity of the gays and the military debate where class and race have often been overlooked in discussions of the subject. For black/working class lesbians and gay men, the military is one promise of escaping homophobia, escaping localities in which there are unfavourable conditions in which to be queer. Jessica Chapin (1998) argues that questions of race were scarcely visibile in the gays in the military debate in the United States. This was despite the fact that, as Chapin notes, the discriminatory policies of the US military have a disproportionate impact on lesbians and gay men of colour. In contemporary discourses of globalized sex, there are dangerous parallels with homophobic discourses on homosexuality and national socialism. There is the equation of male homosexuality with a virile hypermasculinity in which gay men are constituted in discourse as prime agents of globalization – as spreaders of HIV and AIDS; as exploitative sex tourists – penetrating weak vulnerable 'third world' economies and countries.

Likewise, in contemporary discourses on the sexual politics of Hindu nationalism, Paola Bacchetta examines the hypermasculinity espoused by Hindu nationalist organizations such as 'Rashtriya Swayamsevak Sangh' (RSS). She assesses scholarship on the RSS, such as that by Des Raj Goyal. Bacchetta argues that Goyal's treatise on Hindu nationalism represents extreme Hindu nationalists as perverse, as queer. Bacchetta argues that: 'Goyal's argumentative strategy is based on the presupposition that the anti-Hindu-nationalist reader will also be a homophobic reader; he or she will automatically endorse the perverse-politics/perverse-sexuality (and vice versa) equation' (1999: 142). Bacchetta maintains that we should not lose sight of the conservative gender and sexual politics espoused by the RSS and that: 'Hindu nationalism is an expression not of queer sexualities or mentalities but rather of queer phobic ones' (1999: 143).

Nationalism, Homoeroticism and Homophobia

An understanding of nationalism is also useful in understanding homophobia. In certain polities the nation-state is increasingly asserting itself as the protector of the rights of lesbians and gay men. Hence, what are the consequences for our theorizing of the so-called homophobia of nationalism when increasingly lesbian and gay rights are being 'used' or are symbolic in reproducing specific nationalisms, for instance in South Africa and the Netherlands? Vincent Quinn berates the metropolitanism of commentators who generalize or universalize experiences from the particular position of London. In the case of Northern Ireland, Quinn argues that nationalism and unionism have both been hostile towards homosexuality (2000: 260). This points to the specificity of place and the way sexuality is configured within local political structures. Quinn therefore takes issue with the metrocentrism of some queer critiques that assume that queer consumer culture has a uniformly assertive public presence throughout the (contested boundaries) of the United Kingdom. This critique of the metropolitanism of queer commentary leads me neatly on to my next question, which is: can we make generalized statements about the links between homophobia and nationalism? Given the argument made in the introduction to the book about the dangers of asserting an ethnocentric and metropolitan perspective, making such generalizations leaves one open to attack. There are dangers in drawing parallels between Victorian England and the contemporary (former) Yugoslavia. Is it possible to draw together conceptual material developed in one case study of nationalism and apply it to the analysis of another? I would argue that we have no other choice but to construct theory as best we can from the material available to us. Another key issue we have to consider is the extent to which some nationalisms may be perceived as positive towards some sexual dissidents. We have, therefore, to recognize the active agency that many queers play within nationalist politics. Nationalisms do not simply exclude sexual dissidents, the relationship between queers and the nation-state is more ambivalent. Jarrod Hayes is ambivalent about nationalism, arguing that it does not simply exclude sexual dissidents. On the one hand he acknowledges that nationalism may have some progressive potential, for instance in resisting colonization. Are there progressive nationalisms, for instance those that resist colonization? Hayes argues that nationalism normally marginalizes women and is oppressive in its treatment of sexual dissidence. Despite this he admits ambivalence about nationalist politics' treatment of sexuality arguing that despite these misgivings 'national identity has fuelled many struggles for decolonization that I find just' (2000: 11). Can we generalize about the place of sexual dissidence within nationalisms in general? Hayes appears to suggest that in fact there is little difference between the way queerness is configured between western and non-western nationalisms: 'relations between nationalism and sexuality tend to be the same in both budding and established nations' (2000: 16).

This implies that we cannot make a distinction between different types of nationalism and how sexuality is configured within them. For Hayes, it is the utopianism of national projects that marks the impossibility of the co-existence of homosexuality with the new nationalist order, no matter how homosexuals may be tolerated or included in the new national imaginary in the short term. This makes post-apartheid South Africa fascinating as the post-apartheid institution formally embraced the rights of lesbians and gay men as symbolic of a new dawn in South African politics – a new nation. While Hayes readily acknowledges the progressive potential for nationalism within the Maghreb he notes that the search for fixity and purity may be common to nationalism in general. He writes:

Since nationalism often involves a narrative return to national origins that justifies the geopolitical entity of a nation, the return to 'pure' religious traditions exemplified in the rise of Islamic fundamentalism in Algeria and the ensuing civil war could be considered a phenomenon related to the worldwide rekindling of nationalisms. Serbian ethnic cleansing, therefore, and the assassination of those whose who do not fit either official or fundamentalist definitions of Algerian identity operate according to the same logic. (2000: 3)

Hayes appears to be implying that you can argue that there is an essential logic to nationalism. Comparisons can be made between post-communist Eastern Europe and Victorian England. In her incisive study of nationalism in post-communist Eastern Europe, Renata Salecl explains why nationalism took root in post-socialist Slovenia. While communism and nationalism are ideologically poles apart, she argues they do share common traits. She claims that post-socialist societies have been characterized by an intensification of sexism, racism and homophobia, which had hitherto been suppressed in the socialist era. Salecl notes that the gay rights movement in Slovenia was one of the new social movements that constituted the opposition to the communist state. However, with the fall of communism, queers soon became identified as a threat to the post-socialist moral order within the county. Salecl (1994: 146–7) suggests that this was because they threatened the nationalist project of the reproduction of the national population: 'With the end of communism, there has not been any great advance in the public tolerance of homosexuality. In its attempt to encourage a rise in birthrate, the Slovenian moral majority began to attack homosexuals also'. Does post-socialist Slovenia suggest that nationalism must always be homophobic? The homophobic notion that gay men are equated with extreme right wing, nationalist and fascist groups has been based on the assertion of hypermasculinity (Hewitt, 1996). At the same time we need to be aware of the racist notion that black and Asian people are more likely to be homophobic, and there has been some excellent work examining the sexuality that has been configured within African American nationalism (Harper, 1993).

Intriguingly, Hayes turns it around to argue that the nation-state must already be queer given the necessity and the energy it devotes to casting out and expelling sexual dissidence.

> Nationalist discourses that define the Nation by positing marginal sexualities as foreign are not stating what is already the case but actively excluding. If there must be such an effort to exclude the queer from the Nation (queer in both the more recent, sexual sense and its previous meaning as anything out of the ordinary) and show she is an outsider trying to invade, the queer must always be inside already; that is, in some ways the Nation is always already queer. (2000: 15)

The danger in seeing the nation-state as already queer, as Hayes does, can lead to misrecognition of the extent of the homophobia of the nation-state. Is not the nation-state already homophobic, rather than queer? Smith's analysis points towards the mutual construction of race and sexuality as categories of identity. Her work on 'new right' discourse examines the production of purified space, and the heterosexual basis for the nation: British nationalism has constructed a straight non-white nation. Smith's work is significant in making links between the racism, migration policy and homophobia in New Right discourses in Britain, but she does not say much about sexuality and migration policy and discourse. It is the boundaries of the nation that queerness threatens, as Jessica Chapin (1998: 412) argues: 'homophobia becomes a way of expressing anxiety about the (re)emergence of a political unconscious, of the ambiguities and subjugated knowledges that are suppressed by a rigorous naturalization of the boundary line and of the hierarchies that such a line supports'. Sally Munt (1998) argues that nationalism casts out the homoeroticism within institutions at the heart of the nation such as the armed forces and the police. This echoes Eve Sedgwick's fundamental distinction between male homosociality and male homosexuality that explains the homophobic nature of national institutions such as the armed forces. One recent attempt to examine the relationship between homoeroticism and nationalism is Sasho Lembevski's so-called 'queer experiential ethnography' of cruising areas in Skopje, Macedonia. Lembevski's work points towards the mutual constitution of class, ethnicity, gender and sexuality – as his essay powerfully underscores how these identities play out in the often uncomfortable (for some) grubby materiality of public sex acts between men. Lembevski argues that nationalism is a key locus of difference that underscores sexual relations between men in the Skopje 'gay' scene. He speaks of a 'nationalist governance of sex' (1999: 410) whereby Macedonian homosexuals construct Albanian men as the dominant and active partner in sex. Here we are into the area of 'politically incorrect sex' in which Lembevski notes what he argues is a racist desire for the Other. But what of the relationship between desire, (homo) eroticism, nationalism and sexuality within commodity culture associated with 'banal nationalism'? (Billig, 1995; Edensor, 2002). One attempt to think through these relationships is Alan McKee's (1999) essay on Australian porn videos. He analyses the content of gay male porn videos in which the Australian nature of the films is promoted, even though as McKee notes the videos he analyses are produced by non-Australian capital. McKee (1999: 179) argues that the gay male pornography market is so dominated by American products, actors, sites, that it is taken for granted and naturalised: 'Americanness is simultaneously always present in American texts, and so universal as to be often invisible'. McKee notes that porn (as what he terms a 'despised cultural object') rarely features in studies of national identity, which is interesting in itself given the link between nationalism and respectability examined earlier in this chapter in the discussion of George Mosse's work. As porn is the quintessential 'Other' of respectability, perhaps here we should examine 'banal nationalism'. For McKee, claims on authenticity are central to the process of making distinctions between 'the local' and 'the global'. He argues that gay porn videos are interesting as an example of a product produced in Australia 'precisely because they make – and are widely understood to make – no claims to authenticity'(1999: 182). While arguing against the idea of authenticity, McKee seems persuaded of the Australianness of these gay porn films specifically in terms of what he names their 'desperateness'[1], noting the attempt to foster Australian 'mateship' in the videos through the over-the-top, dubbed voice over:

> Australianness is always present so long as the men keep on talking. 'Stick it in my arse – strewth!' exclaims a character in A Sailor in Sydney, keeping the vernacular present as the sex progresses. The insistence on the vocabulary of the 'mate' can again be noted, as the continual conversation insists on inserting this recognizably 'Australian' terminology. 'C'mon mate suck that dick', 'Strewth, yeah, suck it' (Jackaroos); 'Aw, mate, I shot all over you. Yeah.' (Manly Beach) (1999: 185)

Interestingly it does not seem to occur to McKee to read this over-the-top performance as camp. Judith Butler's much studied and quoted work on performativity has often been the focus of critical attention in terms of race but less in relation to nationalism. However, what I am concerned with here is the performative nature of nationalism and popular culture. Does not the inclusion of queer symbolism within the performance of Australian national identity at the opening ceremony of the Sydney Olympics not point towards the nationalist death of camp? This knowing 'nationalization' of camp inevitably points towards the inclusion of queers at the heart of an Australian national identity that was being projected to the rest of the globe. The heart of camp has been the celebration of adversity, the claiming of symbolic space in a culture in which queer culture was devalued. Are these read as a claim for inclusiveness within the national imaginary, or parodies of that very imaginary? To a non-Australian such as myself, it would appear that from the opening and closing ceremonies of the Sydney Olympics with drag queens from the film *Priscilla Queen of the Desert*, and Kylie Minogue singing 'Dancing Queen', that 'camp' is very much a part of Australia's contemporary national imaginary, or at least the 'official' image it projects to the world.

Johannes von Moltke argues that: 'camp *cuts across* distinctions, most notably across those which demarcate boundaries of gender and sexuality' (1994: 83). But what about the boundaries of the nation? Von Moltke discusses the way the relationship between the production and reception of Rainer Werner Fassbinder's films in the United States points towards the production of camp and the way in which Fassbinder's films have been received by audiences in the United States. According to Von Moltke, the production of camp partially depends on 'the loss of complexity of meaning in the crossing of the national border' (1994: 86). 'He therefore argues that there is a link between camp and deterritorialization, specifically in terms of the spatial gap between the production and consumption of cinematic texts. Focussing on the different reception of the film of the New German Cinema in the United States compared to Germany, Von Moltke argues that this can be explained by the: 'gap that separates nationally specific modes of spectatorship and address. This is where the distance between a German audience and a "deterritorialized" American camp spectatorship becomes operative. The transversal, or queer movement of camp [...] serves to highlight not only the tensions between address and reception [...] in addition, it is characteristic that camp should also draw attention to the very boundaries it violates, turning the surreptitious tactics of poaching into an "open secret," exuberantly performed' (ibid.: 85).

In this section I have argued that nationalism has tended to repress sexual dissidence. Homosexuality threatens to destabilize fixed categories of identity, which are fundamental to the fixity of identity within nationalism. However, I have also noted that it may no longer be sustainable to frame sexual dissidents' relationship to the state merely in terms of exclusion and repression. Jarrod Hayes suggests that the nation is already queer and has to expel the queer within. Moreover, Carl Stychin has argued that while in 1980s British New Right discourses on sexual dissidence the queer was framed as an outsider, or Other, the situation changed during the 1990s. Assimilationist politics of gay liberation have meant that lesbian and gay men have gained political and symbolic recognition and have a (limited) place within nationalist politics. Gays have become domesticated within the politics of British nationhood. At the same time I argue that it its important to examine hypermasculinity, which I maintain is fundamental to the distinction between 'normal', 'rational' masculine nationalism, and hypermasculine, perverse ultra-nationalism and fascism. Respectable masculinity is essential for nationalism – this is routinely normalized – whereas as hypermasculinity is framed as queer, or perverse, as the Hindu nationalist case discussed by Bacchetta. 'In terms of banal nationalism and popular culture, while camp has been long been the focus of critical and other attention so much so that writers now speak of the 'death of camp' (Flinn, 1995), few have applied to sought to theorize national identity through the lens of camp. However as we have seen in my discussion of the work of McKee and Von Moltke that camp can be a significant way in which sexual dissidents can potentially disrupt the fixed boundaries of national identity'.

Queer Nationalism: Sexual Citizenship and the Politics of Assimilation

The discussion of camp, authenticity and gay porn in Australia draws attention to the fact that queers' relationship to nationalism is not merely one of rejection and exclusion. What I want to discuss in this section is the way the nation is thought and imagined within queer communities. How does nationalism feature explicitly and implicitly within debates on assimilation and difference and within claims for sexual citizenship? Here this section sets up the discussion about globalization and the nation-state explored more fully in the next chapter – specifically the nation-state as the primary securer of citizenship. Is sexual citizenship not to become globalized? The nation-state still matters despite globalization and the Europeanization of citizenship.

If we agree that the nation still matters, then what narratives of nationhood are spoken by sexual dissidents? In this context the work of Martin Manalansan IV (1995), arguing that Stonewall performs the work of memory, occupies a central place in the mythmaking of the queer nation. However, he also points towards the American-centric character of Stonewall and notes that the Stonewall myth renders invisible the different narratives of sex/nation identity formation – specifically those Filipino gay men in New York City. Perhaps it is the invisibility of the American nation within lesbian and gay studies that requires the most urgent critical attention. This is not to be misrecognised as an anti-American attack, but merely to note that the frustration with the US dominance of all things 'gay' or 'queer' has a long history – reflected for instance in the title of Altman's (1982) book *The Homosexualization of America, the Americanization of the Homosexual*. It sometimes feels like the whole discussion of globalization of sexualities rather than drawing critical attention merely seeks to reinforce the American-centrism. For instance the recently published collection *Queer Diasporas* contains essays which in terms of their geographical range reflect the identities of communities that have become significant within US polity. Carl Stychin (1998) argues that the coming to the fore of rights-based discourses within lesbian and gay politics reflects very much the dominance of rights claims within US political culture. Mark Johnson (1998: 702) notes that 'the language gays use to talk about love is, in large measure, drawn from an imagined notion of American love', a love which after Jean-Paul Dumont, he argues 'signals a performative appropriation of America'. Johnson argued that the adoption of the term 'gay' was: 'part of an attempt to construct an identity, gendered feminine and defined primarily in terms of an imagined America' (1998: 698).

Despite the homophobic beat at the heart of nationalist politics, it is unsurprising that nationalist politicians are labelled queer. Because of the hypermasculinity of nationalism, queers are often said to be attracted to nationalist sentiments and politics. Hence the homophobic notion that the Nazis were queer, despite national socialism's homophobia. In a rather disturbing discussion of the sexual politics of nationalism in Russia, Laurie Essig (1999: 156) argues that some sexual dissidents have become attracted to nationalist-fascist politics: 'as a way to protest the Russian status quo and western imperialism, as well as to protect their national selves from the taint of internal otherness'.

The equating of male homosexuality with fascism and national socialism has a long record, as Andrew Hewitt (1996) has argued. The homoeroticism within nationalism has led many to suspect so-called 'extreme' nationalist politicians to be homosexual themselves. The excess of homoeroticism is seen as evidence for supporting the homophobic notion that a disproprotionate number of nationalist and far-right politicians are themselves gay. While the representation of gays as nationalist fascists is commonplace, there are other ways in which lesbians and gay men and associated activists have sought to lay claim to nationalism by, for instance, using the symbolism of the nation. Moreover there is the work of gay activists such as the Irish nationalist Kieran Rose. Kieran Rose (1994) argues that the local and the global are significant in securing change in the law. Law reform was won through a combination of an effective campaign within Ireland stressing the Irishness of law reform through an appeal to a sense of fairness, with pressure on Ireland at the European level. In 1988 the European Court found in favour of David Norris who had brought a case against Irish laws criminalizing sex between men. The European Court's verdict stated that these laws contravened Article 8 of the Convention on Human Rights. The appeal to nationalism by Irish gay activists such as Kieran Rose is striking. He seeks to articulate an essence of tolerance within Irish society and culture, and that this should be the basis for organization around law reform on issues such as the age of consent (1994:74). Rose's nationalist position is challenged by Kathryn Conrad in her essay on the nationalist and sexual politics in Ireland: 'Rose's history and analysis of the gay rights movement in Ireland attempts to reclaim nationalism as liberatory without explicitly acknowledging the history of nationalist homophobia' (2001: 125). Conrad argues that Rose is too quick to overlook the heterosexism and homophobia within certain formations of Irish nationalism, for instance the conservatism of Irish-American Irish nationalists. Queer nationalism and lesbian nationalism however must recognize the racialized and class-basis of sexual identities and communities.

We might usefully though link this discussion of nationalism and sexuality with current debates on sexual citizenship that have been widely characterised as focusing on the conflict between the politics of assimilation and transgression. When it comes to the right to serve in the armed forces, the argument for assimilation is often based on the assertion that lesbians and gay men are patriots and model soldier-citizens. I do not wish to moralize about the rights and wrongs of lesbians and gay men serving in the military; the presence of lesbians and gay men in the armed forces has clearly troubled and threatens the sanctity of the military establishment in the US and the UK. Campaigns for legal recognition of same-sex relationships and the right to serve in the military are both claims for inclusion with the nation-state (Bell and Binnie, 2000).

There are clear reasons why marriage and the military are lumped together in these lesbian and gay claims on citizenship. To be accepted as families of choice, rather than as the 'pretended families' of Britain's Section 28, means to be symbolically accepted as part of the nation. They are bids for inclusion within the national imaginary. The desire to be virtually normal and be embraced by the nation-state is a deep-seated desire within those claiming their rights to serve their country in the military. This is a complex issue – one in which gender, racialized and classed components tend to be made invisibile on both sides of the argument.

Conclusion

> Historically, as I have suggested, the homosexual may have been constituted as the stranger, the nomad, the outsider, and the excess, in which homosexuality was foreign to the nation-state. However, with changing times, we find that the good homosexual can be incorporated and assimilated into a space that is 'not-marriage' (which remains a special symbolic heterosexual space), and presumably in which children are simply *assumed* not to enter the picture. (Stychin, 2000b: 622)

In this chapter I have examined the relationship between nationalism and sexuality. I have considered the consequences of sexuality for theories of nation and nationalism. In the same way I have examined the consequences of the nation for theories of sexuality. I examined the relationship between homophobia and nationalism, and then went on to critically evaluate work being done on nationalism and sexuality. Specifically I sought to discover whether it is desirable to produce a single theory of nationalism and sexuality – whether it is possible to generalize from different constructions and experiences of nationalism and sexuality. The nation does matter to sexual dissidents and this must not be overlooked within lesbian, gay and queer politics, through I am still undecided whether there is an essential logic to the way sexual dissidence is configured within nationalism. There is considerable evidence to support the assertion that there is no such logic. For instance, contemporary Dutch and Danish nationalisms point towards tolerance of sexual dissidence as key elements within these nationalisms. The discussion of Australian national identity earlier in the chapter also suggests the incorporation of queers into the Australian national imaginary and iconography. While nationalism draws on the notion of an unchanging essence or biological bond, of course, nationalisms are not static. Perhaps we should focus critical attention on how and why nationalisms change over time and how sexuality is configured within these transformations. Having argued against a single logic of nationalism, it is tempting to make certain generalizations about the way sexual dissidence is articulated within nationalisms. It would appear that there are certain commonalities in the way sexual dissidence is treated within nationalist discourses. The fixity of identity and primary loyalty to the nation-state – which lies at the heart of nationalism, can be threatened by sexual dissidence. Same sex desire represents a threat to the national imperative towards reproduction. At the same time we see that in contemporary Eastern European nationalisms that are hostile towards integration within the European Union sexual dissidence represents the threat from outside. In some cases lesbian and gay rights have become important benchmarks in terms of assessing the suitability of Eastern European states for accession. This has inevitably led to tensions in some accession states and others that wish to join the EU. For instance, Carl Stychin has drawn attention to the Romanian case where the issue of the legalization of lesbian and gay relationships, which has been encouraged by Brussels has been a rallying point for nationalist politicians who argue against the interference of the European Union in Romanian politics.

It would appear that sexual dissidence may not be as marginal to certain nationalisms as radicals may think. Lesbian and gay rights are not incompatible with some contemporary nationalisms, with western nationalisms being reproduced as being anti-Muslim or anti-Islamic. Thus it is not difficult to imagine western nationalisms as being pro-liberal, pro-cosmopolitan, and thus upholding a tolerance and respect for women and sexual minorities.

So where does class fit into the equation? What about the issue of authenticity in the discussion of Australian gay porn? The discussion in this chapter suggests that nationalism's power and perniciousness lies in its very capacity for invisibility. Nationalism only makes sense – is only legible – within an international system of states. Nationalism only makes sense within a global framework, as a panicked response to uneven global capitalist development. Where do queers fit within this panicked response? We have routinely been the subject of moral panics, and threats to the sanctity of the nation's borders (see for instance, Edelman, 1992). Queers have never been fully excluded from nationalism. Indeed as Parker et al (1992) state in their discussion of Eve Sedgwick's (1985) critical distinction between male homosociality and male homosexuality, gay men have figured at the very heart of nationalism, in that the erotic bonds between men have to be cast out to reproduce the heterosexual male homosociality at the very heart of nationalist sociality, while sex between men threatens the reproduction of the national line.

Sexual dissidents have not simply been the passive victims of nationalist politics. Many lesbians and gay men have made a considerable investment in nationalist political visions and struggles; indeed struggles for sexual citizenship imply a fight for inclusion within nationhood. This can most clearly be seen in the fight for lesbian and gay equality and the right to serve your country in the military. While Jarrod Hayes suggests queers may be compatible with certain configurations of nationalist movements in the Maghreb, he acknowledges that this presence and agency has been fleeting and that nationalism has tended to suppress these voices. I noted earlier in the chapter how Irish nationalists such as Kieran Rose argue that the struggle for lesbian and gay rights are compatible with Irish nationalism, while other commentators have cautioned against Rose's nationalist position, pointing to the sexually conservative politics at the heart of Irish nationalism. The use of the label 'nation' as applied to lesbian political forces such as 'Lesbian Nation', and to queer activist groups such as 'Queer Nation', point towards a desire for community and solidarity within the notion of nationhood. They also demonstrate the extent of the powerful symbolic appeal of the nation as a means of asserting a political voice. Having examined the relationship between nationalism and sexual dissidence, I now wish to examine the politics of queer globalization.

Note

1. As an aside one wonders whether this 'desperateness' that McKee speaks of in terms of Australian national identity may be more accurately applied as a label to describe much of contemporary gay popular culture more generally. For instance witness gay popular culture's desperate search for the oxygen of glamour; the rush to claim stars as gay icons if they make vaguely non-judgmental public statements about the 'gay lifestyle'; or the ever increasing desperateness of gay popular cultural forms – to claim someone as an honourary gay if they articulate a remotely queer-friendly gesture.

3

Locating Queer Globalization

John Tomlinson has argued that it is tempting for commentators on globalization to lapse into the comfort of theoretical certainties when confronted by the sheer complexity of globalizing processes. In the previous chapter I examined the link between nationalism and sexual dissidence and concluded that nationalism and sexuality were fundamental to formations of both class and capital. In this chapter I argue that the connection between the cultural, the sexual and the economic is one that is rarely made in mainstream discussions of globalization. What is meant by queer globalization? Is it, for instance, the global expansion of a western model of sexuality, or more specifically the Americanization of sexual culture, and of American theories and explanations of sexuality? In order to address these questions we need to define globalization and see how it has been theorized in relation to nationalism. I begin the chapter by discussing the challenges posed by queer globalization to social theory. I evaluate the relative merits of contrasting approaches to globalization and their value in helping to conceptualize queer globalization and then examine the notion of the global gay and the global queer. I outline a critique of these concepts in order to provide a list of key issues that will frame the discussion of queer globalization in later chapters in the book, before going on to trace the parameters of debates about queer globalization that will inform the discussion in the remaining chapters of the book. In my exploration of cyberqueer spaces, I examine the potential for a balanced and nuanced perspective on queer globalization that recognizes agency.

Queer Globalization and Social Theory

How globalization is defined has major consequences for the place afforded to sexuality within theoretical work on the subject. Some definitions of globalization are very narrow and thereby exclude the cultural, as if a separate sphere of 'the cultural' can be detached from the 'the economic' and 'the political'. Where does sexuality fit within theories of globalization? For Neil Smith globalization is the latest phase of uneven development within capitalism. He argues that globalization is satanic or evil and that cuts to the welfare state are a consequence of globalization: 'the crises provoked by privatization and wholesale social service cuts are the social face of globalization' (1997: 177–8). Smith tends to see the nation-state as a passive victim of globalization. Ong (1999) and Holton (1998) on the other hand see the nation-state playing an active role in promoting globalization. For instance, Ong (1999: 21) argues that: 'Asian tiger states have evolved by aggressively seeking global capital while securing their own economic interests and the regulation of their populations'. This points towards the necessity of examining the politics of location when making general claims about globalizing processes. An alternative to political-economic definitions of globalization is suggested by Roland Robertson in *Globalization* who characterizes globalization as 'the compression of the world and the intensification of consciousness of the world as a whole' (1992: 8). This definition is preferable as it points towards 'consciousness', and is thus more immediately relevant for researchers of sexuality. Some definitions of globalization leave out questions of culture and identity altogether, focusing on the narrowly defined political and economic spheres. The global only makes sense in relation to 'the national' or 'the local'. The national and the local are commonly conflated.

While globalization has spawned an avalanche of work on the intersections of global politics, economics and culture, sexuality has been almost completely overlooked. As Ken Plummer notes: 'although globalization is well recognized and much discussed, very few studies ever talk about the connections of this process to the intimate life' (2001: 249). It is only really in the past five years that sexuality has become an object of study for researchers on globalization, and the impetus for this work has tended to come from within Lesbian and Gay Studies rather than mainstream social and political theory. For instance the collection of essays edited by Fredric Jameson and Masao Miyoshi (1998), *The Cultures of Globalization*, fails to mention sexuality at all. While the introduction to *Cosmopolitics* does note the fact that gay men were part of the old class of cosmopolitans (Cheah and Robbins, 1998), there is no further reference to sexuality elsewhere in the collection. Some writers on globalization do, however, make direct reference to sexuality. John Tomlinson's *Globalization and Culture* and Jan Aart Scholte's *Globalization: A Critical Introduction* are among the few that do. Scholte is significant for the way he devotes critical attention to the subject of global lesbian and gay identities, for instance pointing towards the convergence between globalization and the emergence of lesbian and gay

33

politics: 'The historical concurrence of the lesbian and gay revolution with the growth of supraterritorial space is significant [...] Globalization has made room for lesbian and gay affiliations by loosening the hold of territorial communities. In addition, much "coming out" has occurred at supraterritorial locations' (2000: 175). While sexuality has been somewhat neglected within mainstream studies of globalization, definitions of globalization that emphasize the interdependence and interrelation of the cultural, economic and political offer the most to those seeking to explain how sexuality fits into the equation.

The Global, the Transnational and the Politics of Scale

One way beyond the impasse in terms of the dichotomous way of thinking critiqued by John Tomlinson is to focus on the transnational as opposed to the global. This section critically evaluates recent work on the transnational and how it may be useful for thinking through the relationships between sexuality, globalization and nationalism. The transnational has increasingly transplanted globalization as the buzzword when speaking about cultural, economic and political connections across global space. There are good reasons why this has happened. The transnational highlights the resilience of the nation-state in an era of globalization. Aihwa Ong prefers the term transnational to globalism, For Ong noting that 'trans' suggests a cutting across or traversing of national borders which actively transforms the relationships between states and capitalism, thereby drawing critical attention to 'the transversal, the transnational, and the transgressive aspects of contemporary behaviour and imagination that are incited, enabled, and regulated by the changing logics of states and capitalism' (1999: 4). The focus on the transnational as opposed to the global is preferable according to Ong for it draws attention to how the cultural and economic interconnect. Economic processes do not simply determine cultural transformations, but the latter help shape the former. While Ong champions the use of the transnational, other writers are wary of the term. For instance Jarrod Hayes sees the transnational as meaning going beyond or superseding the nation. I don't see it in that way and I don't think Ong intends it in that way – quite the reverse. Conceptually the transnational (as opposed to the global) signifies the resilience of the nation-state. Authors such as Michael Peter Smith (2001) have argued for a less fatalistic view of globalization as omnipotent force beyond our control, calling for a much greater emphasis on agency. And Tomlinson (1999) is critical of what he argues is the one-dimensional approach of authors such as Hirst and Thompson (1996) who are taken to task for their economic determinism. The subtitle of Smith's *Transnational*

Urbanism, 'locating globalization' indicates the reinstatement of agency and resists the economism of accounts that stress the omnipotence of globalizing processes in restructuring the city. Smith is critical of the way the local is represented as authentic and embedded. He is critical of the representation of the local scale as devoid of agency and merely the victim of globalizing processes. I am sympathetic to Smith's position vis-à-vis the global cities approach and share his concern with resisting the totalising narrative of political economy, and his desire to re-instate agency. Smith's notion of transnational urbanism opens more space for diverse readings of the global than the more reductionist, economistic perspectives associated with political economy.

Some discussions of the globalization of culture tend to equate globalization with the homogenization and Americanization of culture. Here the focus is on American dominance of global consumption patterns. It is suggested that whether you are in a shopping mall such as the vast Mall of America in Bloomington, Minnesota, or The Trafford Centre near Manchester, people shop in the same shops (The Gap) and wear the same labels (Levi's, Calvin Klein, Donna Karan) and eat the same food (at McDonalds). This view asserts that indigenous cultures are threatened by the power of global capital. Doreen Massey (1993) takes a very different view on the alleged homogenizing impact of globalization arguing that globalization reproduces spatially uneven development and thereby re-confirms the significance of place, rather than undermining it. The local cannot be understood without reference to the global, as Lisa Rofel (1999: 456–7) writes: 'The local and the global are both acts of positioning, perspectives rather than mere locales, used as signifiers of difference'. According to Massey's perspective, it is evident that globalization has an uneven impact across the globe. For example, access to new technology is highly uneven – not everyone can afford trans-continental air travel or the Internet. Economic and political globalization does not necessarily bring about the homogenization of culture. Globalization has reinforced the importance of space and place precisely because places are differently impacted upon by globalization. Here we can see that globalized practices are located within distinctive national social, economic, cultural and political formations. Ong argues that globalization in the United Kingdom is commonly seen in terms of a perceived threat to the economy and to British cultural identity whereas in Asia there is much more awareness of the positive role of the state in encouraging the development of transnational flows and networks.

It is evident therefore that place does make a difference in terms of how globalization is conceived. An awareness of the significance of location is evident in Alan McKee's essay on national identity and Australian gay porn.

McKee critiques the way in which the local/global relation is configured within some more Marxist inspired perspectives on global culture, arguing that the local is often represented as a privileged site of authenticity. McKee suggests that the local is often conceptualized as a site of resistance to the global which is equated with global capital, arguing that: 'in such a use of the term, the "global" becomes the site of faceless, homogenous cultural production; while the local is the site of authenticity' (1999: 180–1). However I would add that there is also a danger that 'the local' also gets configured as the site of sexuality – the site of an authenticity based on an essentialized, autobiographicial gay identity. McKee draws a number of con-clusions about the way in which 'the local' and 'the global' are thought, conceptualized and studied within international cultural studies. He argues against the local scale as being a privileged site of authentic cultural pro-duction: 'There is nothing "authentic" about the local that is not "authentic" about the global. If we believe that it is important to insist on local identi-ties, whether at street, village, town, country, state or national level, we have to be able to argue why, without resorting to simplistic binaries' (1999: 196). McKee's article is interesting but for my purposes here I thought he could have extended his discussion to focus more on porn as a specific cul-tural form and how it may be implicated within national identity and global culture. McKee appears to treat porn as any other form of material culture (which is refreshing on the one hand). But porn is clearly subject to state control and censorship – like many other forms of material culture. While he mentions censorship in Britain and the sticker on the US tape pro-claiming the right to view porn as a very American practice of citizenship, I think porn may figure more widely as a threat to the nation from without – as a global contaminant to local culture.

It is a touchstone of contemporary cultural studies and social theory that globalization does not lead to homogenization, that globalization has com-plex spatially uneven effects. If we then come to look at the literature on globalization and sexuality one would have thought that these basic lessons would have been learned by now. However a number of writers – particu-larly from a political economic perspective – tend to argue precisely that that globalization has produced an homogenous global gay culture. John Tomlinson argues that globalization shatters the neatly bounded categories of analysis such as the economic, the political and the cultural, and I agree with him. This contrasts with Dennis Altman's approach. Altman makes a clear distinction between each of these elements of globalization, and how each impacts on sexualities. For Altman this is a one-way street: global capitalism is driving globalization forward. Sexualities are produced by capital – they are the outcomes of globalizing processes. The control of non-productive sex and promotion of commodified desire is fundamental to late capitalism, as Donald Lowe (1995) has argued.

Sexuality is commonly seen as synonymous with the local scale – a natural essence impacted upon by global capital. Sexualities are still seen as secondary to the forces of global capital, but it is increasingly impossible to understand global consumption practices (for example) without referring to sexuality and desire. Here there is a danger that sexuality is seen as residing within the intimate sphere of the 'home'. Intimacy is seen as the natural, authentic state where one goes to escape the contaminants of global capitalism, yet as Massey has pointed out, the domestic sphere is witness to oppression; for instance for those affected by domestic violence, the home is a prison, rather than escape (Massey, 1993). Spatial scale is significant because scaling phenomena helps frame what is important and what is not. Often the global scale annihilates other scales such as the body (Smith, 1993). That is why in a sense the global should be treated with some caution by students of sexuality – because it has traditionally been framed in such a way as to trivialize sexual cultures. If Judith Butler (1997) argues that political economists have tended to treat sexuality as a 'merely cultural' phenomenon, then perhaps is it not also the case that those studying globalization have, in their ignorance of sexuality, treated it as 'merely local'?

Locating the Global Gay

Gay men the world over live similar lives and dream similar dreams. The poet WH Auden invented a word for this international homo-culture, 'homintern', meaning the life experiences and innate personality traits that connect gays more closely with gays from other countries than with the heterosexual citizens of their own country, or even their own family. I know I often feel closer to a gay foreigner I've known for five minutes than to heterosexual relations I've known all my life. (Allen, 1996)

As James Allen's statement suggests, the notion that lesbians and gay men across national borders share a common identity and sense of solidarity has a very particular appeal to many. Among erstwhile progressive lesbians and gay men the connection that is felt with lesbians and gay men elsewhere has shaped, for instance, transnational activism, such as when lesbians and gay men in The Netherlands organised and offered support in the campaign against Section 28 in the United Kingdom. A strong disidentification with one's own citizens has characterized many radical elements of lesbian, gay and queer politics and movements. This in turn has helped shape anti-nationalism, and pacifism within these movements. The notion of a common

37

gay identity has been defended by some commentators on queer globalization. For instance, Peter Drucker rejects a postmodern view of sexual identities as fluid, insisting on the commonality of a gay identity. He rejects the notion that it is Eurocentric to criticize Robert Mugabe's persecution of gays in Zimbabwe:

> We can see that LGBTs in the world today, in all our enormous diversity, have converged enough to have a real commonality of identity. This constitutes an objective basis for solidarity in our oppression and in our struggles, past and present, and an objective claim on the solidarity of others. (2000: 37)

However at the same time, the notion of a common identity and bond between lesbians and gays has become as unsustainable as notions of global sisterhood among feminists. The assimilationist tendencies of mainstream and conservative lesbian and gay politics mean that in many national polities, lesbians and gay men may be less likely to disidentify with the nation. While there has been a globalization of 'coming out', Sonia Katyal notes that: 'The recent emergence of gay or lesbian-identified individuals across the globe have created complex ruptures in existing social fabrics, calling into question the universality of legal constructs involving sexuality and culture' (2002: 174).

This has led to considerable debate about whether a global gay subject exists, and if so, how it can be characterized. If one accepts there is a common gay identity, what does it consist of? Who is included and excluded from within this identity? Who is the Other of this global gay identity? To what extent does the the development of gay movements in societies as diverse as Botswana, Thailand and Bolivia represent simply the diffusion, or more sinisterly, the imposition of Anglo-American queer sexual norms, identities and cultures? Speaking of the development of lesbian and gay movements in countries as diverse and different as Liberia, South Korea, Bangladesh and Egypt, Peter Drucker argues that these movements should not be seen as mimicking or copying similar, more established movements in Europe and North America. He argues that these movements should be supported, as they are often isolated in combating the oppressive policies of politicians within their own countries (1996: 93).

Does the development of the global gay reflect an evolutionary model of modernity whereby less developed countries are on an escalator of development that will eventually lead to the recognition of lesbian and gay rights as the end point of modernity, as a final stage of development? What is the connection between identity, rights and citizenship? The strategic essentialism implicit within a common gay identity may be a necessity for recognition by the state. To what extent does striving to achieve modern gay rights reflect a denial of indigenous or folk forms of sexuality? Are indigenous configurations of the relationship between sex acts and identities (such as bofes in Brazil and bakla in Thailand) which are seen as not modern, seen as impediments towards national development strategies to be part of the modern international community? To what extent does the official sanctioning and promotion of certain forms of sexual dissident identity and practice reflect other markers of identity such as race, class and gender? In this context which models of sexuality get to be seen as authentic? How should we conceptualize the development of movements for lesbian and gay rights and the establishment of solidarities and communities within less developed countries? It would indeed be unfortunate to see these as some form of false consciousness, or merely as a result of Anglo-American cultural imperialism. Chong Kee Tan speaks of hybridization whereby selected elements of gay culture and politics have been adopted from the US, but domesticated by Taiwanese tongzhi to form a hybrid sexual culture and politics that cannot be reduced to a simplistic notion of a common global gay identity (2001: 124). Tan is also correct to point out that 'there is no singular American homosexuality – it is fractured by geography, race, gender, class, and so on' (ibid.: 124). Is the strive for gay liberation simply a striving for worldliness or an aspirational cosmopolitanism – or merely a reflection of class distinction within these societies? For instance in the Taiwanese context, Fran Martin's discussion of queer counterpublics in Taipei demonstrates complex configurations of the local and the global. Transformations in Taiwanese sexual citizenship have led to tacit support for tongzhi identity and relationships as a marker of Taiwan's ambition to be seen as a sophisticated developed society and part of the international community. Is therefore the development of movements for gay liberation simply a form of false consciousness and class distinction whereby the upper classes within these societies aspire to be American? Oliver Phillips argues that these movements are significant in their own right and should be seen as vital in providing support in milieu where sexual dissidents are marginalized and oppressed:

> These 'gay/lesbian' names for identities might originate in North America and western Europe, but they have been appropriated by people the world over as they imply a claim to the protection and rights guaranteed under international treaties, and a way out of an almost universal form of marginalization. (2000: 34)

Drucker argues against the view that the development of lesbian and gay liberation movements in the developing world can simply be seen as a result of the diffusion of activist strategies from the West. He suggests the AIDS crisis and the development of links with other indigenous Left-oriented activist groups has been as significant as links with western lesbian and gay groups (1996: 96).

Dennis Altman is probably the one scholar who, more than most, has put questions of globalization to the fore in studies of sexuality. Dennis Altman's (1996a) online essay on global queering stimulated considerable debate about the topic and provoked heated exchanges and a number of replies (e.g. Lane, 1996; Halperin, 1996; Tan, 1996). Further essays (1996b, 1997, 1999), together with his book *Global Sex* established an agenda for the debate on the subject. Altman does come from a very particular theoretical line, for instance suggesting three main ways in which processes of globalization have affected sexualities – economic, cultural and political:

> Economic changes mean that sexuality is increasingly commodified, whether through advertising or prostitution, which, as in the nineteenth century, is closely linked to economic dislocation and change. Cultural changes mean that certain ideas about behaviour and identity are widely dispersed, so that new ways of understanding oneself become available that often conflict bitterly with traditional mores ... And the political realm will determine what forms are available for sexual expression, so that there is a far more overt 'gay' world in Manila than in Singapore, despite the considerable gap in wealth, in part because of different political regimes. (1999: 563)

Altman implies that economic globalization impacts upon sexualities, but not the other way around. He introduces his *Social Text* essay by discussing the proliferation of images drawn from western gay consumer culture in Manila. He argues that: 'in the distinction between the image and the reality lies much of the paradox of the apparent globalization of postmodern gay identities' (1997: 77). Altman (1997: 86) advances a political economic perspective on sexual cultures: 'We cannot discuss the development of modern forms of sexual identity independent of other shifts, which at first glance may not be directly relevant'. I agree with Altman that many of the issues and debates that surround 'non-western' sexualities are applicable to those in the west. Altman concludes his essay on the impact of globalization on sexual identities by arguing that while new sexual identities are being forged outside of the west, the differences in sexual cultures between the west and elsewhere should not be overstated. Moreover, as Chong Kee Tan (among others) has stated, western gay culture should not be seen as a homogenous entity. However, where I take issue with Altman is in his treatment of queer politics, culture and theory. In theorizing the global gay, Altman is severely critical of queer theory, and its relevance for discussing the globalization of sexual dissidence. Queer theory has been criticized for allegedly having nothing to contribute towards the analysis of the global dimension and the social and material. For instance, in the review of the proposal for this book, one referee doubted queer's enduring quality. Queer is seen as troubling, lacking a real political agenda – lacking substance. Thus in some quarters it is criticized for not having academic respectability and weightiness. However, queer is seen elsewhere as having 'sold out', and been safely assimilated into the academic mainstream. In his reply to Altman's paper, David Halperin (1996: 4) argues that the disruptive potential of queer has become assimilated into the mainstream of academic production as queer theory: 'far from posing a radical challenge to current modes of thought, queer theory is in the process of becoming a game the whole family can play'. For Halperin, queer is not being 'in your face' or offensive enough, as opposed to being too offensive. However I believe that we do need to queer globalization, because thus far debates on globalization continue to take place as if sexuality was completely marginal to economic and political processes. We need to explore the relationship between sexual desire and political economy. Particularly if we consider Christopher Lane's pointed question: 'What, for instance, is so compelling about the queer model of desire that numerous lesbians and gay men in different countries have received it with a kind of avidity Altman finds galling?' (1996: 1). Altman lambasts queer culture and politics for supposedly revelling in consumption, for being pro-capitalist and failing to offer a critique of capitalism, celebrating its sexually liberating potential instead. It is thus intriguing how Altman (1997: 77) defines the queer as the following:

> He-sometimes, though less often, she-is conceptualized in terms that are very much derived from recent American fashion and intellectual style: young, upwardly mobile, sexually adventurous, with an in-your-face attitude toward traditional restrictions and an interest in both activism and fashion.

Altman is vehement in his paternalist hostility to queer theory – he describes queer studies as: 'the bastard child of the gay and lesbian movement and postmodern literary theory' (1996: 5). He also caricatures queer theory and is offhand in his complete dismissal of it (1996: 6). In particular he points to the convoluted theoretical language used by writers working in this area, arguing that: 'this theory is almost totally ignored by the vast majority of people whose lives it purports to describe'. While Altman is surely right to point towards elitism within some elements of queer theory, and is correct to suggest there is a gulf between queer academe and the everyday lives and experiences of lesbians and gay men, surely this criticism could be equally levelled at any form of academic enquiry. Much writing from a Marxist perspective is no less opaque than queer theory. Some writing in queer theory has been written in such a way out of a need to legitimate the subject as a serious focus of academic enquiry. For Altman moreover, queer is conceived as being pro rather than anti-capitalist: 'The United States is so consumer-defined that the gay movement was quickly co-opted and turned into an interest group and a niche market (with gay resistance

41

increasingly expressed in aesthetic terms – queer rather than anti-capitalist)' (1997: 85). Altman posits a sexual politics, which moralistically rejects the commercial gay scene, yet the relationship between the gay left and the commercial scene is a long and troubled one, marked by elitism, class hatred, and phobic representations of hedonism. Hedonism is seen as a form of false consciousness and anti-pathetical to some communitarian notion of authentic community untainted by vulgar pleasures of the body. Despite the criticism of Altman's notion of the global gay, there is also considerable support for his standpoint. For instance in *Different Rainbows*, Peter Drucker (2000: 36) argues that: 'measured by Third World standards, Altman's charge that American "queer theory" remains as relentlessly Atlantic-centric in its view of the world as the mainstream culture it critiques' seems valid'. Altman's work has been valuable in bringing questions of globalization to the fore within lesbian and gay studies. He has also sought to bring back issues of social and economic inequality into queer perspectives on sexuality that have sometimes been guilty of being esoteric and lacking relevance. I am concerned however with how we integrate the social and economic into lesbian and gay studies without lapsing into reductionism or moralistic denigration of the erotic. I hope to tread this line carefully in the next section on cyberqueer spaces as these are spaces which have provoked both moral panic and utopian statements about their transgressive nature.

Globalization and Virtual Communities

Technological change is helping to drive the processes of globalization (Franklin, Lury, Stacey, 2000). For sexual dissidents the virtual is an important aspect of globalized sexualities. David Gauntlett argues that sexual dissidents have been at the forefront of experimenting with the possibilities of cyberspace in helping to forge new identities through queer virtual communities. While noting the proliferation of millions of websites, he suggests that: 'the gay, lesbian, bi, transgendered and other anti-gender communities were ahead of the game here' (1999: 327). Cyberspace offers the utopian prospect of escape and self-realization, a means of experimenting with sexual identity and searching for community. It offers the prospect of being elsewhere, escaping the confinement of heterosexuality. Cyberspace is particularly significant for students of globalization and sexuality as it brings into sharp focus the 'here' and the 'elsewhere'. Cyberspace collapses spatial scales – it is where the global is most approximate, most intimate. To what extent does cyberspace render the notion of scale obsolete? In his discussion of globalization, technology and sexuality, John Tomlinson has a very particular notion of intimacy, arguing that: 'the sexual act is intimate knowledge of the Other, combining physical with psychological closeness and bonding. Understood thus, intimacy is the antithesis of distanciation' (1999: 161).

There is a lot to unpack in this quote. Firstly the assertion that the sexual act is an all-embracing act involving 'knowledge of the Other', a one-ness and coming together, when in fact many sex acts involve a partial knowledge of the Other, a fetishism of the Other. How much sex is better for not knowing the Other? Sex can take place as recreational sport; sex can take place without close psychological bonding and without emotion. Problematically, Tomlinson sets up an opposition between the domestic sphere vis-à-vis the public sphere. For sexual dissidents this public–private distinction has been particularly difficult – bound up with the notion of the closet. To what extent can sexuality be seen as residing within the sphere of the domestic when increasingly the public–private distinction has been made meaningless with Operation Spanner (Bell, 1995a, 1995b) and the Bolton 7 (Moran, 1999)? Could it be that the increasing recognition of the right to privacy marks the assimilation of the more respectable marketized aspects of middle-class gay identity? Tomlinson is open to the possibilities of new media technologies facilitating new forms of intimacy. However the net, like the telephone before it, has been represented as a threat to the sanctity of bourgeois middle-class respectable family life. Unfortunately, Tomlinson demonstrates squeamishness when it comes to discussing the erotic possibilities of technology. He suggests a hierarchy of forms of intimacy with the more commercialized forms being seen as less authentic, less intimate, arguing that: 'it would be difficult to find a stronger example of the essential deficit of telemediated intimacy than that of commercial telephone sex' (1999: 163). The implication from Tomlinson's discussion of intimacy is that he sees certain forms of telemediated intimacy as being more valuable and more respectable than others. There are links here with the discussion of respectability from the previous chapter, specifically the production of class distinction. There are correct, respectable, acceptable uses of technology for Tomlinson; those that he sanctions involve the (re)production of the cosy nuclear family. Moreover, Tomlinson makes a highly problematic distinction between intimacy and sexuality:

Furthermore, it might be objected that it is misleading to allow the theme of sexuality to dominate the idea of intimacy. For the sort of 'innerness' that is associated with the close, but not sexualized, relations of family life might provide just as promising a model. A good example of the stretching of this sort of intimacy can be seen in the use of video-conferencing technologies to unite spatially divided families. (1999: 164)

Tomlinson's argument suggests a hierarchy of valued forms of intimacy with some being seen as more authentic than others. For instance consider his disdainful comparison of telephone sex to prostitution outside of the respectable middle-class family. Here we can make a link with the discussion of class, respectability, nationalism and sexuality in the previous chapter. Could not the threat posed by the Internet to the values and morals of the middle-class family become crystallized in controlling access to the net within the family? What counts as authentic intimacy is policed by Tomlinson, for instance in his discussion comparing appropriate, respectable and inappropriate use of the technology of the phone: 'maybe telephone (or CMC) sex could be a more joyous and intimate imaginary encounter where it is practised in a consensual, non-commercial context between two "real" lovers' (1999: 164). In Tomlinson's hierarchy of sex, there is authentic, natural sex that may take place on the phone between real lovers, and there is grubby telephone sex, which takes place within a system of exchange and is therefore labelled as commodified. Tomlinson makes a distinction between unreal commercialized sex and natural, real, authentic love. The relationship between sex and commerce is discussed by Ellis Hanson in his essay 'The telephone and its queerness', in which discussing Susan Sontag's disdain for telephone sex he discerns:

> a more widespread panic about the relationship of sex to commerce. There is an assumption running rampant in our midst that sex can be cordoned off as some sort of transcendent phenomenon, a pure expression of nature that is, or ought to be, innocent of politics and commercial exchange. This edenic illusion seeks to deny the myriad ways in which commercial organization and libidinal organization tend to complement each other, whether one is having sex in a real bedroom or a virtual one. (1995: 34–5)

Hanson warns against cordoning off the sexual as essentially natural, existing outside of politics and systems of exchange. As I argued earlier, the temptation to protect and defend some notion of a private, intimate sphere untainted by commerce appears to be a particularly attractive one in some writing on globalization. In my discussion of Doreen Massey's approach to the domestic sphere and globalization it is the case that the home can come to represent a safe haven, an oasis from the turbulence of global insecurities. The Internet has become a source of cultural anxiety as it threatens to collapse distinctions between the global and the intimate spheres. However, many sexual dissidents have embraced the potential of the new technology. Nina Wakeford notes the hyperbole surrounding the utopian queer possibilities offered by the net within much of the writing on the subject, suggesting the endless possibilities for queer self transformation and realization:

The message, from eulogizing testimonies of on-line experiences in popular print media such as *Gay Times, Diva, The Advocate, The Pink Paper, Girlfriends,* to anecdotal tales of love found or lost in electronic encounters, is that anyone who has not yet encountered the worlds of cyberspace cannot know the wonders which await them: the realization of global community! The remaking of queer identity! The discovery that whichever subculture of a subculture you inhabit there will be a Web page, or discussion group, or real-time chat room just for your kind! (2000: 403–4)

Wakeford though is keen to caution against getting carried away with the hyperbole around the net as a space of freedom for sexual dissidents. She argues that access is the key concern. She comments on a guide to the Internet for lesbians and gay men, in which parallels are drawn between lesbian and gay tourism and uses of cyberspace. There is a synergy between tourism and the net as the latter offers easy access to a maze of images and information about potential tourist destinations. Both tourism and the Internet share a key role in the transmission of queer sexual culture. I think there are clear parallels between lesbian and gay tourism and queer cyber-cultures. In her essay 'cyberqueer' Nina Wakeford comments on some of the publications and guides to the net produced for a lesbian and gay read-ership. Intriguingly the subtitle of one such guide is 'The Travel Guide to Digital Queerdom on the Internet' At the start of his guide Dawson makes the link between tourism and the net explicit:

If you have ever stepped off the ferry on to Fire Island or pulled into Provincetown or any other gay and lesbian enclave, you know the feeling. It's as if a desert dweller had walked through a magical wall into lush tropics. The natives seem exotic and utterly normal. That's what this book is, a door opening into a world where gays and lesbians are the natural majority. (Dawson, 1996: 1, quoted in Wakeford, 2000: 404)

There is a real sense of an insider group being created here, a feeling that you should know what it is like to step off the ferry on to Fire Island. Fire Island is associated with exclusivity and social climbing. It is hardly a tourist destination that can be said to be mainstream or accessible to all. Of course that is the point – the sense of entitlement associated with privilege. Exclusivity may make destinations like these all the more desirable to many of those who cannot afford to go there. The net offers the promise of a secure identity – of a homeland (see the discussion of diaspora in Chapter 5). Wakeford (2000: 404) argues that: 'The key manoeuvre is his suggestion that entering cyberspace can be compared to arriving in an existing place where not only will we feel at home, but we are even the "natural" majority'. Wakeford argues that the hyperbole of Dawson's guide should not blind us to the broader social and economic issues surrounding both the production and consumption of queer online spaces. The economic inequalities that condition access to this technology get overlooked in the rush to acclaim the utopian possibilities of queer cyberspaces. Beyond the economic limitations and constraints on access, there is also the question of language. There is linguistic hegemony within cyberspace and queer online communities clearly reflect this. The ability to speak English is a precursor or given within many online communities and thus renders these spaces exclusive. The Internet however has created new erotic and social possibilities for the sexual margins. Daniel Tsang argues that for some gay men the net has revolutionized their relationship to the commercial scene: 'Personally, I can't tell you how long it has been since I have been to a gay bar, except to pick up gay magazines; like numerous others, electronic cruising has replaced bar hopping' (1996: 155). The technology itself may be a barrier, however. It is certainly an economic barrier. It helps younger gay men and lesbians explore their sexuality in a way unimaginable to men of my generation whose first fumblings and explorations were through gay porn on the top shelf of newsagents, or cottaging and cruising areas. The question of age barriers is significant. While their age prevents them from entering gay bars, Tsang (1996) notes that the Internet may provide a more easily accessible way for younger gay men to explore and experiment with their sexuality. He is optimistic that bulletin boards create a space for Asians and Pacific Islanders to explore and affirm their sexualities (1996: 161). The Internet facilitates queer self-recognition – the feeling that there is someone out there just like me. Whereas in the past this sense of recognition would be mediated through the press and television programmes, increasingly it is mediated through the net. For instance Michael Tan notes:

> I celebrate global queering for the ways it creates space for us in the Philippines. I am reminded of Richard Fung's essay where he describes himself growing up, an 'Asian' in Trinidad and seeing, one day, in the newspapers 'Gay Liberation' as a caption to a photograph of two men hugging 'in front on a statue somewhere in America': 'I had seen the word and I knew that it was to me that it referred'. My yuppie friends have many similar stories, seeing 'the word' in a newspaper or magazine. Today, some young middle-class Filipino adolescent surfing the net will inevitably find QueerNet or GayWeb or even Kakasarian, a Filipino gay website based in the States and know too. (1996: 1)

While ever aware of the socio-economic inequalities associated with unequal access to the new media technologies such as the net, Nina Wakeford embraces the queer utopian possibilities of cyberspace. She argues that cyberqueer spaces constitute a resistance to heterosexism and heteronormativity. Interestingly Wakeford (2000: 410) argues that cyberspace may provide a possibility of escape from more tightly policed lesbian and gay spaces and that cyberqueer discussion lists may be: 'an important "space of refuge" from other lesbian, gay, transgender and queer worlds, some of which are themselves on-line'. The net may reinforce inequalities or further distinctions between queers. As Wakeford intimates, online queer worlds can be as restrictive as offline ones – for instance the policing of who is a lesbian within lesbian chat-rooms. It can also reinforce the notion of distance, when for example the horny prospective sexual partner is on the other side of the world. As Rob Kitchin (1998) has demonstrated there is a real geography to the Internet and its use, and a real inequality in terms of who uses it and where they reside. Wakeford is quick to point out that global capital has not provided the net out of benevolence to the queer underground and community, but rather to make profits, as an attempt to: 'capitalize on the corporate construction of the lesbian and gay consumer' (2000: 410). In order to produce a more inclusive queer cyber citizenship, Wakeford argues that these issues around the inequalities of access must be addressed, though she does not provide much indication of how this redistribution of resources might happen. She suggests that if participation in cyberspace is seen as a citizenship practice, we must pay attention to the specific ways these are shaped within cyberqueer communities. At the same time we must address the social exclusion of those who are barred from participating within these online communities and are thus excluded from this citizenship practice. Wakeford's work hints at the possibility of a nuanced approach to globalization and sexuality, one that embraces the erotic potential of new technologies at the vanguard of the current phase of globalization, while at the same time being carefully attuned to the need for more equitable and socially just queer cyberspaces. The moralism here is not a knee-jerk reaction to the use of technology for erotic purposes, but a wish to see greater access to the technology so that more can participate in the social worlds and queer communities of cyberspace.

In an essay on queer uses of technology, Ellis Hanson states that: 'phone sex allows for the promiscuity and anonymity often attributed to queer sexuality' (1995: 36). Hanson examines the intimacy of queer phone sex in the context of the AIDS pandemic, asking:

> To what extent is the telephone a radical reassertion of queer pleasure in the time of AIDS? Phone sex may be an act of mourning for an idealized sexual freedom rumoured to have now disappeared; on the other hand, it may be a refusal to mourn and a challenge to the validity of the loss itself. The telephone calls up an electrical space that becomes a queer space, a new space of sexual play and sexual imagination. (1995: 44–5)

Hanson draws attention to the telephone as enabling queer pleasure to be produced against the context of the AIDS pandemic, but it is the technologies of the Internet that have really transformed the queer world, providing new electronic spaces for queer sexual citizenship. There are many analogies between HIV and AIDS and the net, for instance the net as viral form of communication, the most common and banal, everyday experience of being infected by viruses transmitted by email. Likewise there is the issue of censorship, and the dystopian realities of the net. Daniel Tsang is thus right to draw attention to the fiction of online privacy. Interestingly he argues that queer users of cyberspace should treat online encounters much the way they should treat prospective sexual partners: 'Like the HIV status of your electronic mate, don't be deluded. Play safe: treat every message as public, and every sexual partner as HIV positive. The BBS challenges traditional notions of privacy and obscures the lines between private and public' (1996: 154–5).

In this section I have examined queer globalization through the focus on queer cyberspace. I have argued that cyberspace has been particularly attractive for queers. New technologies have been at the centre of moral panics over their use for erotic purposes. We see this with the telephone, and my discussion of Hanson's work on the queerness of the telephone demonstrates parallels with the way in which contemporary new media have been treated. As David Gauntlett (1999) has argued queers have been at the forefront of experimentation with this technology and have forged queer spaces online. I have examined the liberatory potentialities and actualities of queer cyberspace in helping young and isolated queers overcome spatial separation and help to forge friendships and relationships without ever having to step into a gay bar. Queer cyberspace also enables specialization and the evolution of new groups as in Daniel Tsang's discussion of bulletin boards to help forge online communities of Pacific Islanders. However, queer cyberspace reflects the social and economic inequalities of the off-line world and Nina Wakeford's research has shown that such spaces exclude on the basis of restricted access to the technology, and also the cultural linguistic hegemony of the English language. Gender is a critical factor in determining the nature and experience of queer cyberspaces, and framing the ability to participate in the development of cyberqueer spaces (Wakeford, 2002: 138).

Conclusion

In this chapter I have argued that with a few exceptions, mainstream accounts of globalization within social theory have tended to ignore sexuality altogether. Within recent years, lesbian and gay studies has embraced the question of globalization as a solution to the impasse in which the relatively young intellectual field of lesbian and gay studies had found itself after the upsurge in creativity and publication witnessed in the early 1990s had subsided somewhat by the end of the decade. The growth of interest in globalization reflects a growing critique of the ethnocentricity of lesbian and gay studies. It also constitutes an intellectual response to criticism of the lack of a material, social and economic critical edge within queer theory. Queer theory had been seen as guilty of ignoring bigger political and economic questions. Dennis Altman has been the scholar who has done the most to champion the study of the globalization of sexualities and has been the most successful in establishing the topic on the agenda of lesbian and gay studies. Having said this, his work has been subject to widespread criticism. In this chapter I have argued that Altman's work is highly problematic in its rather simplistic take on all matters queer and queer consumer culture in particular. Altman's approach towards the commercial gay scene is almost pathological in its representation of gay consumers as passive dupes of the capitalist system. My discussion of queer uses of cyberspace demonstrates the limitations of Altman's ways of thinking through globalization of sexualities. I have argued that there were opportunities to develop a much more nuanced approach, for instance through Nina Wakeford's analysis of queer communities in cyberspace, that acknowledges queer agency while recognizing the structural inequalities in terms of who can participate within these communities. This chapter demonstrates the urgent need to conceptualize the relationship between sexual dissidence and economics. I turn my attention to this in the next chapter.

4

The Economics of Queer Globalization

While economic transnationalism has been embraced by some as a liberating force – usually those who are well off, educated, and mobile – for most people the future is filled with economic and social insecurity. As a consequence, nations and citizens look to sexuality for certainty in a changing world. An appeal to the heterosexual nuclear family becomes an anchor to grab in an increasingly confusing 'new' world order. Carl Stychin, *A Nation By Rights*. (1998)

The interrogation of a transnational queer rhetoric demands a more materialist queer theory than we currently possess. John Champagne, *Transnationally Queer?* (1999)

A central theme in this chapter is the tension between the cultural and the economic. As I argued in the previous chapter, globalization threatens the neat compartmentalization of phenomena into spheres of the social, economic, cultural and the political. In this chapter I seek to examine the economics of the production of sexual identities, cultures and communities as this is imperative if we are to construct the sort of materialist queer thinking that John Champagne is calling for. I start by discussing the relationship between sexuality, production and consumption. I then critique discourses of the pink economy and examine examples of globalized gay consumer culture. I then proceed to examine the specifics of the impact of globalization on a Europeanised sexual politics. In doing so, I aim to tease out the wider connections between sexual identities and communities and macro-economic structures and actors.

Queering Political Economy

I want to begin this section by referring to the exchange that took place between Judith Butler and Nancy Fraser on whether the oppression of lesbians and gay men is 'merely cultural'. Fraser argues that there are material inequalities that are firmly rooted in the political economic sphere associated with the politics of redistribution. She contrasts this with cultural inequalities associated with the politics of recognition. Fraser uses gay politics as an example of the politics of recognition rather than of redistribution. She appears to imply that lesbians and gay men primarily suffer cultural marginalization as opposed to economic disadvantage. According to Fraser, the oppression of lesbians and gay men is primarily cultural rather than economic. After discussing some of the attempts by American multinationals to introduce gay friendly workplace policies, Nancy Fraser argues that this is evidence of the notion that lesbians and gay men do not constitute a specific threat to the contemporary capitalist mode of production. This leads to a confirmation or proof of her position that: 'the economic disabilities of homosexuals are better understood as effects of heterosexism in the relations of recognition than as hardwired in the structure of capitalism' (1997: 285). The theorizing of the link between culture and economics has a particular urgency for lesbians, gay men and queers as discrimination against lesbians and gay men is routinely cast as cultural rather than economic. In writing on queer consumption and sexualized space (Binnie, 1995; 1997a; 2000) and in my work with David Bell (Bell and Binnie, 2000; 2002) I have been deeply ambivalent about these issues. In previous work on the subject, I have sought to challenge and explore the rather simplistic hedonistic and celebratory statements on queer consumption that see shopping as affirming and gay consumer culture as essentially liberatory. At the same time, I have sought to critique the problematic way in which sexuality is framed within debates on political economy. Gay men and lesbians do occupy a particular relationship to capitalism, but as John Champagne argues, this relationship is complex: 'gay subjects have a particularly vexing relationship to capitalism in that, while capitalism is one of the preconditions of a modern gay identity, it also works to "manage" that identity in its own interests, and often in opposition to those of real human beings' (1999: 150). Of course this does not mean that these are uniform categories of identity as I shall demonstrate later in this chapter. Differences of race, class and gender are fundamental in fracturing this relationship, for instance Danae Clark (1993) has critiqued the commodification and domestication of lesbian iconography within mainstream advertising and marketing.

While writers such as Michael Warner (1993) have long since criticised the heteronormativity of social theory and the left's attitude towards sexual politics, it is lamentable that commentators such as Slavoj Žižek continue this tradition. Consider this excerpt from his essay in *New Left Review* on multiculturalism as the logic of late capitalism, in which he argues that:

> Critical energy has found a substitute outlet in fighting for cultural differences, which leave the basic homogeneity of the capitalist world-system intact. So we are fighting our PC battles for the rights of ethnic minorities, of gays and lesbians, of different life-styles, and so on, while capitalism pursues its triumphant march-and today's critical theory, in the guise of 'cultural studies', is doing the ultimate service to the unrestrained development of capitalism by actively participating in the ideological effort to render its massive presence invisible. (1997: 46)

Žižek appears to target cultural criticism for abandoning any critique of late capitalism. He seems to be blaming struggles for the rights of minorities for deflecting critical attention away from the 'real' enemy – contemporary capitalism. After reading Žižek one might despair of the possibility of forging a critically queer perspective on contemporary global capitalism. He argues that the ever-increasing plurality of political struggles serves to displace critical attention from global capitalism. Does Žižek's argument mean that asserting plurality and difference within struggles for sexual citizenship necessarily means a devaluing or downgrading of critical attention on economics and material inequalities in capitalist societies? Sometimes it can be really depressing reading Žižek – especially when he presents an argument in a rather cut-and-dried fashion: the choice between nationalism, totalitarianism or the cosmopolitan liberal free market. The polarization of the debate between those who promote political economic perspectives on sexuality but who are hostile towards contemporary queer intellectual, political and consumer culture (Hennessy, 2000; Altman, 1999), and those who have come to constitute a queer 'establishment' which in recent years has tended to completely marginalize questions of class, economics and redistribution, is particularly irksome for those who argue that both positions are to a certain extent 'establishment' or class-based positions. This is a problem for those who feel neither 'position' or grouping adequately reflects where they are coming from. There are basically two different intellectual camps defending established territories within academia. Roger Lancaster argues that the trivialization of homophobia within Marxism as marginal to production means that: 'With good reason feminists, gays, and lesbians have largely rejected orthodox Marxist attempts to understand gender relations, sexism and homophobia as cultural glosses on economic production' (1997: 195). However, he maintains that that there is a danger of throwing the baby out with the bathwater if political economy is rejected out of hand. If we are to try to construct the bigger picture of how sexual politics are interconnected with wider economic and political structures, arguing that feminists, lesbians and gays: 'have also sometimes less validly dismissed approaches from political economy as "totalizing metanarratives" or discarded "grand theories"' (ibid: 195). Lancaster sums up the tension between political economy and culture in Marxist approaches to sexuality. The main issue, though, is how we resolve the assertion of the sexual without jeopardizing other forms of equality and difference and sidelining the economic altogether. For instance, Anne Phillips suggests that in contemporary society: 'equality is now thought to be a matter of politics or culture as much as (if not more than) one of the distribution of economic resources' (1999: 20). Can the reassertion of the economic add weight and conceptual clarity to the analysis of sexual citizenship? Or must an approach that places economics at the centre necessarily marginalize sexuality, as has often been the case on the left in the past? Phillips argues that: 'The hegemonic status of difference in contemporary social and political thought can make it very difficult to talk about class' (1999: 42). While difference may be hegemonic, some differences are more hegemonic than others. It would be unfortunate if this view fogged the current landscape of sexual citizenship. It is increasingly clear that race, class and gender are becoming central to debates on inclusion and exclusion within sexual communities. Anne Phillips (1999) rails against dominant discourses of difference for neglecting class. In terms of globalization and the politics of transnationalism, there are studies that thoughtfully manage to interconnect the cultural and the economic. Aihwa Ong's *Flexible Citizenship* provides an excellent example of how to marry the cultural and economic in narrating and investigating transnational flows. At the start of her book she notes how researchers in different disciplines have approached globalization in their subject-specific ways with economists focusing more on global business strategies and anthropologists more concerned with understanding diasporic flows of people. Ong, however, is keen to avoid a dualism between culture and economics and stresses how they are interconnected. A political economic view often serves to neglect questions of agency, yet for Ong the questions of motivation and agency are crucial to an understanding of transnational migrations: 'flexibility, migration, and relocations, instead of being coerced or resisted, have become practices to strive for rather than stability' (1999: 19). So migration is not simply an effect of global restructuring, but is also the result of agency and of desire. Of course it is one of the truisms of social theory's engagement with globalization that it is too vast a subject for one discipline or subject to lay claim to. Globalization resists neat compartmentalization into the economic, political and the cultural, for it is precisely one of the key elements of globalization that these are inextricably interlinked. It is imperative therefore that discussions of sexuality and economics acknowledge this. In *Globalization and Culture* John Tomlinson argues that: 'globalization therefore matters for culture in the sense that it brings the negotiation of cultural experience into the centre of strategies or intervention in the other realms of connectivity: the political, the environmental, the economic' (1999: 30–1). Ong's work is significant in the way she conceptualizes culture and economies as mutually constitutive, rather than in opposition. Tomlinson is keen to articulate the links between culture, economics and politics in a way that reinforces their interconnectivity and interdependence. While Altman stresses the political economic basis of globalization and reads off cultural changes as effects of globalizing economic processes, Tomlinson argues that culture is fundamental to globalization: 'culture also matters for globalization in this sense: that it marks out a symbolic terrain of meaning-construction as the arena for global political interventions' (1999: 27). However, he does not see the culture–globalization equation as a one-way street, emphasizing that globalization has had a major impact on the way in which we conceive culture, specifically the disconnection of the idea of culture from an attachment to a fixed locality.

Sexuality, Work and Queer Production

In her essay on the performativity of production and consumption, Miranda Joseph argues that: 'a critique of production needs to look at sign production as well as material production, at the performativity of production, at the circulation of social formations as well as at goods' (1998: 54). The interconnections of culture, politics and economy and how they have become sexualized have become an important focus in research on workplace identities. A considerable body of work has developed specifically on the performativity of production (Adkins, 2000; Adkins and Lury, 1999; Crang, 1994; Holliday, 1999, 2001; Holliday and Thompson, 2001; McDowell, 1995; McDowell and Court, 1994). The question of work and status have often been overlooked in discussions of globalization which focus on questions of consumption – for example, the focus on international tourism (though of course tourism is an industry in which people work). Before going on to discuss consumption, I want to focus on the sexual and queer politics of production. Anne Phillips argues that: 'the association of certain categories of people with certain categories of work has particularly profound effects on a society's status order, and even the most rigorous campaign of cultural revaluation is unlikely to make enough difference to this' (1999: 98). Sex work is one of the most obvious ways in which sexuality and work are interlinked and the one that has attracted the most critical attention. Some authors argue that work is becoming increasingly sexualized. It is impossible to ignore or omit sexuality from the world of work (for instance see Lisa Adkins [2000] discussion of sexualised workplaces). Her essay concerns the commodification of lesbianism and lesbian strategies for survival and self-development at work. Focusing on workers in the service sector she notes the possibilities and constraints for managing workplace performances. Some workers may thrive in work environments where they are able to perform multiple personae, however she argues that not all workers are in a position to do so:

> there are workers with different 'ascribed identities' and 'ascribed characteristics' who, it would seem by their very definition, are unable to play out multiple personae, be inventive in terms of their cultural performances at work and deconstruct true/false dichotomies in relation to their workplace 'selves'. (2000: 208)

In terms of sexual dissidents, we can see a distinction between those who are more able to play with their identity in the workplace and those who are not. Anna Marie Smith (1991; 1994) has drawn attention to the way in which the drawing of distinctions between respectable and deviant forms of sexual dissident identity was fundamental to British New Right discourse on sexuality. Likewise in terms of embodied work place performances of identity, we see a distinction between 'good' and 'bad' homosexuals. For instance in the service industry, those who fail to conform to the required embodied aesthetic may be doomed to failure. The ability to play the performance game at work determines the level of success and therefore wages. The inability to play the multiple personae game in the workplace is particularly acute for lesbians and gay men who may be subjected to harassment and discrimination. Discrimination in the workplace may account for the fact that lesbians and gay men, contrary to general perception, actually earn less than their heterosexual counterparts. Lesbian and gay affluence is one of the myths around the pink economy that has been eloquently taken apart by Lee Badgett (2001). In her book *Money, Myths and Change* she deconstructs the popular wisdom that lesbians and gay men are an economically privileged class within the United States. While deconstructing the notion of queer conspicuous consumption, Badgett's book is notable for the focus on production – specifically on lesbians and gay men not as active agents in the economy but as passive consumers. An excessive focus on queer consumption reproduces stereotypes of queers as affluent and makes invisible the role of lesbians' and gay mens' role as producers. Badgett provides careful critiques of American surveys that have claimed to demonstrate that lesbians and gay men earn more than their straight counterparts. Badgett argues that race and gender are more salient categories in terms of explaining the differences in income. White gay men earn more than white lesbians; both earn more than queers of colour. Having said this, Badgett argues that gay men on average earn less than straight men thereby confounding the notion of the affluent gay. Gay men living in couples are clearly likely to have greater disposable income than heterosexual couples because of gender differences, but this offers little consolation to the single lesbian or gay man. Badgett argues that gay men earn less than straights on average, due to anti-gay discrimination in the workplace, which may for instance make promotion more difficult for out gay men in organizations. Like Badgett, Russell Child has argued against the popularly held view that lesbians and gay men are more affluent than heterosexuals. Child argues that discrimination against lesbians and gay men in the workplace may prevent them earning the same salaries as their heterosexual counterparts. Even in terms of consumption Child argues that: 'some types of consumption are more expensive for consumers who are not part of a traditional heterosexual family unit' (1993: 172). Child's statement points to the complexity of the relationship between queer production and consumption. I have argued that this complexity is routinely ignored in hegemonic discourses of the pink economy that construct lesbians, but especially gay men as economically privileged consumer citizens. Felicity Grace's (1999) work on heteronormativity and credit points to the way in which economic decisions about lending are deeply imbued with heteronormative assumptions about who is a good credit risk. For instance, she points to the emphasis on stability of relationships as an important criterion in the way banks evaluate the credit risk of prospective borrowers. Moreover she acknowledges the impact of HIV testing and status on the ability to borrow. Grace notes how 'misreadings of gay relationships further reveal monogamy to be the other great link between heteronormativity and the provision of credit. Long-term repayment of large debts requires economic monogamy and fidelity' (1999: 443). While queers may face heteronormative values and assumptions in lending practices, it is also significant to note the selling of gay space. For instance take the notion that the development of gay villages is to do with the production of an experience of difference for consumption by straights. (In Chapter 8 I examine the development of 'gay villages' in more detail.) The production of gay villages is significant in producing in positive wealth-creating images to the wider society in order to facilitate assimilation into the mainstream. Gay entrepeneurialism represents a powerful material and symbolic counter to the homophobic notion that gays are associated with waste, death and trash – the view that gays are only passive consumers rather than active producers of wealth and thereby contributing to the wealth of the national economy. Smiegel (1995: 637) argues that: 'Peddling goods, services, and glitzy consumer signs, the gay community as business enterprise begins to sell itself as a product, pushing marketed images expansive enough to entertain, disseminate, and sell all sorts of imaginary contradictions'. The development of gay villages and the higher public profile of gay entrepreneurialism points attention to the role of queers in the creation of value more generally. As Smiegel points out homosexuals have been associated more with consumption, trash and trivia than production. Miranda Joseph argues that gay male sex is a form of 'social production', suggesting that:

> The anonymity and randomness of gay male sexual activity at certain points in gay history seem to me techniques that produce an imaginary expanse of identification, not unlike the newspaper in Benedict Anderson's *Imagined Communities*. This sexual activity has defined and claimed a variety of public places – certain streets, blocks, and parks, as well as bars and bathhouses – as gay communal space. (1998: 33)

This emphasis on social production is significant in the context of camp and death. Matthew Tinkcom (2002) stresses that homosexual camp is a form of queer labour and production. In homophobic discourses gay men have been pathologized as wasteful, as trash – associated with death, disease and the sewer. Gay men have been seen as wasteful, for instance consider the discourses on the profligacy and wastefulness of 'loony left' gay-supporting local authorities in Britain the late 1980s. Support for gay rights was often lambasted as wasteful of public money, hence the counter discourse that gays are an economically active and productive part of the community. Thus gay entrepreneurs play a much documented role in the processes of gentrification and the urban renaissance (Knopp, 1990; Lauria and Knopp, 1985).

In this section I have examined the place of queers in labour and production as a corrective to the notion that queers are simply consumers. There is a much more extensive academic and media debate about the role of queers in consumption and it is to this that I now turn.

The Myth of the Pink Economy

In earlier work on sexuality and consumption I argued that we must tread very carefully when examining gay consumer culture. I stated that we must be ever alert to the potential for homophobia within discourses that ascribe fixed characteristics to lesbians and gay men (Binnie, 1995). Writing about the development of the early 1990s Old Compton Street area in London I admitted by own ambivalence towards the commercial scene. Clearly such spaces of consumption afford possibilities for lesbians and gay men – they also offer employment opportunities for lesbians and gay men. But there is always the danger of representing lesbians and gay men as uniformly affluent and privileged. In terms of Doreen Massey's 'power-geometry' of time-space compression, we are commonly represented as leaders and in control of the processes – of the transnational flows (e.g. as international tourists, affluent consumers, rather than workers and producers of wealth). M V Lee Badgett has argued very powerfully for the critiquing of the hegemonic (and I would argue potentially homophobic) discourses on the pink economy. It is particularly imperative in terms of class and how class distinctions are made from both work and consumption practices. Badgett argues forcefully that gay and lesbian people come from all strata of society and are likely to be as poor as their heterosexual counterparts. The main economic difference between straights and sexual dissidents takes the form of discrimination in the workplace, which impacts on earnings. Badgett's work is significant in carefully critiquing the myth of affluence that characterizes popular and academic discourses on queer communities.

It would appear that this care is absent from some work on the economic basis of the global gay. The figure of the global gay tends to reproduce the old equation of globalization equals homogenization. The superficial appearance from, say, the Gay Games is that gay men and lesbians do indeed occupy a privileged position vis-à-vis the global economic system – but we need to look beneath the surface. Likewise the development of gay villages – commercial districts within cities targeted at lesbian and gay consumers (also significant sites for queer workers) should be treated with caution, particularly by those who have disdain for the vulgarity of commerce. It is clear that without these commercial territories, there would be far fewer possibilities for people to explore their sexuality and come out. As Jeffrey Escoffier argues: 'the visible existence of gay and lesbian communities is an important bulwark against the tide of reaction; the economic vitality of contemporary lesbian and gay communities erodes the ability of conservatives to reconstruct the closet' (1997: 131). There is also a clear class dimension to the pink economy and participation therein. For instance Allan Bérubé (1996) claims that he was excluded from the much of the Castro culture associated with the 'Golden Age' of the pre-AIDS San Francisco scene. Yet there is also a very marked class basis to resistances to the commercial scene. Some of the spaces that are presented as alternatives to the scene are themselves highly class-marked. For instance activism is commonly held up as a privileged site of engagement with a so-called non-commodified self and sexualized space, which, in its moral authority stands in opposition to the scene. Yet activism is not a class-neutral form of activity. Peter Cohen's essay on the class-basis of AIDS activism in New York City (Cohen, 1997), for example, argues that for many middle-class gay men in the city, AIDS meant a severe class dislocation. Commercial territories that are the visible, public manifestation of the pink economy elicit strong feelings of loyalty and ownership and pride on the one hand, and homophobia and hatred on the other. Many lesbians and gay men may also experience a sense of disidentification with these spaces and may feel excluded from them. In Chapter 8 I provide a more thorough examination of the political geography of the queer urban landscape. In this section I have argued that the pink economy myth has been damaging in cementing in the public imagination the view that lesbians and gay men form an economically privileged part of the population. The pink economy myths are particularly damaging when the dangerous assumptions contained within them are deployed to frame discussions of the economic basis of queer globalization. Having outlined and critiqued the myth of the pink economy and the role of sexual dissidents within production and consumption more generally, I now turn to examine the politics of class and consumption within queer globalization.

Class, Consumption and Queer Globalization

While the social-economic inequalities that frame access to the commercial scene are more obviously subject to criticism, this awareness is not always extended to discussions of activism. The class basis of sexual identities is recognised by Carl Stychin, who notes that movements for lesbian and gay law reform also reflect class distinction: 'it has been argued that the construction of sexual identities (and political priorities for a movement) historically has been shaped by the more privileged (in terms of social class) members of the group' (2000a: 293). In the previous chapter I noted that Dennis Altman tends to see the cultural, economic, social and political as separate (if related) spheres, with the cultural and political determined by the economic. He argues that globalization equals western imperialism and homogenization, and there is some support elsewhere for this equating of globalization with homogenization. There are considerable disidentifications with notions of 'gay identity' and the 'global gay', and this does have a class basis; for instance Alan Sinfield (1996: 272) suggests that: 'If you are lower-class, gay lobbying and lifestyle are less convenient and may seem alien'. David Evans (1993) argues that globalization equals homogenization in terms of international gay tourism. He claims that gay consumption territories have become so homogenized that they all resemble Greenwich Village or London's Earl's Court. There is also support for Altman's position from Bob Cant who claims that global gay culture risks becoming so commodified that it could resemble McDonalds in its homogenizing effects: 'What could emerge for the lesbian and gay communities is the spread of McPink – a global pink economy which promotes a series of ever-changing lifestyle options' (1997: 11). Cant's nightmare vision of a conformist globalized McPink, however, should be treated with caution. It is true that there are superficial similarities in queer consumer culture – specifically the gay bar and the gay shop, which look the same in different parts of the globe. However, the clientele in gay bars for instance may be very different, as could the way the spaces are used. Even leather bars and communities, which for David Evans symbolise a virile hypermasculinity

59

and the most commodifed form of queer sexual culture, demonstrate significant differences across the globe. For instance bars aimed at the macho/leather communities in New York are much more ethnically diverse compared to London, yet both are global cities. Leather bars in Amsterdam contain backrooms where sex on the premises is tolerated by the authorities. This is not the case elsewhere, for instance in London where bars have been shut down because the authorities refuse to tolerate such behaviour. Leather bars may superficially look the same, but this doesn't mean that these spaces are used in the same way. I therefore reject the notion that globalization means the homogenization of queer culture, and the view that cultural transformations are simply effects of economic processes. Queer cultures and communities are not simply being homogenized through globalization. Such a reductionist view neglects the question of agency and the specificity of place, as JK Gibson-Graham argues: 'a queer perspective can help to unsettle the consonances and coherences of the narrative of global commodification' (2001: 262). We need to redress the balance in queer commentaries on globalization by focusing on sexual dissidents as active producers and workers, not simply passive consumers as they are commonly represented in political economic accounts of queer consumption. Christopher Lane (1996) has argued that we cannot simply dismiss the desire of many sexual dissidents to embrace a global gay identity as a form of false consciousness.

Major global events such as The Gay Games and the Lesbian and Gay Mardi Gras in Sydney have played an important role in gay liberation, and have a symbolic importance. Such events have been notable in recent years. The success of these events and their economic value has attracted much media attention. Markwell (2002: 82) for instance quotes one estimate of AU$99m in money generated by the three week cultural festival in 1998. While such figures should always be treated with caution (as Badgett reminds us considering the degree of boosterism associated with any aspect of the pink economy) it nevertheless points to an awareness and acknowledgement of the economic value of the pink currency. In an earlier essay (Binnie, 1995), I argued that such an awareness did not always easily translate into tourist policies. For instance, a campaign by the Dutch to attract lesbian and gay visitors to Amsterdam in the early 1990s was seen as risky in terms of possibly damaging Amsterdam's attempts to change its image as an international sex and drugs capital and promote itself as a business-friendly city and a site for conventions and conferences. The campaign was withdrawn after these concerns. Frank Smiegel has argued that the producers of gay consumption districts and gay villages promote a sense of the universalism of gay culture. Such spaces are connected materially and symbolically to others across the globe and they promise a glocalized gay subject:

Following their own gay dollars, localized gay shopping districts promise a mobility beyond their borders: not only that their retail space will physically spread, but also that their AMEX-ed image will guarantee security and recognition the world over. Gay dollars tell us a story of tomorrow's sexual Utopia, not a place of liberated bodies and pleasures where 'love knows no boundaries,' but a time when the Mall of America wraps itself in rainbow flags as if to say 'Welcome Gay Shoppers.' Repackaged, homosexuality would occur in consumer society like any other corporate logo or brand name. And in our world of global capital, such name recognition demands a constant circulation and hard sell. Once incorporated, once test-marketed, the advertizing never stops. (1995: 637)

While Smiegel's discussion points towards the hegemony of the benevolence of gay entrepreneurialism, it is important to note that there are resistances to the notion of the global gay associated with mega-events. For instance some Dutch gays were appalled at the way the 1998 Gay Games in Amsterdam were associated with the ripping off of gay visitors to the city. Opposition to the commercialization of the Gay Games manifested itself in an alternative Gay Games that included sports such as 'handbag throwing'. Markwell notes that many queers in Sydney, particularly working-class queers and queers of colour have felt increasingly marginalized from the corporate direction Mardi Gras has taken in recent years. For instance, he points to the high price of tickets to the main dance party at the festival, which cost over AU$100. Markwell argues that the price of such events constitute an economic bar and reflect a class exclusivity, suggesting that this is leading to marginalization of working-class people. He notes that this may be down to the greater commercialization of the organizers of Mardi Gras: 'The overt "professionalization" of the Mardi Gras Board in the last few years may well have disenfranchised many working-class, suburban gays, as well as gays and lesbians of colour' (2002: 84). At the same time Markwell acknowledges concerted attempts to embrace ethnic diversity at the 2001 parade and the increasing significance of the Sydney Mardi Gras parade to gays from Southeast Asia, pointing towards the presence of queers from, for example, Papua New Guinea, Fiji, South Korea and Thailand (though one wonders how these queers may themselves to a certain extent be privileged in being able to afford to travel to Sydney in the first place.) Markwell argues that while Mardi Gras may symbolize the inclusion of queers within the Australian national imaginary, this is not necessarily translated into an improvement of the condition of all queers in terms of law reform and the social conditions of queers 'a contradiction between Sydney's image as a world-class gay and lesbian city, offering the tourist a multitude of experiences and pleasures, and everyday life for many gays and lesbians, especially in the outer suburbs and in regional and rural areas' (2002: 95). This brings me to the place of class within queer globalization. Chris Haylett (2001: 353) has argued that: 'The "others" which have been accorded such high symbolic status within critical academic theory, for example, are definitely not the white working class poor'. This is significant, for queers are certainly one 'other' who have been accorded such a high symbolic status. How much further off the screen are working class lesbians and gay men?

> The cultural failings of working-class masculinities, pitched as macho, criminal, and redundant, come to mirror the economic failings of traditional heavy and manufacturing industries. The account is reproduced in wider social science literatures, with sexism, homophobia, racism, and social violence generally, used as the markers of unreconstructed, especially male, working-class identities. (Haylett, 2001: 359)

What about the white working-class queer? Such a person does not figure within mainstream accounts of lesbian and gay tourism. The focus in my discussion on gay tourism and consumption assumes that one can participate within it. The focus of Haylett's project is welfare reform at the heart of the New Labour project of modernization of the welfare state. She makes a significant conceptual leap between the abjectification of the white working class and the New Labour project. Here Haylett makes the link with the politics of multiculturalism noting that: 'The identification of the white working-class poor as a barrier to the two-part progress of "multicultural modernization" is pivotal to the contemporary process of national/welfare reform' (2001: 357). Within these middle-class contradictions outlined by Haylett, homophobia is located firmly within the white-working class, while being 'gay friendly' is an extension of one's multiculturalism and a marker of one's class distinction. Of course the 'gay friendliness' associated with middle-class tolerance is a disposition towards the kinds of friendly, cuddly non-threatening representations of gayness that abound in the media. The reality of course is that this middle-class sophistication and urbanity is much more poisonous and is extremely fragile when challenged with more overtly in-your-face and threatening queer imagery.

Globalization and Europeanized Sexual Politics

I feel it is important to say something about the links between globalization and the Europeanization of politics. Here I do not wish to be seen as celebrating the Europeanization of politics, nor reinforcing a Euro-centric or ethnocentric perspective on queer globalization. I would argue that given the American-centric nature of writing on the subject, such a criticism would be perverse to say the least. In this section I wish to examine the relationship between globalization and European identity and citizenship and the consequences of this relationship for thinking through the politics of queer globalization. The emergence of the European Union as a global actor has been well documented (Bretherton and Vogler, 1999; Rosamond, 1999), as has the impact of the development of the European Union on national identities within member states of the Union (Kurzer, 2001). However, the consequence of the European Union for sexual politics and identities has until recently received relatively little critical attention. Economic globalization has multiple and different consequences for queers who are differently implicated within them. For instance, for white, working-class queers in Britain economic globalization may be leading to increased abjection and marginalization. Chris Haylett argues that in Blair's Britain, class has become as 'illegitimate discourse' – with the white working class seen as outmoded and unfashionable relics of a shameful past before multi-culturalism. Haylett argues that what is driving this process of class annihilation is the need for Britain to compete at a global level. In her analysis of New Labour discourses on poverty and class, she argues that the search for global competitiveness produces a supporting logic for the illegitimacy of white working-class agency and politics.

> The role of class within global economic processes cannot be admitted because it ruptures the idea of 'national interest', and however much that nationalistic impulse may contradict the promotion of a modern post-imperial multiculturalism, the idea remains predominant within government discourses of globalization. (2001: 365)

Haylett argues that the promotion of a new erstwhile cosmopolitan British nationalism based on multicultural difference seeks to marginalize those whose differences are less easily assimilated or commodifed. I think we can see some productive links that can be made with queer politics, for the least assimilated and commodifiable aspects of queer culture are in this sense seen as unproductive and wasteful. With ethnic difference certain components of cultures are only assimilated into the mainstream at the expense of others. The middle classes constitute their cosmopolitan distance from the working class 'Other' who are constructed as pathologically racist, sexist and homophobic, as not modern and thereby an embarrassment on the face of the modern cosmopolitan New Britain. As Chris Haylett suggests: 'This middle-class dependency on working-class "backwardness" for its own claim to modern multicultural citizenship is an unspoken interest within the discourse of ille-gitimacy around the white working-class poor' (2001: 365).

Elsewhere within Europe, economic globalization has led to a kind of western European imperialism whereby law reform is foisted on would-be accession states such as Romania (Stychin, 2002). At the same time the demands of European integration shadowed by globalization are used as sticks with which to beat workers and the working classes in the United

Kingdom. See for instance Chris Haylett's work on the way in which New labour's cosmopolitanism and Euro- and gay-friendly stance has created an Other of the white working class, racist, homophobe. The discussion of economic globalization within Europe has tended to focus on the emergence and growth of the European super-state as a distinctive regional response to and an agent of globalization. Threats posed to the nation-state within Europe have been channelled through debates on the development and the future form of the European Union. The European Union meanwhile has become a focus for activism in western and northern Europe, but has limited potential for lesbians and gay men. This is limited due to the economic basis for the legal framework of the European Union. This has profound consequences for claims for sexual citizenship within the European Union; as Flynn notes: 'the culture of the market and principles of market efficiency and competition are central to the creation of the internal market, and to the legitimacy of the legal order founded on it' (1996: 283). While European political and economic integration may lead to a standardization of rights, the economic and social, and regional polarization brought about through creation of a common economic area will mean that there will be winners as well as losers. European economic and political integration is not a win-win situation as far as European lesbians and gay men are concerned.

In a nuanced discussion of the possibilities for a European sexual citizenship, Carl Stychin (1998) guards against seeing the European Union as the panacea to the question of the legal transformations in the position of lesbian and gay rights. Specifically he stresses the economic basis of rights discourses within the EU. While a European sexual citizenship may appear seductive particularly within the UK (which has lagged behind on law reform on sexual rights compared to other EU member-states) the limitations are clear. Stychin is critical of the British pressure group Stonewall for appealing to this free-market economic logic in order to appeal to EU institutions:

> By focusing reform efforts at the institutions of the EU, the tension between an economic free market-oriented Europe, and a conception of European citizenship rights which deepen that vision, is underscored. For example, the English law reform pressure group 'Stonewall' has explicitly pitched its arguments to Europe in terms of economic rights of citizenship for lesbians and gays. (1998: 140)

The focus on gaining rights and recognition for workers may therefore obscure the question of rights more generally. The universalism being sought here is only for the economically active. One wonders where the rights of pensioners, the unemployed and students fit in to this version of European sexual citizenship. As Stychin continues: 'rights struggles around lesbian and gay sexualities may have a growing role within Europe, but they frequently reify a logic of European citizenship that has centred on the economically active' (1998: 144). Stychin (2000a) argues that strategies for lesbian and gay law reform that deploy a rights-based discourse may achieve benefits for some, but he argues that these will tend to benefit the economically advantaged. Those who are less able to take advantage of these rights suffer multiple forms of disadvantage and discrimination. Given the neo-liberal principles that guide the formation of European Law, the less privileged may lose out as the result of the intensification of social polarization that results as the drive towards greater harmonization of European markets. For Stychin, European law is essentially masculinist as it constructs the citizen as a worker in paid formal employment. This thereby devalues and marginalizes those engaged in unpaid domestic labour, which has traditionally been seen as 'women's work'. For Stychin, European law serves to maintain this highly gendered notion of the citizen. For this reason he sees dangers in lesbian and gay law reform strategies that base claims for sexual citizenship of the European Union on the citizen as economically active, to the extent that they buy into this highly gendered notion of citizenship.

It is also important to note the key role now being played by European institutions and the growth of a European 'identity' in terms of the sexual politics of particular member states of the EU. For instance, it is widely acknowledged that law reform and the changing climate towards sexual diversity within the Republic of Ireland was in some part influenced by the closening of economic, political and cultural ties with the European Union. In her discussion of the sexual politics of Irish nationalism, Conrad (2001) reflects upon this changing macro-economic and political climate and the degree to which it has been responsible for helping to change the climate enabling law reform. She argues that membership of the European Union has been fundamental in changing the social and cultural climate in Ireland, suggesting that the boom in the economy in the 1990s has helped to assuage doubts about the changing nature of Irish national identity associated with law reform. Conrad's argument posits the profound importance of economics to law reform in the Irish case. However the subtlety of her argument demonstrates that the relationship between sexuality and the economics of queer globalization is a complex one. In asserting the importance of class and social exclusion in discussions of queer globalization I wish to explore how these are racialized.

Conclusion: Race and the Economics of Queer Globalization

While Chris Haylett's work on social exclusion is primarily about class and the way in which it has become an 'illegitimate discourse' within contemporary British politics, her argument does stress the way class is racialized. She argues that the white working class is racially marked as 'white'. Key to whiteness is its invisibility – its naturalness. While I broadly agree with her argument about the abject place of the white working-class within British political discourse, abjection is multiply racialized. Working-class Black Britons and British Asians are also clearly illegitimate subjects within British politics. Not all forms of cultural difference are sought after, or easily assimilated by the new middle class. Neville Hoad argues that the politics of class, race and sexuality are inextricably intertwined with the economics of globalization. The legacy of apartheid in South Africa means that white gay men there are in a relatively advantageous financial position, and are therefore in a better position to make rights claims based on consumption. Hoad suggests that this accounts for the great media profile of white gay men and may therefore explain the popular equation of gay culture with whiteness (1999: 564). While Hoad discusses the adoption of the pink economy discourse within South African sexual politics, it is also clear that race and consumption are central to sexual citizenship struggles elsewhere.

This chapter has demonstrated that globalization does not necessarily equal homogenization, and that we need to learn from cultural studies and social theory writing on globalization to be highly suspicious of claims of a universal gay identity. In the next chapter I develop some of these concerns about the racialization of the global gay in my discussion of queer post-colonialism. The European Union demonstrates the necessity of an economic underpinning to the understanding of the formations of queer globalization within Europe and without. The EU's policies, for instance towards Romania, demonstrate some of the conflicts and contradictions of the economic basis of queer globalization. In this chapter I have argued that sexuality is not simply an effect of global economic processes but is rather integral to their operation. This is an important observation, as globalization (as we saw in the previous chapter) is commonly seen as a merely economic entity. Insights about the sexualized nature of globalization have consequences for how we imagine economic globalization. So here sexuality is not supplementary to economic processes but core to underlining and legitimating economic processes. The marketized identity politics of the 'global gay' are not just being questioned and resisted in South East Asia and the post-communist societies but also in North America and Western Europe. As Neville Hoad's intervention suggests, it is imperative that we see queer globalization as racialized and classed. In the next chapter I will address concerns that questions of race and colonialism have been sidelined in attempts to understand global queer solidarities.

5
Queer Postcolonialism

The study of the postcolonial nationalisms of the so-called Third World continues to be quasi-uniformly based on the presupposition of an unexamined totalizing signifier: universalized heterosexuality. Paola Bacchetta, *When the (Hindu) nation exiles its queers* (1999).

The consumation of an early marriage between queer theorizing and the dominant methodologies of post-structuralism in the United States academy, have almost emptied these disciplines of any attention to the histories of colonialism and of race, which could point the way to a radical activist scholarship anchored in a sexual politic of anti-colonial and anti-racist feminism. M Jacqui Alexander, *Imperial desire/sexual utopias: white gay capital and transnational tourism* (1998).

In the introduction to this book I stressed the need to be aware of the dangers of producing a globalizing discourse on the contemporary transformation of sexual identities, communities and cultures. Discussing and critiquing the notion of universalism and the global gay, we need to be attuned to the dangers of collapsing the local and the distinctive into a globalizing discourse informed by a particular conceptual framework. In this chapter it is postcolonialism that I want to take issue with, specifically the way in which sexualities have been conceptually configured within postcolonialism. Moreover, what I shall attempt to do here is to provide a critique of the way in which some of the key concepts of postcolonial writing (e.g. questions of diaspora, hybridity) have sometimes been uncritically adopted and used by scholars in lesbian and gay studies. Having done this I will discuss the interconnections between the development model of Rostow (1994) associated with modernity, and models of homosexuality. What theoretical insights are to be gained from a thinking-through of parallels between the conceptualization of the homosexual as 'arrested development' and a failed developing country?

The homosexual has been commonly pathologized within medical discourse as a case of arrested development. Conversely, counter-discourses associated with modern gay liberation movements are bound up with the same distinctly modern discourses around development (for instance, see Ashman, 1993), namely that certain countries are more 'developed' than others in terms of how they treat sexual diversity. Does the emergence of movements and cultures associated and linked to modern western lesbian and gay cultures provide the evidence for this thesis? Do such phenomena constitute a global gay or global gay consciousness – a kind of sexual political 'trickle-down effect' whereby these societies 'copy' movements and communities that have developed over a longer period elsewhere? (Butler, 1990).

In addressing these key questions I shall critically evaluate the work of Dennis Altman and specifically his conception of the 'global gay'. I shall argue that while superficially there is much evidence of the globalization of sexualities, we should also pay critical attention to the globalization of homophobia (see for instance Zimbabwe). The two key points I go on to address at the end of the chapter relate back to the global gay. Altman tends to present the global gay as a form of 'false consciousness' and denies agency and subjectivity to those who are deploying and re-working symbols and images associated with the global gay to help fight their own struggles for self-determination, rights and resistance to violence and the production of spaces and territories. I argue that we need to recognize the allure of the global gay – what makes it so desirable in the first place? Why do so many lesbians and gay men identify with the 'ethnic' model of sexuality, which many academics have come to regard and disdain as essentialist? I argue that it is imperative to at least recognize agency and questions of desire and not trivialize them as examples of false consciousness. What I am trying to get a handle on here is the notion of allure. Why is the global gay such a desirable entity? How is this reflected in strategies for movement and migration to the north? I argue that the displacement of homophobia on to the south is a real possibility – witness Zimbabwe. There is a real danger of a new racism emerging whereby rights around sexual diversity become a marker of a nation's level of development – that tolerance and recognition becomes a measuring point of a nation's success at developing. Of course this new racism masks the extent to which so-called 'progress' on matters of sexual diversity has been achieved in the west. Moreover, it obscures the very real and meaningful differences between nation-states (e.g. member states of the European Union), and the extent to which the rights that have been won are for the economically active few and reproduce distinctions between those who are socially included or excluded. In Chapter 2 I argued against the American-centric nature of lesbian and gay studies/queer theory. I argued that this particular form of insularity is particularly significant when discussing globalization and the transnational. In examining the ways in which the links between postcolonial and queer theory have been examined in current work, the critique of American-centrism must come to the fore and be developed. However, before I discuss American-centrism it is necessary to begin by examining the ethnocentricity of queer theory/lesbian and gay studies.

Ethnocentrism in Lesbian and Gay Studies/Queer Theory and Politics

I now wish to consider criticisms of the ethnocentricity of lesbian and gay studies. I then discuss writing on queer diaspora. In doing so I wish to articulate my concern with the ways in which terms from postcolonial theory such as 'diaspora' and 'hybridity' have been adopted within lesbian and gay studies/queer theory. Before I continue, I feel it is necessary to address the notion that lesbians and gay men constitute an ethnic group – a queer folk. Alan Sinfield (1996) argues that while conceptualizing lesbian and gay men as an ethnic group goes against the tide of constructionist and deconstrutionist perspectives on sexuality which dominate lesbian and gay studies, the notion that lesbians and gay men constitute a quasi-ethnic group has wide appeal to many lesbians and gay men. The danger of conceiving lesbians and gay men as an ethnic group or a queer folk is that it risks reproducing the universalism of gay identity and marginalizes 'ethnic' gays and lesbians. It also solidifies categories rather than challenging the power relations that lead to their production in the first place. Conceiving of lesbians and gay men as an ethnic group is significant particularly when we come to examine the globalization of gay identity. There are real problems with the way Sinfield constructs his notion of race contra lesbian and gay politics. The implication from reading his work is that you have race and ethnicity on the one side, and lesbian and gay identities on the other. For instance, borrowing from postcolonial theory, Sinfield suggests that gay culture is hybrid 'to the point where it is difficult to locate anything that is crucially gay – either at the core of gayness, or having gayness at its core' (1996: 279). To what extent is gay culture hybrid? Is gay culture becoming less diverse, less hybrid – in effect more homogenous? In Sinfield's essay 'gay' is assumed to be synonymous with 'white', as 'African diaspora' is compared with the queer diaspora. This renders black queers invisible:

> ... for lesbians and gay men the diasporic sense of separation and loss, so far from affording a principle of coherence for our subcultures, may actually attach to aspects of the (heterosexual) culture of our childhood, where we are no longer 'at home'. Instead of dispersing, we assemble. The hybridity of our subcultures derives not from the loss of even a mythical unity, but from the difficulty we experience in envisioning ourselves beyond the framework of normative heterosexism. [...] If diasporic Africans are poised between alternative homelands – in mid-Atlantic,

> Gilroy suggests – then lesbians and gay men are stuck at the moment of emergence. For coming out is not once-and-for-all; like the Africans, we never quite arrive. (1996: 282)

The critique of ethnocentricity has equally been applied to authors whose work is much more sophisticated and more informed by queer theory. For instance, consider the daddy of queer theory – Michel Foucault. The irony with Foucault of course is that many postcolonial writers have found his analyses of sexuality and power highly useful and appropriate, while he is supposedly found wanting in his failure to discuss colonialism and racism in depth in his work (mirroring similar criticisms from feminists who, while critiquing his failure to discuss gender explicitly, have found much in his writing to develop their critiques of gender and power). One example of the criticism of the ethnocentricity of lesbian and gay studies is provided by Gayatri Gopinath who argues that certain writing on sexual citizenship from a queer perspective fails to take into account questions of race and ethnicity. She is critical of some writing on sexual citizenship for the superficial treatment of nationality and questions of citizenship:

> Berlant and Freeman state that 'disidentification with US nationality is not, at this moment, even a theoretical option for queer citizens', disregarding the fact that identification with either nationality or citizenship is not an option for many queers (particularly queers of colour) in the US. (1996: 125)

Dennis Altman's work tends to produce a 'globalization equals homogenization' argument, which has been rejected as far too simplistic in cultural studies debates on the globalization of culture (Tomlinson, 1999). Altman's work which tends to equate gay culture with an homogenous consumer culture can be contrasted with the work of Martin Manalansan who demonstrates an awareness of the way in which globalizing tendencies are present within gay culture, politics, criticism and theory. While Altman has been much criticized for his evocation of the label 'global gay' as a reflection of: 'the apparent internationalization of a certain form of social and cultural identity based on homosexuality' (1996b: 77), he does recognize that a uniform homosexual identity – a queer equivalent of global sisterhood – is a myth. In this sense his work does pay respect to difference and the conceptual violence of the universal homosexual identity. He is keen to distance himself from the evocation of a utopian homosexual identity which can transcend other markers of identity: 'the romantic myth of homosexual identity cutting across class, race, and so on doesn't work in practice any more than it does in the West' (1996b: 89). He argues that urban/rural distinctions, class, age, are among the factors that cut across the myth of a unifying lesbian and gay consciousness and community. However, his work tends to produce a conceptual violence in terms of the global gay. The term may have potentially harmful consequences as it tends to reproduce the myths about lesbians and gay men being a particularly affluent and privileged group of actors within transnational space. In Chapter 4 I argued that myths of the economic power associated with the pink economy were dangerous fabrications fuelling homophobic discourses. Martin Manalansan IV argues passionately that the other stories (which counteract this myth) need to be heard. His work has been at the forefront of contesting what he sees as the harmful universalizing tendencies of gay culture and politics: 'in the shadows of Stonewall lurk multiple engagements and negotiations. Conversations about globalizing tendencies of gay identity, politics, and culture are disrupted by local dialogues of people who speak from the margins. These disruptions need to be heard' (1995: 436). However, there is a danger here that Manalansan tends to constitute the global as the scale of powerful forces (i.e. global capitalism and the local scale as the authentic site of resistance to these forces).

I have examined the view that queer theory as well as lesbian and gay studies has been guilty of ethnocentrism. Moreover, the cartography of this ethnocentricity is more complex than simply the west versus the 'rest', for instance there is considerable American-centrism as discussed in Chapter 2. Later in the chapter, I examine the relationship of homosexuality to broader issues of modernity and development, but before that I examine the notion of postcolonialism and its complex relationship to queer theory.

Postcolonialism as Universalizing Theory

I now wish to address the problems with postcolonial theory and the difficulties therein of articulating a theoretical position, which critiques the universalism of the global. Aihwa Ong suggests that postcolonialism may be a metropolitan discourse arguing that such a 'metropolitan theory of third-world subalternity tend[s] to collapse all non-western countries (except Japan, of course) into the same model of analysis in which primacy is given to racial, class and national dominations stemming from the European colonial era' (1999: 32). The danger with the way postcolonialism has become assimilated into the academy is that it undervalues agency. Subalternity tends to get translated into passivity and victimhood. The danger of writers such as Altman is that they are doing precisely this – denying the agency of activists – via the notion that their attraction to symbols of the global gay is a form of false consciousness. Ong critiques the unitary discourse of the postcolonial as it has become appropriated within American academia to refer to a whole range of contexts and circumstances across the globe. This unitary discourse of the postcolonial is dangerous because it tends to reproduce the globalization-equals-homogenization hypothesis. It also denies agency and specificity to the local. Specifically the label 'postcolonial' gets applied to all manner of social and political conditions and transnational actors which may be more accurately labelled transnational rather than postcolonial. Postcolonialism as a brand of theory tends to drown out all other discourses concerned with charting transnational power relations and relationships across the globe – for instance those between Western and Eastern Europe. Ong argues that postcolonial theory has sometimes been used rather indiscriminately to apply to what are often vastly different social, economic and political contexts across a wide range of geographical areas. In this sense the term postcolonial annihilates difference, rather than being sensitive to the local and the different. She suggests that postcolonial theory as applied by western scholars demonstrates imperialist tendencies in attempting to encapsulate the experience of postcolonial 'Others' through a single lens of postcolonialism, rather than engaging with work produced outside of the west. Of course I acknowledge that I leave myself open to such criticism. I have deliberately set out in this book to try to avoid speaking for others. Where I find Ong's study of Hong Kong immigrants in California useful is her analysis of power. She recognizes that this transnational community is simultaneously shaping and being acted upon by processes of globalization. The subjects in Ong's study are transnational actors who both benefit and suffer from processes of globalization – they are not merely victims of it. Her work is also valuable in questioning where the centre is in terms of the politics of location and position:

> The hegemonic Euroamerican notion of modernity – as spelled out in modernization theory and theories of development – locates the non-west at the far end of an escalator rising toward the west, which is at the pinnacle of modernity in terms of capitalist development, secularization of culture, and democratic state formation. (1999: 31)

Ong argues that it is also misguided to speak about a single logic of modernity within Europe and North America. Ong is correct to point out that there hasn't been a single trajectory of development – a single evolutionary narrative of modernity in the west. She calls for studies that are more attuned to the specificity of non-western cultural forms, and work that does not simply read off developments in the non-west as less developed copies of western original paths to development. The model of 'development' is very similar to the notion that homosexuals have arrested development – that they are not fully formed, mature human beings, that homosexuality is a phase one goes through, like Rostow's stages of development and economic growth. Ong notes that the term 'postcolonial' has limited theoretical application in many Asian countries that are actively driving globalization and in many cases are themselves now involved in economic processes which can be seen as colonizing. For instance, she points to business people from Asian tiger states such as Malaysia, Singapore and Hong Kong operating in South East Asia, South America as well as the UK and the United States. She argues that these transnational agents confound the use of the label 'postcolonial' to describe south-east Asian countries. Ong argues that universalizing theories of the postcolonial cannot account for the evidence on the ground where former colonized countries in south-east Asia are now engaged in economic practices that are seen as another form of economic colonization. Seeking to challenge what she sees at the universalizing tendencies of postcolonial theory, she proposes 'alternative modernities' rather than 'postcoloniality', to describe many Asian economies whose modernization has taken a different trajectory to the 'escalator' of the development model. While Ong's critique is aimed at postcolonialism in general – how might it be applied to the way in which scholars of sexuality have deployed the theoretical and conceptual language of postcolonialism into their discussions of transnational sexual communities? This is the key question I address in the next section.

The Queer Postcolonial, or the Postcolonial Queer?

In this section I examine the ways in which the relationship between postcolonial theory and queer theory has been examined within lesbian and gay studies. Here I revisit the criticism of American-centrism I developed in Chapter 2. Questioning the American bias of much writing in lesbian and gay studies, the Canadian writer Terry Goldie makes the following telling observation:

> 'Postcolonial' is now a body of literature in the American academy, replacing a quite minor category called 'Third World'. As this homology has spread, like so many Americanisms spread, there is no room left for any cultures which might be post-colonial but are not 'third world,' 'developing,' or whatever is the latest euphemism for the poor and racially other (in the perception of the west). (1999: 14)

Goldie backs up this assertion by referring to two key works on postcolonial and queer theory, namely *The Post-Colonial Studies Reader* (Ashcroft, Griffiths and Tiffin) and *The Lesbian and Gay Studies Reader* (Abelove, Basale and Halperin). Presenting a scathing attack on the American bias of the latter Goldie points to the fact that the overwhelming majority of the chapters in the collection (thirty-nine out of forty-two) are written by scholars resident in the US at the time of publication, arguing this domination is so evident that: 'It is as if the Americanness of gay and lesbian studies is a given that requires no justification, no explanation and no apology' (1999: 15).

73

Goldie's criticism supports the critique of the Americanness of lesbian and gay studies made in the introduction to the book. This represents one problem in attempting to promote a critically queer take on postcolonialism, as part of the hegemony of postcolonialism lies in its dominance within American academia. Bringing together the insights of queer and postcolonial theory is therefore not without difficulties as John Hawley notes in the introduction to *Post-Colonial Queer*: 'Some queer critics at times find themselves resistant to the seemingly deeply ingrained homophobia of much postcolonial culture and discourse; many of those in postcolonial studies decry gay/lesbian studies as 'white' and 'elitist' (2001: 1). It could be argued that elitism marks both postcolonial and queer theory, and not all work within lesbian and gay studies could always be said to be anti-homophobic given that the label and accusation of homophobia (like racism) is all too often used to silence those who put forth unorthodox views. Not all work within queer theory is 'queer' – as the term is so highly contested. Much queer theory is obfuscatory and anti-desire or at least is not very sexy. Much of queer theory is a real turn off to lesbian and gay students, who feel that it does not reflect their lived experience. Queer theory, often rooted in the most abstract post-structuralist thought and based on psychoanalysis, has become assimilated into the academy – and has lost a radical cutting edge. It is rare to find much discussion of pervy sex and bodily fluids. Nowadays you would struggle to find much that is challenging within queer theory – or much to make 'straights' squeamish. Commenting on the elitism of both postcolonial and queer theory, Goldie argues that 'too much of both postcolonial and queer theory gives the impression of a nose well-elevated' (1999: 19). Lisa Rofel attacks the universalizing tendencies within Altman's global gay thesis, arguing that: 'For Altman, invocations of universalism, whether by Westerners or by Asians, appear to be self-evident and self-referential rather than rhetorical strategy, double-voiced dialogism, the locational politics of representation, or strategic essentialism' (1999: 455). Rofel's criticism of Altman mirrors that of Christopher Lane, who poses the question: what is the attraction of the global gay – why does it have such an appeal? Lane argues that the appeal has to be examined in closer detail, not merely dismissed as a form of false consciousness. Ong is similarly keen to pay critical attention to agency and avoid the way in which the west is seen as all-seeing, all-conquering and suggests that we need to beware of the dangers of postcolonial criticism that fails to address questions of agency. In this section I have examined some of the issues involved in attempting to bring together queer and postcolonial theory. I have argued that both demonstrate elitist tendencies. As queer theory has become assimilated within the academy, it has tended to eschew or skirt around questions of lust and raw fucking and it has lost its cutting edge. I now wish to focus on one specific term, namely the notion of diaspora, and the way it has been approached from a queer perspective.

Modernity, Development and the Homosexual

> ...histories of homosexuality often read like narratives of progress towards the western model of egalitarian homosexuality, wherein both partners can be active as well as passive regardless of any masculine or feminine identification on either's part. [...] Although such observations may have sociological or anthropological validity, they leave little room for dissidence and are remarkably similar to the narratives of progress that established between Europeans and the rest of the world a pseudoevolutionary hierarchy that justified the civilizing mission and, therefore, colonialism. (Hayes, 2000: 5)

Robert Holton (1998) argues that there is a danger in an evolutionary approach towards globalization that would see it in terms of an underlying logic of development. Concerning the development of a modern gay identity, I am also suspicious of a single logic of a universal gay identity, or that tolerance of lesbian and gay communities are a marker of a country's development. We saw in the previous chapter that 'progress' on lesbian and gay rights has become necessary for the admission of would-be accession countries such as Romania into the European Union (Stychin, 2002). In the previous chapter I made it clear how much I valued Aihwa Ong's work on the economic and cultural dimensions of transnationality. Here I think her arguments about their mutuality – the impossibility of separating the economic and cultural – are reinforced. For it is cultural difference (and a maintenance of it) that is crucial to a critical perspective on the understanding of the way in which the emergence of sexual communities and politics is conceptualized, specifically what I said in my introduction to this chapter about the stages of development and of homosexuality/gay liberation. Ong helps us to counteract any tendency towards reading off events in non-western societies against trends in the west – i.e. that they will follow the same pattern of growth of a subculture, community and identity formation and production of territory. She argues against the harmful notions that: 'the rest of the world will eventually be assimilated to an internationalized modernity originating in and determined by the west; and that multiple modernities arise only through resistance to the west's universalizing trajectory' (1999: 53). These considerations seem eminently applicable to lesbian and gay studies and to developmental narratives (Hoad, 2000). There is an inextricable link between modernity, development and sexual politics. In modernity the control and regulation of population was a necessity for the reproduction of the modern nation. Lesbians and gay men have not been granted full citizenship status within modern nation-states.

In modernity, homosexuals and non-whites were the uncivilized other and constituted as threats to the moral order of the nation-state. The degree to which this developmental narrative of lesbian and gay rights has emerged alongside the development of the new racism is interesting. The logic goes something like this: you are less developed than us because you treat your gays badly. Thus the western state becomes guarantor of lesbian and gay rights versus the threat constituted by the savage brutal other, for instance Robert Mugabe. Carl Stychin makes an important connection between the increasing assimilation of lesbians and gay men as sexual citizens within states in the west, and the construction of non-western states as unsophisticated and uncivilised in their treatment of sexual dissidence. In this sense he argues that: 'the colonial discourse of the civilizing west comes to be replicated as the recognition of formal legal rights signifies progress, modernity, and western "civilization"' (1998: 200). I have encountered this attitude myself when living in Denmark and the Netherlands. Such discourses are crucial to the formation of Nordic and Dutch nationalisms (see also Kurzer, 2001, on Nordic and Dutch cultural norms and moral regulation). The idea is that we are superior, more developed than you. The logic of the argument is that we are more civilized than you because we give more rights to lesbians and gay men. In this context, the internationalization of lesbian and gay rights activism could be seen as part of a civilizing mission of modernity. Discussing sexual citizenship and the push for law reform in Romania, Carl Stychin (2002) fascinatingly notes the central role played by Dutch politicians and activists in supporting and promoting law reform in Romania. This again points toward the complexity of transnational movements and actors and the role of agency. The Dutch-Romanian axis demonstrates that we cannot conceive of queer globalization as simply the Americanization of queer life. The transnational links between the Netherlands and Romania demonstrate the power of the European Union as a global actor (Bretherton and Vogler, 1999), and the economic basis of queer globalization. Stychin (1998) argues that as law reform generally speaking becomes more successful in Western Europe and North America, there is a danger that such achievements will be used in a racist sense to preach to states in the South. Stychin's nuanced anti-essentialist position contrasts with Altman's conception of modernity, which completely relegates cultural questions, which he subordinates to economic issues and questions. We need to move beyond Altman's view of the global gay as depicted in his discussion of the development of organized lesbian and gay movements in societies such as Indonesia, Japan and the Philippines in the 1990s, which leads him to ask whether such societies are following a modernising trajectory established by the west:

The basic question is whether these developments suggest a fundamental change equivalent to the creation of powerful gay communities with economic, social, and political clout as in North America, Australasia and northern Europe. Is there, in other words, a universal gay identity linked to modernity? This is not to argue for a transhistoric or essentialist position ... but rather to question the extent to which the forces of globalization ... can be said to produce a common consciousness and identity based on homosexuality. (1996b: 79)

While Altman argues against essentialism, the problem with his statement is the way the west is seen as the original, and 'the rest' seen as the 'bad copy' (Butler, 1990): the notion that sexuality follows a path of the development of global capitalism, with a liberated gay consciousness as the highest point of 'development'. It is also relevant to point towards the evolutionary narratives (Hoad, 2000) within lesbian and gay studies whereby 'the homosexual', is supplanted by the 'gay' and 'lesbian', followed by the 'queer' as the most developed form of sexual dissident subjectivity and politics. Likewise, it is necessary to mention the metropolitan biases of these narratives in which the metropolis – London, New York, Paris – is placed at the centre of analysis. It is not simply the case that many rural or non-metropolitan sexual dissidents may not be empowered to come out into a gay or queer identity, community or lifestyle – but rather that they may wish to reject these as markers of a metropolitan arrogance and condescension or a lifestyle and politics that says nothing to them about their lives. The previous sections in this chapter have discussed postcolonialism and queer diaspora, this section is significant because it argues that it is homophobia that has been exported as much as a global gay consumer culture.

The Globalization of Homophobia

While there has been much discussion of the globalization of sexual cultures and specifically the global McPink associated with the most visible and affluent public manifestations of lesbian and gay consumer culture, it is imperative that we also focus on what could be termed 'the globalization of homophobia'. One could make a very good case for stating that it is homophobia that has been most successfully globalized, not global gay consumer culture. Jarrod Hayes argues that homophobic sentiment has been effectively deployed within nationalist discourses: 'nationalist rejections of homosexuality that inspire critiques of sexual tourism rely on a constructionist model of homosexuality as western and bourgeois, which is exported to the rest of the world' (2000: 35). Yet this homophobic sentiment is a product of colonialism. Hayes notes that both the homosexual and homophobia are products of colonialism. Heteronormativity is exported to Africa through colonization. He argues that while heterosexuality was a colonial import, no African nationalism mobilizes against fighting heterosexuality as a western imposition. Oliver Phillips (1997) makes a similar point in relation to legal discourses on homosexuality in Zimbabwe. Neville Hoad (1999) in his discussion of the sexual politics of post-colonial southern Africa posits that the constructed nature of homosexuality/homophobia is masked by the essentialist appeal to nationhood. He argues that Christianity (which has been a western imposition) is constituted as authentically African in mobilizing against the citizenship claims of lesbian and gay men in contemporary southern Africa. It is significant and deeply ironic that religion – specifically Christianity – is used to valorize and give legitimacy to homophobic sentiments in southern Africa, particularly as Christianity itself is a colonial import, whereas homosexuality is decried as western, decadent and alien – un-African. So here we can see how homophobia has been exported through colonialism. Hoad argues that the Zambian government denouncing homosexuality as a 'Norwegian conspiracy', while sounding surreal and ridiculous to many in the west, is logical given Nordic states' involvement in transnational activism and organization around lesbian and gay politics (1999: 573). Earlier I noted that activists from Nordic States via the International Lesbian and Gay Association (ILSA) were among the most articulate and vocal in international lesbian and gay rights activism. Hoad implies that there is a logic to the Zambian government's position given the Nordic tinge to international lesbian and gay rights activism. For Hoad this statement points towards the transnational basis of activism for lesbian and gay rights reform within Zambia. Hoad argues that globalization leads to a defensive reaction by the Zambian state to protect its citizens from what it perceives to be a foreign threat. In the same way indigenous lesbian and gay rights activists within Zambia seek to forge alliances with international lesbian and gay rights activists in order to defend against the homophobic Zambian state.

In this section I have argued that the modern evolutionary narrative that global society is witnessing a trajectory towards ever-greater liberation is a myth that has great resonance for many lesbians and gay men in the west. It serves to legitimize transnational movements for lesbian and gay rights and for law reform. As a coda here I should add that what we mustn't do in critiquing the imperialism of western narratives of gay identity and community is throw the baby out with the bath water. There is a very real danger when rightfully condoning the imperialistic tendencies of some international gay rights activists, that we lose sight of the lived experiences of homophobia in the south. Thus, as Hoad's quote reminds us, we need to pay attention to the invisibility of heterosexuality within anti-gay narratives that are articulated within political formations such as those in Southern Africa. There is also a very real danger that western gay men are singled out for particular attention by critics of imperialism as they represent a very real visible minority. As I have argued in the previous chapter, the surface affluence of lesbian and gay men is often little more than skin deep. While essays critiquing the imperialistic tendencies of gay men – particularly within studies of global gay tourism – abound it is rarer to find essays bemoaning the globalization of heterosexuality. In the next section I go on to examine another narrative associated with the development of the modern global gay, namely that of the universal closet.

The Universal Closet

We can see the impact of universalism (and resistance to it) when we witness one of the touchstones of queer theory coming under scrutiny when considered from a transnational or postcolonial approach. Katie King has argued that western sexual categories fail to encapsulate the complexity of cartographies of acts, identities and communities outside the west: 'The coming out story as a technology to reconstruct sexual identity does not work when feminist life histories – not only from EuroAmerican centers but from transnational locations as well – increasingly cannot be captured by the three names "heterosexual", "lesbian" or "bisexual" (1993: 87). However, the coming out story as the basic narrative of sexual dissident identity has come under threat in the west. This makes us turn to the notion of knowledge and epistemology, for how do we know what constitutes a sexual dissident identity, and how has epistemology been transformed in postmodernity? Among authors' pioneering work on transnational, post-colonial sexualites, Tom Boellstorf has problematized the notion of the closet as applied to dissident sexualities in Indonesia. He notes that the closet is framed around notions of confession, which are associated with the export of the Christian religion to Indonesia. Boellstorff argues that the concept of the closet has limited application there:

> Lesbi and gay Indonesians are open not to the whole universe but to the gay world; confessing to other worlds in society is irrelevant. We find not an epistemology of the closet but an epistemology of life worlds, where healthy subjectivity depends not on integrating diverse domains of life and having a unified, unchanging identity in all situations but on separating domains of life, and maintaining their borders against the threat of gossip and discovery. (1999: 496)

Thus the closet may not be the most relevant theoretical framework for examining dissident sexualities in Indonesia. Writers such as Boellstoff and Manalansan argue that core terms within lesbian and gay studies/queer theory such as the closet have a limited use and application within the communities they have studied. Indeed they may have a limited application more generally in the west as well. For instance, for working-class and rural gays the closet may not be the central organizing principle of their lives. As Alan Sinfield notes: 'If you are lower-class, gay lobbying and lifestyle are less convenient and may seem alien' (1996: 272). This statement leads to the question of whether there is not also a conceptual imperialism operating within queer theory, for instance, which by its very nature is metropolitan, cosmopolitan and above all North American in focus? As I argued in Chapter 4, queer theory/lesbian and gay studies have become increasingly prone to accusations of elitism and class bias.

In terms of the limited conceptual reach of a term such as the closet, consider the excellent work by Martin Manalansan IV on the transnational sexual imaginings of Filipino gay men in New York City. He argues that among the men he interviewed for his study, the closet did not assume prime importance or centrality in their lives: 'For many of my informants, the closet is not central to their personal narrative. They see "coming out" as the primary preoccupation of gay men from other ethnic and racial groups' (1995: 434). Manalansan argues that many of the gay Filipinos he interviewed did not seek to publicize their sexuality for fear of deportation, and that they felt excluded from the commercial gay scene. Manalansan's work serves as a challenge to writers within queer theory/lesbian and gay studies who have a tendency to see 'coming out' as the primary basis of gay liberation politics. Here I should add a strong element of self-criticism as a previous paper rather pompously sought to provide a 'coming out of geography' (Binnie, 1997b). Those who do not come out are seen as occupying a position of 'false consciousness' – they have not been 'saved' by gay liberation politics, again hinting at the role of religion in the production of sexual selves. Narratives around the centrality of coming out and the closet are based on the idea that gay liberation is the highest form of modernity and progress. The failure to come out and conform to somebody else's notion of what a gay or lesbian identity is is a reflection of one's failed subjectivity or spoiled identity. Indeed, as Jarrod Hayes has argued, coming out narratives are not un-problematic in terms of how they are applied to the analysis of sexual cultures and identities in the west:

> In the US one can think of a number of men who consider themselves straight because they are always the active partner in sexual intercourse with men. Many histories of homosexuality would claim these men are holding onto an 'outdated' model of identity. Is it coincidence that working-class men or men of colour are characterized as embodying this model more often than middle-class white gay men? (2000: 6)

Hayes' statement acknowledges the class basis of sexual dissident identities and a growing focus within queer social theory on the limits of the closet as a model for organizing and regulating desire (Bech, 1999; Seidman, 1998; Seidman, Meeks and Traschen, 1999). Hayes' statement points towards a general tendency within the postcolonial and transnational turn within lesbian and gay studies/queer theory. This is the way in which studies of sexualized subjectivities in the postcolonial Other are to a certain extent a reflection of crises within sexual dissident cultures, communities and politics in the west. Is it the case then that debates about queer globalization are more often than not reflections of conditions in the US (or the UK)? Many of the questions about the authenticity of gay identity and culture are as applicable in Boston as they are in Manila. Hayes stresses that the mode of egalitarian 'pure' modern homosexual relationships (as described by Anthony Giddens ([1992]) is as much a myth in the west as it is elsewhere: 'It is also important for us to render less destructively presumable homosexuality (and heterosexuality for that matter) as we know it in the west' (2001: 84). I have argued that a homosexual or gay identity is as much subject to criticism and deconstruction in the west as elsewhere. Indeed our current concern with all matters postcolonially queer, is partially a reflection of uncertainties within queer/sexual politics in the west. Now that there is a perception (particularly among the metropolitan elite) that many of the battles for lesbian and gay recognition associated with modernist gay politics have been won, what role for activists, what does community and a gay identity mean? The discussion in this section posits that we need to make sure that we do not lapse into 'particularism' as well as universalism. This links to the next section in which I examine postcolonialism as universalizing theory.

Queers in Diaspora

A growing body of work has recently emerged on the notion of queer diaspora (Eng, 1997; Fortier, 2001, 2002; Sinfield, 1996; Watney, 1995; Sanchez Eppler and Patton, 2000). To speak of a queer diaspora is both necessary and highly problematic. It is necessary in order to challenge the heteronormativity of thinking on the politics of diaspora. It is rare to find any mention of queers within the vast volume of literature on diaspora. For instance consider Robin Cohen's book *Global Diasporas*, which examines a wide range of diasporas but overlooks sexual dissidence. It is also imperative to speak of queer diasporas in the plural. Some diasporas are more diasporic than others and I would argue that the term has more salience for some queers compared to others. Perhaps we need to define the term before we can move the discussion on a bit further. Clearly what we mean by 'queer' and 'diaspora' is up for grabs – the meanings of both are not static or un contested.

> In fact, for lesbians and gay men the diasporic sense of separation and loss, so far for affording a principle of coherence for our subcultures, may actually attach to aspects of the (heterosexual) culture of our childhood, where we are no longer 'at home'. Instead of dispersing, we assemble. (Sinfield, 1996: 280)

If one accepts the ethnic model of lesbian and gay identity, there is a very real sense in which queers as a folk can be seen as in diaspora. The very real dislocations as a result of the process of the production of a sexual dissident identity for instance – the (often) forced movement away from family, home, homeland. On the other hand queer cultures could be considered as anti-diasporic in the sense that diaspora depends on some notion of a homeland that one has been forced out of. The notion of diaspora is dependent on some notion of shared cultural values, which are often rooted in notions of authenticity. Questions of authenticity have a particular resonance within queer culture because our cultures have commonly been derided as inauthentic, or bad copies of straight originals. Authenticity is something that may be craved because of an absence of roots and fixity, and in Chapter 8 I examine queer claims on the city in terms of authenticity. Michael Warner argues that queer culture cannot be in diaspora because it is not rooted in a particular locality from which to be uprooted: 'It cannot even be in diaspora, having no locale from which to wander' (1993: xvii). It is my contention, however, contrary to Warner, that queer culture does have locales from which to wander and that the spatial is paramount to queer culture. It is one of the touchstones of the geographies of sexualities that it is only possible to be queer in certain places and spaces. The search for fixity is one in which lesbians and gay men participate endlessly. While pomo queer theorists may celebrate the deconstruction and pulling apart of identities and categories and embrace fluidity and ambivalence, many queer folk demand certainty, structure, order and the attachment to specific localities where sexualities can be performed, celebrated, recognized, made public and legitimized. As Martin Manalansan argues, fixity may be essential when confronted with overwhelming difference on arrival in a new country:

> ...while many studies on transnationalism and diaspora emphasize displacement and the unbounding of borders, transmigrants' experiences in certain moments point to some kind of provisional fixing or mooring that is necessary to a sense of belonging in a new land. (2000: 192)

It is also important to recognize the economics of queer diaspora, as Sonia Otalvaro-Hormillosa notes:

> The dangers and difficulties in conceptualizing hybridity in terms of queer diaspora due to the unequal power relationships existing between members of the same diaspora, some of whom are located in more economically privileged sites. (1999: 103)

As I mentioned earlier in this section, many lesbians and gay men identify and ascribe to the 'ethnicity' model and the global gay bemoaned by scholars as essentialist and exclusive. While Warner's essay was written at the height of queer theory, the politics of space have now come to the fore within lesbian and gay studies (e.g. Bell and Valentine, 1995; Bell et al., 2001; Binnie and Valentine, 1999; Brown, 2000; Duncan, 1996; Ingram, Bouthillette and Retter, 1997). Clearly formations of queer diaspora cannot and should not be homogenized. There are different lines and very different forms of queer diaspora, where questions of race and religion may play a fundamental role. For instance Gopinath argues that: 'as queer South Asians in the diaspora, "citizenship," queer or otherwise, is not something that we can ever take for granted' (1996: 120–21). The form and meaning of queer diaspora experienced by South Asians in the United States will be rather different from that of white Irish in that while the latter may be subject to discrimination in the UK, they may be permitted freedom of movement within the EU, whereas queer South Asians will have greater restrictions on their movement because of racism. Gopinath speaks of 'diasporic pleasure', and is ambivalent about the term: 'current articulations of diaspora tend to replicate and indeed rely upon conventional ideologies of gender and sexuality; once again, certain bodies (queer and/or female) are rendered invisible or marked as other' (1996: 121). While Gopinath speaks of diasporic pleasures, Martin Manalansan argues that the condition of diaspora is resisted by his informants who 'play with the world' through cross-dressing, arguing that 'For many of my informants, cross-dressing was one way of confronting the vicissitudes of diasporic living' (2000: 191). Reflecting some of the points made in Chapter 1 of this book about cosmopolitan subjectivities of queer intellectuals, Ong is keen to link the discussion of diasporas and the diasporic subject with the status, position and location of diasporic intellectuals, noting that: 'Academic interest in how diasporas shape racialized, gendered, sexualized, and oppositional subjectivities is often tied to scholars' attempts to shape their own cosmopolitan intellectual commitment' (1999: 13).

I now return to the closet and the earlier-mentioned critique of the universalism of the closet. Where is the queer diasporic experience located? Sinfield, discussing Simon Watney's work, argues that a gay bar may be the place where we can find the queer diasporic subject:

> The nearest equivalent to a queer diasporic experience, Simon Watney remarks, is 'the sense of relief and safety which a gay man or lesbian finds in a gay bar or a dyke bar in a strange city in a foreign country'. Considered as a model for the good society, a gay bar lacks quite a lot, but for a gay man it is a place where he is in the majority, where some of his values and assumptions run. (1996: 287)

This statement assumes a secure sense of self and 'being at home' within gay bars in one's own city. The immediate question that springs to mind is 'what about that feeling of dislocation experienced by many on the gay scene 'at home'? What about those non-metrosexuals who do not feel comfortable within the gay bars within the borders of one's own country?' For many men and women who disidentify with a gay identity or the commercial gay scene, a gay bar may well constitute a foreign country or an alien territory. There are a large number of men and women who do not share the 'values and assumptions' associated with the scene, or for that matter the lesbian and gay political elite. Lesbian and gay communities and political organizations can be as off-putting and alienating as the commercial scene. What are the alternatives to the models of queer diaspora I have been discussing in this chapter? Does diaspora presuppose some notion of origin and authenticity? If so, how can we authenticate queerness. Who can speak as queer? Some queers are more privileged than others.

In this section I have examined the notion of queer diaspora. I have argued that while we have to challenge the heteronormativity of much of the material on diasporic identities, it is equally urgent that we reflect long and hard about how appropriate, useful or accurate the term diaspora is when approached from a queer perspective. I now round off the chapter with a discussion of borders, mobility and migration.

Framing Queer Mobility

In this chapter I have examined the links between race, ethnicity and queer globalization. I have discussed ethnocentricity within lesbian and gay studies. I have examined the notion of queer diaspora, which I argued demonstrated some of the problems in attempting to queer postcolonialism. In the section on queer diaspora I argued that many queers have no home from which to wander and are locked into a continuous struggle to find a secure sense of self and home, place and identity, while finding that many of the identities on offer lead to a sense of disidentification. The notion of diaspora is a tricky one, as already discussed. There is an important distinction to be made between the notion of all queers (as an ethnic group) being in diaspora (which is a dangerously universalizing and ethnocentric move), and the recognition of the multiplicity of queer diasporas. Accordingly, migration is clearly a more pressing issue for some queers than others. The ability to move across borders is obviously gendered, classed and racialized. The border has become a fetishized object within postcolonial writing on difference. It is almost as though the border is romanticized, in the same way that the margins have been romanticized as privileged sites of radicality – rather than concrete structures that police, contain, control. While the border may be commonly seen as a privileged site of radicality or liminal space, we know it's tough to be an outsider in different communities. In his discussion of sexual politics in Northern Ireland, Vincent Quinn argues that borders reinforce fixity and strengthen loyalties: 'Ireland's border zone continues to be a site of violence rather than of playful inversion [...] living on the border does not in itself unfix rigid loyalties; if anything it strengthens them' (2000: 273). For Quinn, borders symbolize division, fixity and separation. They are spaces where identities are not in flux, but rather, rigid, discrete, exclusive and bounded. Quinn argues that living on the border can create conflict and reinforce rigid identities rather than the fluidity of the postmodern self.

Migration is essential for many queers to participate in queer culture, to be full citizens in the queer world. In Chapter 3 I argued that technological changes associated with the Internet are transforming this somewhat – but, in certain respects, further reinforce these spatial divisions. Bob Cant supports Michael Warner's view that the queer have no homeland, and argues that this makes queer migrants different: 'lesbians and gay men differ from other groups of migrants in that there is no homeland that can validate our group identity' (1997: 1). But Cant's statement is of course problematic given the discussion earlier in this chapter of the links between homosexuality and modernity.

In this chapter I have argued against the notion that 'gay liberation' represents the high point of modernity. In so doing I have sought to challenge the idea that the development of a gay identity, culture and politics reflects a developmental model whereby cities outside of the west are in a process of becoming ever more tolerant and accepting of modern gay identities. In discussing the plurality of queer diasporas, we need to be aware of the very real practicalities of moving across national borders. Here we need to bring the state back in and examine questions of transnational citizenship. In discussions of queer diaspora, movement across national borders is assumed to be unproblematic, yet there are very real obstacles and barriers to movement, in the form of heteronormative and homophobic migration policies, for instance, as well as the very real economic and emotional costs of migration. In the next chapter I examine what is at stake in moving across national borders. I also develop ideas raised here about queer postcolonialism through a discussion of queer tourist practices. Queer mobility across national borders cannot and should never be taken for granted.

6

Queer Mobility
and the Politics of
Migration and Tourism

I begin this chapter by examining the furore surrounding the financial collapse of Sydney's Mardi Gras. The event has become immensely significant in drawing media and scholarly attention to the financial clout associated with the pink economy (Markwell, 2002). The 2002 Mardi Gras witnessed a loss of AUS$400,000 (£140,000) and recriminations abound regarding the reasons for the deficit. Fewer people turned up compared to previous years and there has been much debate in the media about the reasons for this – focusing on a perception that Mardi Gras had become too commercialized and 'too straight' (evidence backed up by Markwell's (2002) analysis of the event). Similar reasons have been used to explain the financial losses of London's Mardi Gras event in 2002. The collapse of Sydney Mardi Gras points towards the volatility of the tourist market. It also points very clearly towards the limits of the pink economy discourse. In Chapter 4 I examined the whole set of discourses around the pink economy, and I concluded my discussion by arguing that the affluence of lesbians and gays was not only over-stated, but also that the continuing trope of the affluent queer was damaging to a liberatory sexual politics. Representing gays as being a particularly economically privileged group runs the risk of reinforcing homophobia. In this chapter I examine queer mobility by focusing on movement and migration in relationship to queer identity, space and location. I focus on migration policies and the possibilities for queer citizenship.

Migration occupies a central place in coming out narratives, for example. It represents a key way in which space and place play a significant part in the formation of sexual identities, cultures and communities. Discussions of global capital assume that freedom of movement of persons is a reality, yet for queers this can be intensely problematic. The discussion of diaspora and universalism in the previous chapter must be linked here with a much broader discussion of questions of movement across national borders, hence my agenda for this chapter. First I discuss migration in general. Then I examine the gendered nature of migration. I then go on to discuss international migration. While I discuss the shifting landscape of legislation and legal discourses on the matter I maintain that a narrow focus on rights can lead us down a theoretical cul-de-sac. While some lesbian and gay migrants move to secure the protection of the state in their host country, it is clear from other accounts and narratives of the migration process that the legal dimension is only a part of the equation. The chapter concludes with a critical discussion of the sexual politics of international tourism. I maintain that queer tourism and migration should be examined together conceptually. There is a clear overlap between them. For instance, the desire to migrate to a city or country may be inspired by a tourist visit. Holidays are associated with sex and romance, the desire for unity, sameness as well as otherness. It is to the economics of queer mobility and migration that I now turn.

The Economics of Queer Mobility and Migration

Before we can examine queer mobility and migration it is necessary to contextualize the discussion in terms of the recent growth of interest in mobility within social theory. John Urry (2000b) has argued in his discussion of mobile bodies and global citizenship that mobility is increasingly seen as a right. It is also imperative to recognize that many migrations are not voluntary, not a matter of choice, but are rather matters of economic necessity and compulsion. For instance there is the well-documented case of women who are 'forced' into migration as sex workers and mail-order brides (Tolentino, 1996), and refugees (Bhabha, 1996; Pettman 1996). I feel ambivalent about these gendered and sexualized transnational flows. One may feel revulsion about the sexualized exploitation implicit within sex work, but I also recognize the danger in making knee-jerk moralistic statements about these issues. In Chapter 4 I argued that work in late capitalism is becoming increasingly sexualized so it becomes more difficult to delineate a separate sphere of work as sex-work. This highlights the need to understand the complexity of power relations and avoid labelling people as passive victims of sexualized transnational flows. In this context, Roland Tolentino argues against any simplistic representation of Filipina mail order brides as passive victims (1996: 51). Thus far I have argued that globalization has had an uneven impact on sexual cultures. One key area of concern is that of migration. While I share some of Altman's ideas of 'global queering' (however problematic that may be), it is clear that there are barriers to stop the transmission of a global gay culture; there are specific limits to the mobility of sexual dissidents. Despite the media's glamorization of international lesbian and gay tourism, there are limits on the movement of sexual dissidents across national borders. While access to capital means white middle-class gays and lesbians may enjoy and participate in neo-colonialist economic structures of the global tourist industry, there are limits to this line of enquiry. Escaping place to travel somewhere else in order to discover one's sexuality is the major trope within coming out stories. The wish to escape the boundaries of one's own nation is likewise a familiar trope within gay literature. In many instances the need to migrate is not so much borne out of the desire for pursuit of the American Dream but out of the very real fear and threat of persecution in the country of origin. Migration is not always a choice but a necessity. Thus we are not talking here of economic migrants but political refugees, people for whom being a sexual dissident is either illegal, or makes one vulnerable to brutal attacks, persecution or the threat of death. Given the very real threats to one's life within some states that persecute sexual dissidents, it is easy to understand the attraction of states where laws protect sexual diversity. However, as I wrote in an earlier essay about migration between the UK and the Netherlands (Binnie, 1997a), there are much more complicated factors at work here. In that essay I argued that in the early–mid 1990s the legal status of lesbians and gay men was markedly different between the two states, despite their membership of the European Union. Lesbians and gay men in the Netherlands have enjoyed much better social and legal protection under Dutch Law than their counterparts in the United Kingdom. Given this I noted the irony of the fact that London was developing as a focus of lesbian and gay tourism and immigration. Clearly we have to recognize that being a vibrant, complex global city is an attraction in itself, and also that there was much in London to attract people. For instance, Cherry Smyth's (1995) essay on the emigration of Irish lesbians mentions one lesbian from Cork who said the reason she left home was to find more women she was attracted to, as there was a very small lesbian community in Cork. We therefore have to get under the skin of the reasons why people are attracted to cities and nations and stimulated to migrate, either as tourists, or temporary or permanent workers. It is clearly much more than the freedom from restrictive laws. It is also the freedom to become something, someone else – the elsewhereness of belonging. The media proliferation of the symbols and practices of global queer consumption outside of the west may provide a strong attraction. Is it really so surprising this 'global desire' and the dreams of queer perfection promoted by gay and other lifestyle magazines and media leads queers to attempt to migrate to Los Angeles, Paris, Miami, New York, London? See for instance this statement from the Filipino writer Vicente Groyon III, quoted by Dennis Altman:

You are reading the latest copy of *Interview,* one of the trendy fashion-slash-lifestyle monthlies that tell you what to wear, what to talk about and how to live. You are under the impression that you belong to the world the magazine describes, and not in this tropical, underdeveloped, unstable country. You dream of escaping to this world full of perfect people, with perfect faces and perfect lives and perfect clothes and perfect bodies. (1996b: 86)

Migration is of particular significance for sexual dissident populations because of the need to 'get thee to a big city' (Weston, 1995). In order to survive – to produce an identity – one needs to migrate to a big city in the first place. It is impossible to separate the economic from the social and the sexual, but this is not a case of economic reductionism – it is not a one-way street: the desire to escape to a big city (and I would argue that this is a relational term) has economic consequences too. For many newly-arrived migrants the easiest jobs to get will be in the service sector where there is fast staff turnover and demand for large numbers of low paid workers. The desire to produce a queer self means people are willing to make economic sacrifices to leave settled lives and jobs behind to relocate to the big city and make do with temporary, less well-paid jobs. These difficulties are obviously multiplied for those sexual dissidents crossing national borders. There is also an age factor here, as it is the young who often have the greatest need to migrate, but who possess the least capital to do so. As Gayle Rubin (1993) notes, migration may involve financial sacrifices, and that burden may be most difficult to bear for the young, who may experience the greatest urgency to migrate in the first place. In her research on 'families of choice' in the Bay Area, Kath Weston (1995) is quick to acknowledge the economic component of migration. Indeed the booming economy of the Bay Area provided opportunities for the men and women she interviewed in the expanding service sector in the 1970s and 1980s. Economic motives were therefore also significant in the decision to move to San Francisco as well as greater opportunities for sexual freedom. Indeed Weston noted that in their discussions of their reasons for moving to the Bay Area, some of her informants specified economic motives rather than sexual ones. There is a danger, however, that Weston's research is merely seen as confirming the widely-held belief that gay men are a uniformly affluent and highly mobile part of the population. In Chapter 4 I argued that this assumption is false and highly damaging. The limited research on gay men's mobility supports the widely-held view that gay men are a particularly mobile part of the population. In their survey of gay men in London, Kelley, Pebody and Scott claim their statistics demonstrate that 'Gay men appear to be an extremely mobile population' (1996: 13). Their study of gay men in the capital found that 77 per cent of gay men in their sample did not originally live in London and migrated there from elsewhere (1996: 6). However such a study can only reveal a part of the picture. Such studies inevitably attract those who have the capital to be out and visible in gay spaces within the capital (see also Hindle (2000) on gay migration to Manchester city centre).

In the previous chapter I examined the notion of queer diasporas. I argued that there was an important distinction to be made between the notion of all queers being in diaspora, and the multiplicity of queer diasporic communities. Clearly migration is a more pressing issue for some queers than others. The ability to move across borders is obviously gendered, classed and racialized. This means that migration is essential for many queers to participate in queer culture, to be full citizens in the queer world. Bob Cant (1997: 1) reinforces Michael Warner's view that queers have no homeland, and argues that this makes queer migrants different from other migrants. This points to a need to conceptualize queer migration and to ponder why migration is significant to so many sexual dissidents. Migration is of centrality to nationalism and citizenship as it brings into focus questions of sovereignty – of the symbolic enclosure of the space of the nation, discussed by Anna Marie Smith in *New Right Discourse*. Smith's book is significant for the manner in which she analyses the discourses surrounding British post-war immigration policy and the debates around Section 28 in late 1980s. The point of Smith's project was to articulate connections between racism and homophobia within new right discourse. The attempt to promote a purified, original, white, national space within these discourses was based on the exclusion of immigrants and gay men from the New Commonwealth. In these discourses immigration represents a threat to the boundaries of that enclosed space. In a similar way, in her discussion of the migration of sexual dissidents across the Mexico–United States border, Jesscia Chapin (1998) argues that homophobia reflects anxieties about the threat posed by migrants to the security of territorially bounded identities. Of course, biphobia and transphobia are significant in terms of queering the boundaries and rigidities of national identity. David Bell (1994) has critiqued the notion that bisexuals are tourists in lesbian and gay culture – not truly committed – just here on a day trip and then they can go back to the safe, supportive world of heterosexuality.

Having discussed the relationship between migration and queer mobility and migration at a general level, I feel it is important to try to separate the different formations of queer mobility and migration. There are many different kinds of migration as part of the time–space management of identity (see Valentine, 1993). These occur at different spatial scales, from the daily commute to work to a different city from where one lives and socializes, to international migration. The most common is rural to urban within the same country. Those trapped by poverty in places unsupportive of their sexuality are least likely to have the resources to be able to migrate to the queer homelands in the first place. There are clear economic brakes on migration. Having examined the relationship between migration and queer mobility in general terms I shall now examine one particular form of migration: namely between the rural and the urban, and show how that structures the queer migrant experience.

Queer Migration and the Rural–Urban Binary

The historical urban basis of modern homosexuality means gay identity is first and foremost an urban identity. Industrialization enabled the formation of gay identity in the cities of Western Europe and North America in the nineteenth century. Industrialization brought about dislocation and facilitated movements from rural areas and small towns into large cities though again migration was for multiple reasons – economic as well as sexual. As Gayle Rubin (1993) notes, movement and migration has been fundamental to the establishment of urban concentrations of lesbians and gay men in Europe and North America. Thus the formation of modern homosexualities was the result of industralization and urbanization, which enabled men and women attracted to the same sex to congregate and form communities within cities. Economic motives for migration were as significant as opportunities for sexual freedom, meaning that we should always be attuned to the economic basis of sexual cultures and identities. Any discussion of sexuality must be aware of the broader social and economic context. For instance, George Chauncey notes that migrations of gay men to New York should be seen in this broader context: 'gay men's migration was clearly part of the much larger migration of single men and women to the city from Europe and rural America alike' (1994: 135). Economic motives for migration to New York were intertwined with the desire to escape the constraints of family life, but what of contemporary motivations for migration?

Studies of the present and recent past demonstrate continuity in terms of the dovetailing of the economic and the sexual. Kath Weston's work shows the symbolic value of the urban/rural opposition. Weston argues that these spatial contrasts are fundamental to the way they discussed their sexualities, noting that this was a much more complex pattern than a simple contrast of the rural as oppressive, the urban as liberatory. She argues that symbolic space is equally significant in attracting lesbians and gay men to migrate into these neighbourhoods and cities from rural areas. For Weston the distinction between rural and urban life is symbolic in framing coming out narratives: 'the gay imaginary is not just a dream of freedom to "be gay" that requires an urban location, but a symbolic space that configures gayness itself by elaborating an opposition between rural and urban life' (1995: 274). In contrast to the moral constraints of small town life, cities offer anonymity and the opportunity to meet like-minded people. Weston suggests that this urban–rural distinction is embedded within the gay consciousness. For lesbian and gay migrants within national borders, the primary shift is from rural to urban; provincial to metropolitan. Weston has shown how the rural–urban distinction has been central to how migrants make sense of their sexuality. If, as Weston argues, the symbolic opposition between rural and urban lies at the heart of many narratives of identity formation, then it follows that this applies equally to those who migrate from the urban to the rural (Bell and Valentine, 1995). What lies at the heart of the rejection of the urban in favour of the rural among sexual dissidents? There are also significant national differences in the migration of sexual dissidents, as Bob Cant, speaking about the role of London as gay capital argues: 'migration does not have the same role in the consciousness of people in Britain as it does in the United States' (1997:10). This begs the question, which British people? For Black Asians and Black Britons, the experience of migration does play an important role in the cultural memory and consciousness. The social, cultural, political and economic contrasts within a densely populated country such as the United Kingdom, or the Netherlands and Belgium are fewer than within a country such as the United States. Likewise the physical distances between rural communities and major conurbations are significantly less. It follows that it means something very different to be rural in these densely populated countries than it does in the United States. North Dakota and Montana are sparsely populated, compared to the Belgian Ardennes or rural parts of the Netherlands, such as Friesland. Other work on urban–rural migration reveals the complexity of migration patterns. See for instance Meredith Raimondo's (2001) essay 'Corralling the virus'. She examines the discourses around the media coverage of AIDS in rural US states. She notes that the urban–rural distinctions and place-making reproduce the myth of the rural heartland. One of the dominant narratives Raimondo examines is that of the gay man with AIDS returning home from the big city to die. She calls this the 'coming home to die' narrative. Urban life enabled these men to be come out and be openly gay, something they felt unable to be in the rural heartland. Raimondo notes a second major urban–rural trope, namely that of the gay man with AIDS who leaves urban areas in search of an AIDS-free rural utopia. Raimondo quotes from an article in *Newsweek* that labelled 'gay refugees' who actively seek out the rural. She argues that this group of men are represented as a threat as they may seek sexual partners in the homeland, and are thereby constructed as a threat to rural communities.

Movement from the country into the city does not of course solve all of one's problems. The idea of coming out suggests that you are born again as queer, you enter the promised queer homeland. In her study, Kath Weston notes that the city provides migrants with as many problems as opportunities: 'homelands can be easier to desire from a distance than once you arrive on their figurative shores' (1995: 275). As Weston suggests, many of those who arrived in the mythic queer homeland experienced a sense of disenchantment. The discovery of queer communities and media hype of the lesbian and gay business also foster this image of a correct and objective way of being gay. It is at this point that one may experience multiple forms of disidentification (Munoz, 1999) with the range of queer lifestyles and identities on offer. As Allan Bérubé (1996) noted, the newly arrived migrant, more likely to be young, may not have the capital to participate in the newly available social spaces on offer to him or her. Meredith Raimondo argues that the media narratives of gay men returning from the big city were highly gendered, thus reinforcing the gendered nature of the migration of sexual dissidents. Raimondo examines the gendered narratives of homecoming in which gender roles are essentialized, with the focus on maternal love fixing women very clearly in the role of keepers of the heartland: 'maternal compassion represented a place-making force that brought such migrations to a close' (2001: 9). She argues that this fixity also performs an aspect of nation-building in response to the AIDS crisis and a powerful symbol of American nationalism as well as reproduction of heterosexual norms: 'emphasizing the power of maternal compassion as a model for the national response to AIDS, these stories imagine heterosexual domesticity as a means of fixing sexuality in place' (2001: 12–13). The visibility of immigrant gay men in London and the supposed hypermobility of gay men should not mask the real economic costs of migration, and the gendered way in which these costs are borne. As Eithne Luibheid notes, speaking about the migration of Mexican lesbians to the United States: 'It is important to note that lesbians do cross borders. Immigrant lesbian lives remain little documented or understood, however' (1998: 501). The gendered political economy of migration means that this is more difficult for lesbians. There are considerable gender differences in migration. One significant attempt to document the lives of immigrant lesbians has been Oliva Espin's *Women Crossing Boundaries*. As Espin (1999) argues, the experience of migration is a gendered one as it may reinforce gender roles, but also offer an opportunity to subvert them. For women, migration represents both threat and opportunity, as Espin claims that for women of whatever sexual orientation 'the crossing of borders through migration provides the space and "permission" to cross boundaries and transform their sexuality and sex roles' (1999: 5).

In this section I have argued that the rural-urban binary plays a key role in framing coming out narratives, but also the management of sexual identities more generally. The predominant movements of sexual dissidents are rural to urban to escape the constraints of rural and small town life. However, there are also significant movements in the other direction, for instance reflecting disenchantment with the structures and institutions of urban commercial lesbian and gay life. Moreover, As Raimondo's work on AIDS and gay men in the rural heartland of the United States demonstrates, movement of sexual dissidents is highly gendered. Having examined the place of the rural–urban binary in framing the migrations of sexual dissidents, I now turn my attention to queer migration across national boundaries.

Transnational Migration and Queer Citizenship

As Elman (2000) and Bhabha (1996) note, family life and the intimate sphere are areas that are very much fundamental to the nation-state's sovereignty. The area of international migration of sexual dissidents brings to the fore questions of national identity, citizenship and belonging. For transnational migrants, coming out narratives are framed in terms of national difference (though this may also interconnect with the rural–urban distinctions I have discussed). The distinctions between country of origin and host country may become central to the management and formation of identity. The lesbian migrants to the United States interviewed by Oliva Espin often expressed this in terms of language. Significantly, some respondents felt more comfortable discussing transformations in sexuality in English rather than Spanish, Dutch or German. Espin suggests that it may be easier to come out or explore one's sexuality in a foreign language, noting that 'the exclusive preference of one language over another may compartmentalize the contradictions inherent in being an immigrant' (1999: 141). Espin observed that while the women she interviewed said they were more comfortable discussing their new sexual identity in English, they often resorted to their first language in sexual scenes. Like Weston, she argues that migration is central to identity formation. She argues that the migrant experience has many similarities with the process of coming out in that it may involve considerable dislocation, emotional cost, a mixture of fear and joy in forging and developing new social networks and creating a distance between old and new life and identities. In thinking through Espin's work I am minded of the issues I discussed in the previous chapter concerning the universalism of the closet. I argued that coming out of the closet may not simply be the be-all-and-end-all of being gay or a sexual dissident. Many people may reject the notion of a gay identity completely. Espin's work tends to reproduce the notion that these women will simply develop a lesbian or gay identity, rather than challenging or contesting the whole notion of identity politics, or the notion of gay identity.

In any discussion of queer migration it is important to understand that the legal status of lesbianism and male homosexual acts is only one factor in the equation. A sense of freedom, and ability to produce a queer self may be easier in societies where one is strictly speaking less free than the society of origin. Thus, what is significant and interesting in Oliva Espin's discussion of lesbian international migration is that some of her respondents from the Netherlands and Germany found more freedom in the United States, while they in fact enjoy better social welfare provision and enjoy a much better legal status in their states of origin. She noted that even where lesbians had not been subject to persecution in their countries of origin, they said they felt more comfortable away from their families. For instance Espin cites the example of a Dutch lesbian who said that they felt much more liberated in North America, even though the Netherlands had more progressive social policies towards lesbians. This echoes my discussion of the early 1990s boom in queer London, which saw a major growth in the visibility of queers in the capital, and saw the city emerge as one of Europe's gay capitals despite the backdrop of legal setbacks such as Section 28 and Operation Spanner. Espin's respondents reinforce the point I have made about the rejection of simplistic explanations for queer migrations. It is not simply the case that queers migrate to somewhere where they may benefit from greater state protection and enjoy more rights and entitlements.

All that has been said thus far applies to migration in general. This section has focused on the economic costs of migration, but in the next I will focus on the particular issues associated with migration across international boundaries, for it is here that issues of rights and citizenship come to the fore. The debates around migration of sexual dissidents and the rights afforded sexual citizens are crystallized at the national scale. This does not mean that political economy can take a back seat, for one has to understand what the underlying economic forces shaping and moulding migration policies are, for instance the case of the European Union discussed in Chapter 4. Most states do not recognize same-sex marriages for the purposes of acquisition of citizenship or immigration. The United Kingdom has recently joined an ever-expanding list of states which now recognizes persecution on the basis of homophobia as grounds for granting asylum. This is related to the UNHCR in which persecution based on 'membership of a particular social group' is recognized. Derek McGhee (2001) argues that there has been a fundamental transformation in the treatment of gay men as political refugees, specifically in terms of how gay men are considered to be part of a 'social group'. While one may celebrate legal victories and advances in the rights of lesbians and gay men, it is imperative that we recognize how the law privileges certain forms of same-sex relations to the exclusion of others. This leads to a discussion of how the state recognizes sexual dissidents as lesbians or gay men and same-sex relations for the purpose of awarding rights. I then move on to a discussion of what I term the queer epistemologies of international migration.

Queer Epistemologies of International Migration

Migration policies that marginalize queers and deny migration are contested in a number of ways. Of course there is resistance to these policies, for instance in 'passing'. In this section I discuss two recent essays examining the question of sexuality and international migration. The first, by Jessica Chapin, examines the history of monitoring at the US–Mexican border. In the article Chapin focuses on one Mexican woman and how her case was dealt with in US immigration law. The second by Derek McGhee examines the recent case of a Romanian – Ioan Vraciu – and his application for asylum in the United Kingdom. McGhee's (2000) essay focuses on the question of the authenticity of his homosexuality before the law. What links these essays and what makes them fascinating is their common focus on questions of knowledge and truth. McGhee's paper raises a number of pressing issues about intelligibility, authenticity and legal technologies. Vraciu was denied asylum because he could not prove that he was gay. Chapin speaks of migration as a form of passing, bringing in to focus questions of the performativity of migrant bodies: 'like the homosexual, the undocumented immigrant opens an epistemological gap by exercising the power to dissemble, to pass' (1998: 414). Vraciu's attempts to pass as straight, argues McGhee, meant the law failed to recognize him as homosexual. By passing to avoid hostility and the threat of imprisonment if expelled to Romania, Vraciu sought to defend his privacy. While passing is commonly seen as a retrograde manoeuvre to protect one's status and power, Vraciu's case suggests that passing means that the law failed to recognize him as gay and therefore rejected his claim for asylum because he could not prove he was gay and therefore subject to persecution. This question of how the law recognizes and constructs knowledge about queers is explored by Chapin who argues that the drive for certainty and proof reflects both homophobia and xenophobia: 'xenophobia and homophobia converge in a search for secure knowledge, a reactionary effort to regain an epistemological footing by targeting and expelling such indecidable and therefore threatening figures as "illegal aliens" and "queers"' (1998: 414–15). Vraciu's case provides a counterpoint to the commonplace assumption that it is those who choose not to pass as straight, and those less easily assimilated aspects of queer culture, for whom crossing the border is hardest, as Chapin notes in her discussion of Mexican vestidas attempting to cross the border into the United States (1998: 418). The 'queerer you look', the more vulnerable you are to being hassled on the basis of your sexuality (see also Eithne Luibheid's (2002) discussion of rape at the border). Chapin notes the link between performativity, crossing the border and passing:

> ...crossing becomes an exercise in passing – a kind of mimetic subversion. People in Ciudad Juarez talk about crossing the border illegally in terms of dressing up, dissembling, and manipulating their appearances through changing the ways they walk, talk, or dress. The goal is to construct a closet that will make them invisible and help them avoid being 'read'. (1998: 416)

This passing to avoid being read is something queers do in everyday life. As the Vraciu case demonstrates, there are troubles in passing and being closeted. Such immigrants are more likely to be closeted out of fear thus proving their sexuality before the law is fraught with difficulties. Passing can be seen as form of resistance, parody, and subversion of laws designated to discriminate against sexual dissidents. In this context we should see the use of mutually beneficial arrangements between host and immigrant partners as a means of circumventing restrictions on migration. As Leo Flynn notes, a considerable market has developed in recent years for unmarried lesbians to marry foreign gay male nationals for money: 'In London and other large cities located in Member States with strict immigration laws, a market in EC (as opposed to host state nationals) workers who are unmarried lesbians has emerged in recent years' (1996: 297). Lesbian citizens of the European Union living in London may then trade on their European Citizenship, which Flynn argues thereby becomes a tradable commodity.

I have argued that lesbians and gay men have historically been denied the right to migrate across national borders. This is most commonly associated with the Cold War, when policing of national borders and identities, especially in terms of sexuality, took on a particularly restrictive form (see Katrin Sieg [1995] on sexual dissidence and the Cold War in the German Democratic Republic; for a discussion of the Cold War, nationalism and sexuality in the United States, see Lee Edelman's [1992] essay on the epistemology of the water closet). However in the post-Cold War period, a number of states have begun to recognize persecution on the basis of homosexuality as a basis for the award of refugee status. Moreover, a number of states have begun to recognize same sex relationships for the purpose of citizenship claims of the foreign partner. However, the focus on a monogamous same sex partnership is very much the basis for the award of citizenship status. The notion of same sex marriage serves to reinforce the sanctity and social status of marriage within our society (Bell and Binnie, 2000).

In terms of both asylum claims and recognition of same sex relationship for the basis of claims for residence and citizenship, homosexuality has only very recently been recognized as a valid variable. There have been significant changes in a range of countries in the 1990s. The questions we have to pose are why? Why then? Why now? We cannot assume that simply because this a growing issue of concern in the United States, the UK, Australia and the Netherlands, that it is the case elsewhere. Why in certain countries and not others? Of course on a basic level the growth of awareness of globalization has meant that there have been more concerted efforts for law reform. With more people involved in international tourism and business, the greater the chance of relationships being forged across national boundaries is. The awareness of globalization or a 'global gay' community elsewhere may spur people to migrate to some queer promised land in Sydney, London, Paris, New York, Barcelona or Los Angeles.

The growth of recognition of same sex relationships as the basis for residence and citizenship reflects a growth of interest in the human rights records of less developed countries more generally. In this context we see the British media focus on Zimbabwe where the state's oppressive treatment of gays (rightfully) receives plenty of column inches in newspapers in London. Another example of this is the whole controversy over Jamaican ragga music in the early 1990s (Skelton, 1995), when artists such as Buju Banton's and Shabba Ranks's virulent homophobia received plenty of media attention, thereby rendering visible the squeamishness of educated middle-class broadsheet readers. We can see very real parallels between the treatment of gay men and women in international human rights law in terms of the way that they are a benchmark, or reflection of a state's human rights record. As Jacqueline Bhabha notes: 'This is the era when the west is championing one of its prize exports, respect for universal human rights, as part of its new assault on the "the rest" and in tandem with its foreign policy strategy of "good governance"' (1996: 5). The international human rights system seeks to protect gays in the way that many nation-states fail to. Therefore it is not too difficult to see the superficial attraction of international human rights and the language of globalism within lesbian and gay rights discourses. Bhabha (1996) suggests there is a double standard in the way western states treat human rights, arguing that western states label abusive treatment of women in the developing world as primitive, while failing to give women equal rights within their own jurisdictions. In a similar vein Jasbir Puar (2002) speaks of the double standard of western states in her discussion of the controversies surrounding queer tourism in the Caribbean. Puar argues that while the UK government was outspoken in its condemnation of homophobia in the Carribean, it failed to grant protection for such tourists at home: 'Ironically, the United States and British states advocate protection for cruise ships in the Carribean while granting no such rights when cruisegoers return home' (2002: 102). Bhabha recognizes that the universalism associated with international human rights may be imperialistic, and notes that feminist ideals around greater rights for women can serve to bolster anti-Islamic sentiment. However, she suggests the language and rhetoric of human rights may be valuable in helping to promote recognition of claims of refugee women for residency and citizenship, arguing that: 'the application of a uniform standard informed by human rights norms can provide the basis for a defence of the right to differ and a critique of persecutory practices imposed on individuals which a relativist perspective may preclude' (1996: 31). As Bhabha suggests, the notion of universal human rights, no matter how flawed, has a rhetorical power and symbolic value in helping to legitimate claims for refugee status. However, in terms of sexual citizenship we cannot assume that European, global or international activism will transplant the national community as the prime basis for activism, organization and political struggle. You have to make changes where possible. There is nothing inevitable about change and law reform, and we must not see law reform as something we can ever take for granted, or merely as an inevitable part of a modern escalator of development of greater and greater rights. Speaking about the frustrating pace of legal transformations in the status of lesbians and gay men within the European Union, Amy Elman (2000) observes that in some member states this had led to a focusing of lesbian and gay activist energies on the national scale. I have noted that an increasing number of western countries have now legislated to include persecution on the basis of sexual orientation as grounds for recognition of asylum claims. More states are also recognizing same sex relationships for the purpose of claims for citizenship of the foreign partner of a citizen of that state. While recognizing that these represent valuable legal victories in the cause of lesbian and gay equality it is important to acknowledge the multiple contexts of law reform. In this context we should bear in mind the claim by Arnaldo Cruz-Malavé and Martin Manalansan IV who argue that:

> Another trope of globalization discourses is perhaps potentially more sinister: the appropriation and deployment of queer subjectivities, cultures, and political agendas for the legitimation of hegemonic institutions presently in discursive crisis, institutions such as the nation-state or US imperial hegemony. (2002: 5)

Queer Tourism

In the previous section of this chapter I discussed whether citizenship is restricted to queers who migrate across national borders. I argued that movement across national borders is restricted for some sexual dissidents because of heteronormative and homophobic migration policies. These

99

restrictions of course are classed, racialized and gendered. In terms of consumer citizenship, John Urry has focused on tourist practices in terms of the rights of the consumer, suggesting that 'the right to travel has become a marker of citizenship [...] Citizenship rights increasingly involve claims to consume other cultures and places throughout the world' (1995: 165). However, this right is increasingly contested by, for instance, groups campaigning for indigenous rights and environmental groups who point to the pollution associated with tourism. For lesbians and gay men the right to travel and partake within tourism has been highly contested. Many hoteliers still refuse lesbian and gay tourists or make them feel unwelcome. Having to assert one's rights in order to be treated with respect in service encounters within the tourist industry is something to which many lesbians and gay men have become accustomed.

It is important to bear in mind the real restrictions on migration for sexual dissidents when it comes to sexualized consumption practices like tourism. Notions of desire and longing are fundamental to tourism (in addition to cosmopolitan consumption discussed in Chapter 8). What both discussions share is an understanding of how desire both shapes and is constrained by economics. In an earlier chapter we saw the centrality of the desire for elsewhere, specifically the desire for an idealized, romanticized view of America. We saw, for instance in Mark Johnson's study of the Philippines, how America performed a role as an imaginary space where people aspired to live, to be – where a particular notion of love or romance could be realized. Johnson notes that it is this romanticized view of queer life abroad, passed on through gossip which is significant in shaping this imaginary space: 'translocality is as much about fantasy and imagination, a traversing of conceptual spaces, as it is about the actual movement of goods or people' (1998: 696). Tourism is a sexualized phenomenon. However, the literature on sexuality and tourist practices tends to be dominated by discussions of sex tourism. This can sometimes pathologize gay men's tourism depicting western gay men as predatory paedophiles. This masks the fact that all tourism is sex tourism to the extent that tourist practices are sexualized – most commonly in that they embody notions of heterosexual romance. There are certain types of tourist experience, and certain tourist gazes (Urry, 1990) that are represented as 'normal' – namely the family (in the narrowest, straightest sense) package tour. Other tourist experiences such as global lesbian and gay events like the Gay Games are sometimes treated with bemusement by the mainstream media. Much of the discussion of the economic power of lesbians, and most especially of gay men focuses on queer tourism. Queer tourism represents perhaps the most visible and distinctive form of queer consumption. In *Virtuous Vice: Homoeroticism and the Public Sphere*, Eric Clarke notes the role of travel and tourism within lesbian and gay consumer culture. Noting the prevalence of advertisements for the travel industry within the lesbian and gay magazines that have proliferated in recent years, he suggests it is lesbian and gay oriented businesses that promote their economic visibility, thereby perpetuating the myth of the pink economy examined in Chapter 4:

> As if to emphasize the potential for such activities to transform self-representation into a profound sense of entitlement, indeed a transformation of identity literally into propriety, the latest 'international gay travel magazine' is called, simply, *Our World*. (2000: 146)

This sense of entitlement that Clarke speaks of is redolent of imperialism. In the previous chapter I mentioned the body of work examining same sex tourism as a reproduction of colonial power relations. For Clarke these advertisements and the development of the niche market in international lesbian and gay travel represents: 'both a continuation and a rearticulation of the exoticizing, vaguely erotic adventure that ... undergirds a nineteenth-century legitimation and inclusion of male homo-erotic self-representations which erotically exotic romps across the globe' (2000: 147). It is clear that this should not be read at face value, for what is wrong with a sense of entitlement about being able to travel? Lesbians and gay men still face considerable discrimination within the tourist industry, so what is wrong with a sense of entitlement at being able to travel without discrimination? If one accepts Pheng Cheah's (1998) vision of cosmopolitanism as a more genuine universalism, or Ulf Hannerz's (1996) argument that cosmopolitanism is a more genuine 'engagement with the Other', why should not lesbians and gay men share a sense of entitlement to travel across national borders without harassment? Heterosexuality is still naturalized as normal; straights still have a sense of entitlement to cross space without having their heterosexuality called into question. Of course the very authenticity of heterosexual relationships is routinely questioned by immigration authorities, when it is suspected that heterosexual marriage may be merely a front to obtain residence and citizenship for the migrant partner. The right to travel associated with global sexual citizenship must be accompanied by responsibilities, for instance in terms of ethical tourism and respect for indigenous cultures. In terms of rights and cosmopolitan authority, who has the authority to legislate which forms of queer tourism, which queer tourist practices are authenticated, and involve a genuine engagement with the Other? For instance in Jasbir Puar's discussion of queer tourism in the Caribbean, she acknowledges that there is evidently an overlap between ethnography and tourism, but I wonder who has the right to legislate between non-authentic and real experiences of otherness? She has a sense of entitlement to carry out research as an ethnographer but applauds Caribbean states' rejection of lesbian and gay tourists. She appears to be suggesting that she has cosmopolitan critical authority, as opposed to other lesbians and gays who wish to partake in tourist practices. Why is being a researcher any less exploitative than being another tourist? Wouldn't other tourists contribute more towards the local economy? Her work also raises the question of representation. Adopting the position as ethnographer tourist, she feels no compunction about presenting herself as an authority on gay men's sexual cultures. Lesbians and gay men (like heterosexuals) partake in the tourist industry as consumers, but many are also involved in the tourist industry as producers, doing low-paid work in the service sector. Earlier in the chapter I noted that many queer migrants may settle for poorly paid jobs in the service sector when they first arrive in a new space in order to a get a foothold in a new city or country. I maintain that what are often highly exaggerated claims about the economic strength of lesbian and gay tourism serves to reinforce and reproduce the pink economy discourse. Moreover, as perniciously, it reinforces the notion that lesbians and gay men are not only hyper-affluent but also hyper-mobile. This is a dizzying cocktail of misrecognition that has dangerous consequences for how we think through questions of queer mobility.

Some work on queer tourism does trouble me in terms of representation. There is a tendency to take at face value some of the promulgations and wild claims about the economic power of lesbians and gay men. This is dangerous as Carl Stychin argues that this perception of queer affluence can be deployed by others for homophobic purposes: 'The perceived frequency of lesbian and gay travel has been deployed in the construction of gays as an "undeserving" (because privileged) minority, who do not "deserve" what are described as "special rights", because of their upward mobility' (2000b: 605–6). In this context, Puar (2002) quotes figures about the money generated by lesbian and gay tourism as evidence to bolster her claims about the post-colonial power relations of international gay tourism. The focus of many of the discussions of gay tourism is on firms that specialize in package tours addressing the gay market, whereas the reality of queer tourism is that many queers take part in tourism in an independent way, do their own thing and encounter the everyday homophobia of hoteliers. Another point that seriously bemuses me is the way Puar expresses relief and joy at the way the authorities in the Cayman Islands and elsewhere refused landing rights to the cruise ship and refused to be persuaded otherwise by statements from politicians such as Blair. I must admit I feel uncomfortable about the line she adopts in her discussion of this matter, for it appears to seriously downplay homophobia. This is common within representations of gay men as tourists, as Jarrod Hayes argues. There are of course major links here with the discussion of queer postcolonialism in the previous chapter.

A number of authors have argued that sex (and other) tourism reproduces colonial and imperial power relations. For instance, Pettman (1996: 196–7) argues that sex tourism: 're-enacts colonial and contemporary power relations, which are "raced" as well as gendered'. In much of this work, women are represented as passive victims, men as aggressive and penetrative. However, there is some complexity as she acknowledges that western women also participate as international sex tourists (1996: 201).

As I mentioned in the previous chapter, when discussing the relationship between postcolonial and queer thinking there is a real danger that postcolonial theory can reproduce homophobia – specifically in terms of the denigration of any form of sexual relationship across national or racial boundaries. On the other hand the romanticization of difference and otherness has long been a part of queer utopianism. Hayes is insightful about the relationship between representation, sexuality and tourism, arguing that hegemonic discourses and critiques of sex tourism are inflected by a homophobic sentiment:

> Most critiques of sexual tourism, while pretending to condemn colonialism, end up being more about an anxiety about desires that cross racial, cultural, or class boundaries. These critiques often single out homosexual sexual tourism (which I shall call 'homo sexual tourism' hereafter) for a particularly vehement criticism that tropes homosexuality as essentially exploitative. (2000: 26)

As Hayes argues, what he terms homosexual sexual tourism, and I would argue homosexual sex per se, has been subject to fear and loathing because it threatens to destabilize these very borders and boundaries. 'Hayes' statement demonstrates the urgent need to articulate an anti-homophobic postcolonial position on sex and queer tourism:

> Critiques of sexual tourism or Orientalism have been levied against homosexual and heterosexual tourists unevenly, without any consideration of differences between dominant and marginalized western sexualities as they are transplanted into the Orient. That homophobia should be related to homo sexual tourism is never suggested. Such critiques, often inspired by Said, are thus far less nuanced than Orientalism, which at least suggests a relation between sexual repression at home and tourism abroad. Often condemnations take on a puritanical tone: what is insidious about sexual tourism is that it involves sex; never is there any suggestion that tourism in itself might merit interrogation and the sexual tourism might only be a smaller part of a more general exploitation. Instead, characteristic critiques rely on a phobic reaction to homosexual encounters that cross national and racial boundaries. (2000: 29)

I have argued that any discussion of queer tourism must not take at face value some of the statistics, facts and figures that are bandied around about the lesbian and gay tourist market. Discourses of gay affluence that abound in work on queer tourism parallel those of the pink economy more generally.

Now that these have been expertly de-bunked by writers such as Badgett, we have to be very wary of such discourses and what they serve to do. Western lesbian and gay male tourists (like their heterosexual counterparts) participate in global structures of economic inequality that reproduce power relations that reinforce the poverty of the South. However, work in this area needs to be sensitive to the potential for pathologization of gay men in discourses on sex tourism.

Limits to Queer Mobility

In this chapter I have examined the notion of queer mobility. I have done this by focusing on movement and migration and the relationship to queer identity, space and location in general. I have argued that it is extremely difficult and dangerous to conceptually separate queer migration and queer tourism. Discourses and discussions of the latter often overstate the ability of queers to cross national borders. Likewise discourses on queer migration can tend to emphasize the victimhood of passive queers acted upon by the repressive oppressive nation-state that denies access to racialized Others. I posit that there is a racialized distinction between on the one hand (active) hypermobile white queers participating in global gay tourism, and the (passive) queers of colour who are subject to barriers, borders and breaks on their movement across national borders. As Aihwa Ong has reminded us, migrants come from a variety of backgrounds and national political formations. Not all queer migrants are poor, impoverished Others, but may equally be part of a transnational elite.

In this chapter I have argued that migration should also be considered in terms of two key facets: namely the rural– urban binary and the gendered nature of migration. International migration should therefore be examined alongside rural–urban migrations within a nation-state. Likewise queer migration must take account of the difference that gender makes. Lesbians face additional barriers to migration compared to men, namely access to the capital to migrate in the first place. I then went on to discuss migration policies and the possibilities for queer citizenship. Having done this I examined the notion of queer tourism. The spectre of AIDS haunts each of these discussions, and the relationship between migration, identity, sex and the pandemic will be examined in the next chapter. We can see that queer migrations across national borders constitute a threat to the fixed categories of identity, specifically national identity. Queer relations are often characterized by engagements across racial and class lines and it is this that promotes anxiety in those who see themselves as guardians of these boundaries. Jarrod

Hayes has made an important intervention in condeming highly moralistic denigrations of queer tourist practices, which often reflect a profound squeamishness about sex. This explains the particular concern with gay men's tourist practices as gay men are constructed as being hypermasculine and predatory. Thus we see the moralistic denigration of gay men's tourism by some feminists that parallels and mirrors the disgust at gay men's sexual practices that lies at the root of Mugabe's (for example) homophobia.

The critical focus on the globalization of queer tourism says much about homophobia in the west and a displacement of anxieties about sexual identities in the west in the bodies of gay men travelling to the developing world. In her critique of Altman's writing on the global gay, Lisa Rofel argues that Altman takes at face value the assertions and claims of a global gay identity that is being claimed and promoted. But I would argue that this is as true of sexual cultures in the west as it is in the developing world. For instance the entitlement claims for gay men wishing to engage in international tourism discussed by Eric Clarke reflect in many cases a lack of power and recognition. I argue that despite the growth of visibility, status and publicity of lesbians and gay men, it is clearly far from the case that it is 'Our World'. The experience of living as a gay man or lesbian is still very much the experience of being an outsider, of a sense of disenfranchisement, rather than entitlement. Where does class fit into the picture? It comes in terms of the class-marked distinction between queers. For working-class queers their sense of transnational tourist flows may be more restricted, and shaped by financial constraints. Thus, in this sense, what does 'entitlement' mean? Entitlement means the same opportunities for tourism as straights. Class also comes into the equation in terms of the attempts in queer criticism to mark a distinction between queer intellectuals and activists and the mass of queers as Other. Lesbian and gay anthropologists constitute themselves as travellers – as the expert or knowing Same that projects their own imperialistic tendencies, traits and guilt on to the bodies of those queers engaged in package or mass tourism. Here for example see the work of Peter Gurney (1997) on mass observation in Blackpool and its pathologization of working-class sexualities. The work displays prurient interest in the sexual habits, customs and cultures of working class Boltonians in the seaside resort of Blackpool.

Writing the conclusion to this chapter I feel a deep unease and ambivalence about queer migration and tourism. I acknowledge and recognize the racist and imperialistic tendencies of many lesbians and gay men engaged in international tourism. However, I feel very uncomfortable about some of the criticisms of these tourist practices that tend to revolve more around the self-righteousness of the moral guardians of sexual purity. One should strive for the eradication of all power relations and inequalities between sexual partners, whether in the west or the developing world. However, as Jarrod Hayes, Eric Rofes and Samuel Delany argue, (sexual) contact across racial and class boundaries cannot simply be marked by exploitation.

7

AIDS and Queer Globalization

In the previous chapter I argued that despite the popular discourses of queer hypermobility, sexual dissidents actually face considerable barriers to movement across national borders, specifically in terms of rights of residency and citizenship. Cindy Patton (2000) argues that the migrant's body is key to discourses in which AIDS is represented as an alien threat to the indigenous body. Mobile actors associated with transport and communications industries are commonly held responsible for the transmission of HIV from elsewhere, whether they be truck drivers, or airline stewards. HIV and AIDS are routinely represented as a threat from elsewhere, particularly a virile threat to the sanctity of borders, as William Haver argues: 'the Human Immunodeficiency Virus is the first true cosmopolitan, respecting neither geographic, cultural, sexual, class, nor racial boundaries' (1996: 7). In addressing the threat posed by HIV and AIDS, we have to consider boundaries at different spatial scales, whether national, or as in Meredith Raimondo's (2001) discussion, the imaginary boundary of the rural heartland. AIDS threatens to collapse spatial scales, as a threat from elsewhere may be constituted as simultaneously a threat to the nation, the planet, the rural and the body. Spatial metaphors abound in discussions of AIDS.

In this chapter I argue that the AIDS pandemic represents a particular challenge to social theory, particularly in relation to globalization. AIDS is often seen as a metaphor for globalization and the relationship between AIDS and globalization has been conceptualized in a variety of competing ways using the language of diaspora through to cosmopolitanism. Building on the discussion of queer diaspora in the previous chapter, I will now examine the notion that experience of living with AIDS represents a form of diaspora in itself. The use of diaspora to describe the experience of living and dying with AIDS is an interesting one but potentially problematic given what I have said in earlier chapters about the dangers of essentialising a single experience of queer diaspora. After examining the challenges posed by AIDS to the way social theory has approached globalization, I will then examine national formations of AIDS and sexual citizenship. I argue that the experience of AIDS has in many respects reinforced the significance of the nation-state. I develop my discussion through an examination of two national formations of AIDS and sexual citizenship and I conclude my discussion by focusing on AIDS as a cosmopolitan virus.

AIDS as a Metaphor for Globalization

The HIV pandemic has an especially problematic relation with frontiers and boundaries of all sorts. The spread of the virus is evidence of much more that the struggles to manifest and resist national sovereignty along territorial borders. The nexus of HIV transmission across this territory is a metaphor for the globalization of investment, trade, and cultural identity. Although the dominant realist tradition in studies of international relations conceives national territorial space as homogenous and exclusive, what is referred to as the 'new global cultural economy' must be seen as a complex, overlapping, disjunctive order, which cannot be adequately understood in terms of center-periphery, inner-outer, state-border models of the past. (Porter, 1997)

AIDS, like globalization, is seen to challenge the very limits of working and thinking within a national framework. As Michael Warner (1993: xii) puts it: 'nowhere has the need for transnational comparative thinking been clearer than on the subject of AIDS'. In terms of globalization and social theory, AIDS is significant, as it is a global pandemic. As Manderson and Jolly note, the transmission of HIV in Africa along trucking routes is: 'gruesomely metaphoric of a process of globalization across national borders' (1997: 20). Theorizing around globalization, moreover, has accelerated as the AIDS pandemic has assumed global proportions. Angus Bancroft argues that in the context of Southern Africa, the economic development of transport and health infrastructure associated with modernity, and associated sexual freedoms have enabled HIV to spread. In this sense he argues that: HIV/AIDS resulted from globalization and the impact of modernity, modern medicine and modern nation-state structures on Southern Africa (2001: 92). Much of the work on lesbian and gay studies has been financed or funded through research projects linked to AIDS. Many writers and commentators have argued that AIDS is symbolic of globalization itself and I now proceed to examine this idea.

While AIDS may be powerfully symbolic of the process of globalization, we should still be aware of the dangers of representing AIDS as a symbol or metaphor. In terms of globalization, AIDS has sometimes been written about in a highly problematic manner. HIV/AIDS is seen by many as contributing towards the sense of the erosion of the real and symbolic borders of the nation. The human rights of people with AIDS to cross international borders have been denied on a daily basis. The mobile person with AIDS is seen as a threat to the national body. The sense that national borders have become much more permeable with the current focus in social theory on mobility (Urry, 2000a). In representations of AIDS, the virus is commonly associated and linked with international transport, so that the fear of AIDS is transposed onto the architecture and technology of transport. AIDS has brought into focus the relationships between migration and sexuality, particularly in Southern Africa (Hoad, 1999). For a select few – those who have made careers out of it, AIDS has led to social mobility. However, for the overwhelming majority, AIDS has led to immiseration and downward social movement. Peter Cohen (1997) has examined the class dislocations produced by the pandemic in New York City, arguing that, for the affluent white, middle class gay men who dominated AIDS activist groups such as ACT-UP, AIDS represented a fundamental challenge to their sense of entitlement. Having bought social acceptance through successful participation in the capitalist system, this very system was now unable and unwilling to provide solutions to the crisis. Cohen's work thus demonstrates the fact that there is a class dimension to the pandemic, a dimension that had hitherto been lacking in analysis.

The global AIDS pandemic has been crucial in bringing questions around the globalization of sexuality to the fore in debates within social theory. AIDS has led to draconian laws on movement, for instance the US ban on people with HIV and AIDS entering the country. Increased mobility has been blamed for accelerating the spread of HIV and AIDS – see for instance the case of 'Patient Zero', the gay Canadian air steward who was seen as single-handedly spreading the virus around the world through air travel. In many instances, HIV/AIDS is seen as a threat to the sovereignty of the state. Many states are unable to cope with the pandemic thereby threatening a crisis of legitimation. AIDS reinforces the interconnectivity of social relations, and also threatens to collapse spatial scales, as it is a threat to the boundaries of the body. For Dennis Altman (1999) and Doug Porter (1997), AIDS represents a threat to the sovereignty of the nation-state. AIDS is deeply implicated in the way we think about globalization, specifically in terms of the politics of spatial scale and the threat to national sovereignty.

AIDS as Globalizing Panic

I now turn to a key early essay on the subject of AIDS, globalization and sexuality by John O'Neill. It contains so much that is worthy of further consideration and examination for helping us to think through the relationships between political economy, AIDS, globalization, sexuality and the representation of each of these. 'AIDS as a globalizing panic', is one of the most significant essays conceptualizing and examining the links between AIDS and globalization. We should, however, be attuned to the dangers of using AIDS as metaphor (Sontag, 1989) In the essay, O'Neill speaks of 'the development of a framework for the study of AIDS which sets national and local concerns in the context of the global political economy' (1990: 332). I agree that any discussion of AIDS, globalization and sexuality must have a material basis. But I differ from Altman and O'Neill in my approach, in the way that we set about doing this. Theoretically this is significant as it is rooted in political economy. The relationship between queer theory and political economy has been a rather fraught one as I argued in Chapter 4. O'Neill appears to suggest that the global panic of AIDS is producing cultural homogenization in the same way as Coca-Cola: 'By a *globalizing panic* I understand any practice that traverses the world to reduce the world and its cultural diversity to the generics of Coca-Cola, tourism, foreign aid, medical aid, military defense posts, tourism, fashion and the international money markets' (1990: 332). O'Neill claims that AIDS represents a threat to particularity and difference. AIDS therefore threatens to become a universalizing and homogenizing force much like Coca-Cola. Unfortunately, in O'Neill's argument same sex culture is equated with the global consumer culture he castigates. Writing that AIDS may lead to the homogenization of global culture, he argues that may simultaneously be a threat to that same culture based on the nation of consumer choice and that sex has become detached from reproduction and can be enjoyed in its own right. The unfortunate tendency within O'Neill's otherwise useful and innovative essay on is the way in which he discusses gay consumer culture in a moralistic and somewhat patronizing manner:

> The experience of AIDS panics the sexual culture of global capitalism in several ways. In the first place, it has 'disappointed' those who were most committed to its ideology of sexual freedom. To its credit, the gay community has learned that sexuality cannot be played out in the anonymous intimacy and extraordinarily high rates of casual contact which were enjoyed in the bath houses. (1990: 335)

O'Neill sees sexual freedom as ideological – as a form of false consciousness. We see in his writing a moralistic denigration of bath house culture. He suggests that globalization (i.e. global consumer culture) has spread sexual freedom and hedonism around the globe – these are now out of control but threatened by the AIDS pandemic. Sexual freedom and globalization do not sit as comfortably as O'Neill's argument would suggest. Spaces devoted to sex – such as commercial venues – have been squeezed out by major multinational corporations and actors, who have sought to promote their own products and desires. This is not to argue for some untainted mythic state or queer utopia of pre-AIDS bath house culture – the sexual libertarianism was only ever on offer to some. San Francisco's golden age was also on the back of an economic boom, which provided jobs for sexual dissident immigrants. Both pre-AIDS and post-AIDS sexual cultures in the US and UK have excluded people on the basis of racism, gender, and class – but also in a Bourdieuvian sense on the basis of possession of the various forms of capital – social, bodily, economic (Binnie and Skeggs, 1999). O'Neill makes a conceptual distinction between the experience of AIDS in the developing world, and North American experiences of the pandemic. He speaks of US AIDS, which he associates with urban gay men and drug users. O'Neill argues that 'gay sub-culture has been a highly articulate ideological element in North American society. The imperial dominance of American capitalism within the global system, of course, diffuses American "life-style" ideologies through global mass culture, tourism, commercial and military travel' (1990: 338). It is significant that O'Neill highlights gay culture as being ideological to begin with. Therefore gay sub-culture is inauthentic – is a form of false consciousness. Having stated how this so-called 'ideological' culture is a particularly powerful and influential one in North America, he then proceeds to decry the imperialism of American consumer capitalism. It is dangerous to suggest that gay culture is so powerful, especially at the time O'Neill was writing, which was at the height of the hysteria around HIV and AIDS in North America. Having made the equation between gay culture and American consumer capitalism, he proceeds to argue how so-called 'American lifestyle ideologies' are dominating the world. Gay sub-culture is not named explicitly – but is surely implied in the link made in the previous sentence. It is not simply the case that there are unfortunate representations of gay consumer culture in thinking around AIDS as a global pandemic. There are very real concerns around the way in which sexual acts, identities and communities are configured within discourses on (global) AIDS. In the next section I consider the notion that AIDS has been the first postmodern virus. I go on to argue that questions of knowledge are fundamental in these discussions.

AIDS and Queer Diaspora

And now he was here, participating in his own worst nightmare: to be in a foreign land and ill.

He had worked it out at home before he left what was so peculiarly threatening about this thought: to be ill in a foreign country was simply to experience in advance the reality of all illness, which is to be homeless. It was to be in a permanent foreign land – one where the language used is barely comprehensible, or at least where words seem to match, only clumsily, what they stand to represent. Worse still, you had to adjust to customs you barely comprehend in a place which you never can be, you never actually want to be, at home. It was to be in permanent exile from the world you knew. You were a refugee before you even knew it. A refugee on your own world too, perhaps. (Wells, 1995)

In Chapter 5 I examined the notion of queer diaspora. I suggested that there were multiple ways in which diaspora could be queered. I argued against the idea that the label 'diaspora' could be applied equally to all sexual dissidents. The label is much more appropriate for the experience of some sexual dissidents more than others. Not all queers experience the same level of dislocation and displacement as a result of their sexuality. For those involved in transnational queer communities the term has a greater valency, though I also noted that the term, with its roots in postcolonial theory, had a limited applicability and could only partially encapsulate the complex cartographies of queer transnational communities. The New Zealand writer Peter Wells has written of AIDS as a diaspora. He speaks of the condition of 'homelessness' engendered by the illness. AIDS has brought about homelessness and severe dislocation, which have led to movements across space.

I have already mentioned the rural to urban, and urban to rural migrations within the United States in my discussion of the work of Meredith Raimondo. In terms of homelessness in a practical as opposed to existential sense, see for instance Philip Brian Harper's essay in which he discusses homelessness in New York alongside the epidemic. Some of the best work on the impact of AIDS on queer diaspora comes from Martin Manalansan IV. In his interviews with Filipino gay men in New York, he suggests that for these men, AIDS, in addition to being a medical crisis, was also a crisis of legitimacy in terms of their relationship to the United States: 'coming down with the disease was seen by some as a failure on their part of attaining the American dream, particularly those whose who found out as part of their naturalization (citizenship) process' (1996: 59). We therefore see that there are additional crises suffered by these men in that they risk deportation from the country, and as Manalansan notes, for some it represents a failure of their making it in the United States, and may lead to further dislocation. Here we see the distinction between Brennan's cosmopolitan being 'at home in the world', and the literal homelessness associated with AIDS. Manderson and Jolly (1997) argue that AIDS also has a class dimension. They suggest that research on HIV and AIDS has brought questions of race and class to the fore in research on sexuality. AIDS does not simply lead to dislocation and abjection but has also led to the production of new spaces of transnational activism. For instance in a paper on Puerto Rican gay men's responses to HIV and AIDS, Frances Negron-Muntaner argues that the transnational basis of this community shaped activism in Puerto Rico. In San Juan strategies to draw attention to AIDS in Puerto Rico such as marches and 'die-ins' reflected many Puerto Rican men's experience of AIDS activism while resident in the United States:

> This form of activism was predicated on a sense of belonging to multiple locations and on an ethnical imperative to all Puerto Rican spaces. In using the air bridge to share information, resources, and strategies in the fight against the epidemic, Puerto Rican gay men enacted a globalized political consciousness firmly rooted in New York communities, panethnic identifications, and the American queer movement. (1999: 523)

I have suggested that there are clear parallels between the experience of living with HIV and AIDS and the experience of being in diaspora. For queers in diaspora, HIV and AIDS may reinforce the acute risks and vulnerabilities in being an outsider, or immigrant within a host society. However, as the Puerto Rican example discussed by Negron-Muntaner shows, AIDS activism may help forge a transnational community, and may produce a transnational sense of solidarity.

In this section I have argued that on the one hand AIDS reinforces the abjection of many sexual dissidents who are marginalized as outsiders within the national polity because of their citizenship status. In this sense the experience of living with HIV and AIDS acutely reinforces the sense of powerlessness, homelessness and loneliness associated with being an outsider within a political community. However as Manalansan's and Negron-Muntaner's work demonstrates, the political responses forged as a reaction to HIV and AIDS may help constitute a transnational sense of solidarity and community.

AIDS, Modernity and Postmodernity

In this section I discuss the notion that AIDS represents a challenge to the notion of modernity and that it is the first postmodern virus. AIDS constitutes a legitimation crisis for capitalist societies and also a threat to faith in modern science. For John O'Neill AIDS constitutes a threat to modernity itself, he argues that 'nothing represents the postmodern moment in our history more sharply than the transformation of our sexuality in its encounter with the HIV virus' (2001: 181). In Chapter 5 I argued against the evolutionary narratives of modern gay liberation. I critiqued the notion that in modernity, we are on a path towards ever-greater gay liberation. Gay identity is a modern identity, which presupposes an evolutionary theory of sexuality and development. I concluded that globalization, rather than leading to a simple transmission of gay identity and culture across the globe, is instead leading to greater challenges to the notion of what we mean by a modern gay identity based on confession and the closet. Does postmodernity mean the end of sexual categories, or specifically to what Henning Bech has termed 'the disappearance of the homosexual' (Bech, 1999)? AIDS has both challenged and reinforced the notion of the modern gay subject. It has called into question evolutionary approaches to sexual subjectivity (i.e. the focus on coming out and the closet) and the confessional nature of western subjectivity. For instance, Larvie's (1999) work on AIDS and sexual citizenship in Brazil argues that responses to AIDS on the one hand have led toward an institutionalization of sexual citizenship for those who conform to the modern gay identity. On the other hand it has revealed the complexities of sexual acts and identities beyond the simplistic notion of the closet and coming out associated with modern gay identity, subjectivity and politics. Thus the 1990s witnessed the coming to the fore of bisexual, transgender and transsexual politics which constituted a challenge to received notions of gay liberation. AIDS has enabled the transfer of transnational activism on gay rights and the transmission of the model of the global gay through, for instance, world AIDS conferences. Unfortunately there is a dichotomizing tendency within thinking on global gay identity, where a gay identity based on public affirmation of sexual preference is equated with the west.

AIDS is putting severe pressure on the development of strategies of some developing countries. The very notion of development itself has been critiqued from a queer perspective, as we saw in the previous chapter. We must be ever aware of the way in which the establishment of a lesbian and gay community and movement can be read as a measure of a society's level of sophistication and development. O'Neill's essay suggests a globalizing, universalizing response to the 'society with AIDS' – he presupposes a uniformity of the state's response to the pandemic. However, what is clear from the best work in the area is the multiple nature of the state's responses to HIV/AIDS. For O'Neill, AIDS is seen as symbolic of the loss of faith in modern medicine to find a cure, a medical, technical, modern solution to the pandemic. AIDS is clearly implicated in this loss of faith in the future and the heightened sense of living in the ever-present – the notion that history has come to an end, associated with postmodernity. Is there not a danger, however, in AIDS being an epidemic of oversignification? O'Neill writes at a time before there had been significant medical breakthroughs in the treatment of HIV/AIDS. Combination therapies have led to rather more optimistic discussions and prognoses recently.

I have argued that AIDS constitutes a challenge to social theory, specifically the way we think about the configuration of sexualities, acts, identities and communities. In addressing this challenge, however, there is a danger of fetishizing the local. As I argued in earlier chapters, are the local and global not mutually interdependent constructs? For instance, in Brazil we see the North American sex researchers imputing the authenticity of non-gay defined alternative configurations of sex, gender and identity, while locally in Brazil we see a representation of Brazilian gay culture and community as part of an international gay identity and community. The local and global are interconnected in terms of the globalization of the modern homosexual – the claiming of a modern gay identity in the south on the back of global and national responses to HIV/AIDS, while in the north we have witnessed the highly contested notions of post-gay identities. Here there is a very close and strong link with the notion of modernity developed in Chapter 4. So the history of homosexuality is essentially the history of modernity – homosexual identity is a modern invention. Hence also the link with the colonial and imperial constructions of sexuality that was discussed in Chapter 2.

I have examined the relationship between AIDS, globalization and sexuality. I argued that AIDS represents a powerful symbol of globalization. Work by O'Neill (and Dennis Altman) was significant in arguing for the materiality of sexual identities, communities and politics but at the same time the political economy has been problematic in the way it represents desire. I then went on to examine the notion of the relationship between AIDS, modernity and postmodernity. This led to a discussion of the links between these and questions of knowledge and epistemology. I maintain that each of these brings into focus questions of nationhood and national identity. I argue that national formations of sexual citizenship are still significant and should not be underestimated.

National Formations of AIDS and Sexual Citizenship

AIDS activism points towards the limits of applying one political discourse and response from one national polity to another. AIDS activism itself is form of globalizing culture – witness the proliferation of the symbols associated with it, such as the red ribbon. In his discussion of AIDS activism and practices of citizenship in Vancouver, Michael Brown argues that the politics of AIDS are simultaneously local and global:

> In the case of World AIDS Day, the global nature of AIDS is not dichotomized with a fixed set of local responses in Vancouver. Instead, local responses in Vancouver are compared and contrasted to those in other places like Mexico and Nicaragua, as well as rural British Columbia. In this way, the local politics of AIDS in the city are simultaneously – and self-consciously – global politics as well. Moreover, the week-long string of events allowed thousands of Vancouver citizens to reflect on their own relationship to HIV risk, while constantly situating themselves in the global context of the AIDS crisis. (1995: 257–8)

From the discussion in the previous section we can see that in many respects AIDS is deeply symbolic of globalization. However, while AIDS is globalizing and is a truly global pandemic, we must not lose sight of the highly uneven impact of the pandemic on specific regions and states. In this section I wish to stress that AIDS has in many respects reinforced the importance of the nation-state, rather than its irrelevance. In Chapter 2 I argued that we must acknowledge the resilience of the nation-state and that any discussion of queer globalization must take this into account. I shall now go on to examine two distinctive national formations of sexual citizenship, Brazil and the Netherlands, and assess the way the relationships between AIDS activism and globalization have been configured within each. Elsewhere, we have seen conscious transnational comparing and contrasting of local responses with those in other national polities. One could argue that as with the theory of the relationship between globalization and the nation-state discussed in Chapter 2. The threat posed by HIV/AIDS to the national polity has led to distinctive national political responses. This reinforces the point made by Manderson that HIV/AIDS is both real and symbolic. From Manderson and Jolly we can see that each national polity has therefore a different and distinctive 'discursive constitution' (1997: 19). While I am in general agreement with Manderson and Jolly's argument that the discursive construction of HIV and AIDS is different outside of Europe, North America and Australia, I would add that HIV/AIDS is also different in its discursive construction within Europe; for instance, compare Dutch, British and French responses to the epidemic. Jan Willem Duyvendak (1996) has argued that the response to HIV and AIDS in the Netherlands was marked by a significant and conscious comparison of responses with those of elsewhere. Thereby these specific local responses constitute and reconstitute a Dutch nationalism – a specific reproduction of Dutch nationhood. AIDS therefore did not lead to the destruction of national borders or consciousness, but instead reproduced them. In this sense the threat posed by AIDS offered an opportunity for the production of nationalism. Duyvendak has examined Dutch sexual polities, specifically in his *De Verzuiling van de Homobeweging* ('The Pillarization of the Gay Movement'). In addition he has compared different national political responses to HIV and AIDS in the Netherlands (for instance he has compared policy responses in the Netherlands with those in France). Duyvendak argues that responses to the AIDS crisis in The Netherlands, reinforced and reproduced the Dutch political-cultural values of tolerance and political accommodation.

AIDS represented a challenge to the Dutch nation, and the response reproduced and reinforced Dutch social, cultural and political values and norms. Duyvendak (1996) argues that the paucity of activism around AIDS, at least relative to the United States, can be explained by the Dutch political model of accommodation and inclusion whereby the authorities actively engaged with the organized lesbian and gay rights movement and sought their input into policies to tackle AIDS within the community. While the state produced a policy based on the system of pillarization[1] and to a certain extent gave the Dutch gay movement considerable influence in determining policies aimed at reduction of rates of transmission and infection, the grassroots activists' response to AIDS reflected a very Dutch moral concern with the epidemic beyond the boundaries of the Netherlands. Duyvendak writes about the campaigns of the Dutch chapter of ACT-UP and notes the strong international dimension to their protests and campaigns: 'It is also interesting to note that the political authorities that were criticized were usually either abroad or the targets of international campaigns' (1996: 428). He argues that an international focus characterized the actions of the Dutch chapter of ACT-UP, referring to campaigns organized against Philip Morris, for instance. This international dimension to AIDS activist politics was significant as it again reproduced a Dutch national identity. The implication was that the Dutch had responded well and had involved the gay community, which was seen as a progressive step when compared to other countries. However, as Duyvendak notes, this in itself did not mean that Dutch measures and policies to stop the spread of HIV and AIDS had been more successful than other countries (1996: 424). Duyvendak suggests that despite the inclusion and participation of the Dutch gay movement in helping to formulate policies to prevent the spread of HIV and AIDS, these policies have not been any more successful than neighbouring countries where the gay movement was excluded. Dutch policy responses to HIV and AIDS were also conditioned by a fear of the infection of the Dutch national polity from outside forces. Fears were expressed that the Netherlands could find itself in the same predicament as the United

States. The implication was that the Netherlands should be scared of the American progression of the epidemic, but also that the Netherlands ran the risk of being infected with US welfare and treatment policies that reflected social polarization. This fear could have reflected the participation of US activists within the Dutch organization. Duyvendak quotes from Rumke an ACT-UP activist who reflects a concern that AIDS could be the trojan horse of neo-liberalism, leading to US style welfare policies in The Netherlands:

> The Netherlands is threatened with circumstances similar to those in the United States, where people with AIDS die in the streets because only the wealthy can afford medication and care ... At present the hospitals are still able to foot the bill, but there are ever louder rumours that they will soon be unable to raise the 350–500 Guilders that is required per AIDS patient per month. This means that American conditions are on the way. (Rumke, quoted in Duyvendak, 1996: 428–9)

Thus we see a clear example of the way in which AIDS represented an Americanization of the Dutch polity, a threat to the Dutch way of doing things and the Dutch welfare state. Larvie argues that there is a key link between the politics of recognition and AIDS prevention and citizenship. Larvie's work suggests that the closet and the US model of citizenship has indeed been globalized and imported into Brazilian society and political culture. Dutch responses to AIDS reproduced a Dutch national political formation and identity. The specificity of the Dutch model of pillarization is contrasted with the way acts, identities and citizenship are configured in the Brazilian case. In his essay, 'queerness and the spectre of Brazilian national ruin', Larvie argues that the notion of gay identity and culture in Brazil is associated with modernity, progress and development. Gay identity is therefore seen as a marker of the nation's progress in becoming a modern developed state. The association of the gay identity and movement with modernity was seen to be significant in developing strategies to prevent the spread of AIDS. Larvie notes that a gay identity is based on 'coming out' and publicity makes a gay community visible to policy makers and thus more accessible in terms of AIDS prevention. Citizenship rights are attached to those who ascribe to this gay identity, which is seen as modern and progressive. The modern gay identity, based on confession, the closet and western notions of subjectivity, is contrasted with sexual dissident identities that do not conform to this configuration of desire and identity and association. Thus Larvie discusses the outsider group, who are constituted as the Other of the modern gay. 'Bofes' who are represented as a Brazilian folk model of sexuality are seen as a pre- or anti-modern embarrassment to this vision of progress and modern gay subjectivity and politics:

> Like the 'irrational' or prepsychologized object of preventional initiatives, bofes are represented as constitutionally impaired, with a diminished capacity to assimilate and act on the scientific information necessary to prevent the spread of HIV. Worse, because they are unable or unwilling to organize a community or even a group, they are excluded from the ideal of political modernity articulated by the NPSTD/AIDS. Unlike gays or transvestites, bofes will never acquire full sexual citizenship, unless they adopt a new consciousness with respect to their sexual desires and political subjectivity. (1999: 548–49)

Thus we see how the rights for gays have been based on the exclusion of bofes, who Larvie argues are seen as shameful reflections of a lack of modernity and as 'embodying the antithesis of nationalist development and civilization' (1999: 549). In a similar vein, Chris Haylett (2001) argues that the abject white working class are constituted as a threat to Blair's vision of a globalized, Europeanized modern New Britain. White working-class men are constituted as violent, uncivilized and in this way they are racialized and sexualized. These distinctions between a supposedly progressive cosmopolitan gay identity and abject other are fundamental to the reproduction of the class and racial basis of sexual politics in the west, as well as Brazil. Jarrod Hayes argues that many of the statements that are applied to non-western contexts and polities, cultures around the limits of a modern, western approach to gay subjectivity and identity are also applicable to the west as well. Larvie's essay on sexual citizenship in Brazil is especially useful in that it presents a careful and nuanced examination of the relationships between modernity, Brazilian nationalism and the development of sexual citizenship. It is interesting the way homophobia gets configured in the Brazilian state's policy responses to the AIDS crisis. Homophobia is seen as un-modern, and therefore something to be challenged in the drive to modernization. In the same way, Larvie argues that indigenous constructions of sexuality were seen as backward and unprogressive.

> In the era of AIDS, Brazil's 'folk' models of sexuality have been seen as a threat to the establishment of a modern public health technocracy. The absence of properly organized communities of sexual others has been imagined as symptomatic of a backward mentality toward sex that is said to hinder the country's advancement toward civilization. When reviewed through the lens of nationalist science, homophobia has emerged as an impediment to the attainment of a new and great national civilization. The nation's sexual others have been called to action, asked to join activist groups to promote sexual tolerance and prevent AIDS. (1999: 552)

National political formations demonstrate that the nation is still important and should not be seen simply as a passive victim of global AIDS. While in many cases this is true, context is everything and we should be aware of the complexity of transnational flows and connections. There are also nations taking an active role as transnational actors, for instance the Dutch involvement in European Union politics and pressure on Romania to reform its laws on lesbian and gay affairs (Stychin, 2002). Duyvendak's work demonstrates how the Dutch response to the crisis very clearly reflected and reproduced the Dutch political system and structures – specifically the notion of '*verzuiling*' (pillarization) by which an elite is given control and responsibility for managing their own people – certain structures are put in place to facilitate this. The AIDS crisis demonstrated how the national polity reproduces itself. The national debate on AIDS contrasted local and national concerns with what is going on elsewhere. However, in asserting that national identity should be recognized within discussions of globalizing AIDS, it is important to note, as we saw in Chapter 2, that nation-states have never existed in isolation. As John Urry reminds us, nation-states have never been separate from a system of states and asserts that: 'it is through this interdependence that societies are constituted as partially self-regulating entities, significantly defined by their banal or vernacular differences from each other' (2000a: 189). Duyvendak's comparative studies of the different national responses to the AIDS crisis – in terms of activism, the gay movement and the state – demonstrate the futility and (annoying essentialism) of terms such as Euro-American, especially as they tend to be to used by scholars from the United States and the United Kingdom.

In this section I have considered the appropriateness of the modern basis of gay subjectivity and identity. This model has been challenged as a basis for examining sexual dissident cultures and communities outside of the west, but I have argued that this model is increasingly challenged from within the west, most significantly on the basis of class and race. In fact, I have suggested that the whole turn towards thinking through the global dimension, for instance in the form of the global gay, is a reaction to these challenges and to the whiteness of the global gay. Haylett has argued that in Britain the white working class are illegitimate political subjects, and as such are racialized and made visible as white. Thus, in this liberal, multi-cultural discourse, poor whites are an abject Other on which whiteness projects its liberal homophobia and racism. White working-class and black sexual dissidents may not be able to or willing to conform to the strictures and norms of a gay consumer culture.

AIDS as Cosmopolitan Virus

In this chapter I have examined the extent to which AIDS is symbolic of globalization. Specifically I addressed the extent to which it is a symptom of a globalizing panic, the virus reflects fears about the decline of national sovereignty and external threats to the body politic. I examined the notion that the experience of living with HIV and AIDS reflected a particular form of queer diaspora. I argued that in the United States AIDS represented a particular threat to immigrant sexual dissidents who tended to be most vulnerable and lacked the resources to cope with the pandemic. However, I suggested that the transnational framework of AIDS activism also led to the development of transnational spaces of solidarity and community. In the section on national formations of AIDS and sexual citizenship I argued that while AIDS represents a challenge to the ability of many nation-states to cope with the pandemic, it has in many cases helped to bolster the power of the nation-state. The very real national differences in terms of the political response to the pandemic, mean that far from implying the death of the nation-state and the insignificance of the national scale, AIDS has rendered nationalism and national identity as significant as ever. In *The Body of This Death* William Haver argues that the technological advances, particularly in transport, associated with globalization have made the AIDS the first true, genuine cosmopolitan virus. While O'Neill argues that AIDS represents the postmodern, other writers have argue that AIDS is also the first true cosmopolitan, moving freely across national borders, without restrictions. Is AIDS the first cosmopolitan virus as well as the first postmodern one? This is an interesting use or deployment of the term 'cosmopolitan' for it implies that the cosmopolitan does not respect boundaries and difference – but annihilates them. In the US, AIDS has been represented as an urban pandemic and constructed as one associated with otherness, as opposed to the sanctity of the imagined white familial sameness of the rural homeland (Raimondo, 2001). The AIDS pandemic has served as a rationale for the crackdown on public sex in North American cities such as San Francisco and New York (*Dangerous Bedfellows*, 1996) leading to the displacement of non-affluent sexual dissidents. This particular alignment of corporate and local political interests has led to, for instance, the re-invention of Times Square in New York as a family friendly consumer space. In the next chapter I focus on the global city, and AIDS has had a significant impact on the contemporary sexual geographies of cities.

Note

1. For a discussion of the Dutch political model of pillarization see Andeweg and Irwin (1993).

8

Queering
Transnational Urbanism

Cities are attractive to businesses because of transportation, availability of
materials, and skilled workers. Cities are attractive to people because of the
pleasures the city holds. Much of that pleasure is cultural, certainly. Jobs are
necessary to afford those pleasures. But when the average male thinks about
sex once every thirty seconds and the average female thinks about sex once
every three minutes, pretty much throughout their lives, it is absurd to think
that sexual pleasure and sexual opportunity are somehow exempt from the
equations that make city life attractive and livable. Samuel Delany, *Times
Square Red, Times Square Blue.* (1999)

Samuel Delany's quote brings us back to basics. What is it exactly about
cities that attract people? How do these attractions bring people into
opposition, as well as bring people together, and how does this relate to
transnationalism? There are a number of clear links between this chapter
and earlier ones in the book. For instance the question of mobility, migration and tourism discussed in Chapter 6, that cities are major receivers (as
well as generators) of national and international flows of queer migrants as
well as tourists. The question of the development of global cities is significant for sexual citizenship as these are receivers of migrants whose loyalty
may be greater to that city than to the state. Loyalties may also be multiple and transnational. Queers who migrate to come out in such cities may
feel a great sense of loyalty and investment to those cities as places enabling
of their sexuality (though these loyalties, identifications and attachments
must also be balanced by disidentifications; as we saw in Chapter 6, queer
migration patterns are complex). Global queer cities such as New York,
San Francisco, Paris, Sydney and London exert a tremendous pull for
would-be queer migrants and tourists alike. Likewise there are clear links
between AIDS and the city, ahistorically cities have been represented
as diseased, unhealthy places. There are also connections between the

regeneration of major cities and the desire to produce a cleaner, healthier city through the purification of space. AIDS has also led to practices of urban citizenship that have a clear transnational basis in, for instance, candlelit vigils.

In this chapter I wish to think through the relationships between queer, transnational connections and the city. I consider which of the theoretical frameworks and approaches for studying these relationships is most useful for queers. Are some of these frameworks more useful than others in helping to shed light on these links from a queer perspective? Are some approaches more harmful than others towards queers? Having provided some answers to these questions I derive a framework for thinking through these relationships that will guide my deliberations in the remainder of the chapter. Having done that I go on to discuss two specific ways in which these relationships are being reproduced in contemporary capitalism. The first is 'queer place promotion', which I discuss in the broader context of city marketing and place promotion. The second is the contention that globalization is leading to a purification of urban space.

Globalization and the City

In this section I examine the relationship between social theory, sexual citizenship, globalization and the city. In discussions of the relationship between globalization and the nation-state, the global city has come to the fore. However, thus far, what has been lacking in work on the relationship between sexual citizenship, globalization and nationalism, is sustained discussion of the role played by the city. There are three main points that I think are key to developing a framework for thinking through these relationships, and the consequences for reworking them from a queer perspective. These are: the structure-agency debate as applied to globalization and the city; the question of the politics of spatial scale; and the question of how global cities are conceptualized more generally. Much of the discussion in earlier chapters of this book was concerned with the agency of the state in globalization. In this section I examine the agency of the city within globalization, for cities are becoming significant actors within globalization. Michael Peter Smith (2001: 168) argues that 'cities are not to be viewed as empty containers of transnational articulations'. Smith's statement echoes a key essay by the geographer Neil Smith (1993), in which he berates the way space has been conceptualized within social theory as passive and simply the blank canvas on which social processes are drawn. Cities are not simply the empty containers or backdrops where social, economic and political events take place. Michael Smith notes that the state still has agency. The question is: what kind of state and what kind of agency? Here we have to think about the transformation of the role of the state. For instance, Brenner focuses on the re-scaling of the state. In an earlier chapter I argued that what is most significant is not so much the decline of the power of the state under the threat of globalization, more the transformation in what the state does. As Marcuse and van Kempen (2000) argue cuts in the state's welfare provision do not so much reflect the decline in the power of the state, but rather a shift in emphasis away from redistribution towards the promotion of business. Engin Isin and Patricia Wood (1999) argue that there are two main features of what they term the global city that are particularly important in terms of thinking through the relationship between citizenship and identity, namely the growth of transnational classes and new groups to provide goods and services for them. Who are these groups? Who are these transnational classes? The question is what do Isin and Wood mean by transnational classes? There are parallels here within the work of Leslie Sklair (2001) in his 'The Transnational Capitalist Class'. Sklair equates the transnational capitalist class with cosmopolitan professionals working in finance whose cosmopolitan sense of place is structured by their working patterns and practices that are increasingly transnational. But are the working classes increasingly transnational? Pnina Werbner (1999) suggests that working-class cosmopolitans may be more genuinely cosmopolitan in their membership of multiple communities that extend beyond national boundaries. Here I wish to distance myself from the 'global cities' discourse, which is most clearly associated with geography. The main problem with this discourse is that they tend to over-state the power of global capital. Likewise, they understate the agency of the state, plus other actors. Michael Peter Smith has done an excellent job critiquing the global cities discourse. The issue of agency is central to Smith's deliberations. Moreover he argues that agency does not simply reside at the local scale:

> Since human agency operates at many spatial scales, and is not restricted to 'local' territorial or sociocutural formations, the very concept of the 'urban' thus requires reconceptualization as a social space that is a crossroads or meeting ground for the interplay of diverse localizing practices of national, transnational, and even global-scale actors, as these wider networks of meaning, power, and social practice come into contact with more locally configured networks, practices, and identities (2001: 127).

So agency does not simply lie at the local scale, with the global scale being the structure that determines and constrains the possibilities for the agency of the state. The big question is how cities are being transformed and how are they implicated within these transnational flows of people, capital, products and media messages, and transnational networks? Smith (2001: 13) is keen to assert that transnational processes cannot be reduced to the affects of transnational capital: 'Transnational social space is a contested terrain rather than an exclusive preserve of multinational capital'. Any discussion of agency clearly has to examine the politics of spatial scale. There are clear links between the structure–agency debate as applied to globalization, and the next section, which deals with the politics of spatial scale. Neil Brenner examines the changing relationship of cities to states and to transnational flows of capital and people. In his essay on scale and urban governance Brenner (1999) argues that it is a truism of contemporary urban theory that cities are connected through transnational flows and networks of goods, services, capital and labour. And Nigel Thrift stresses that: 'even (or especially) in imperial systems cities are points of interconnection, not hermetically sealed objects' (2000: 245). Brenner discusses the approach of globalists such as Martin Albrow and Kenichi Ohmae, who argue that the increasing globalization of capital has meant that the state is severely weakened in its capacity to intervene and control economic activity within its own borders. He also considers the opposing view, articulated by Hirst and Thompson (1996), among others, who argue for the continued resilience of the state. Brenners argues that the state is changing in terms of spatial scales, with transformation in the role of the local and regional scale. He argues that local and regional levels of the state no longer act primarily to manage collective consumption programmes pre-determined at the national level. Instead, their prime focus is on promoting the desirability of their own city or region as entrepreneurial spaces and locations for outside investment. This focus on entrepreneurialism is relevant, as I will go on to discuss later in the chapter in relation to queer enterpreneurialism.

Smith argues that his transnational urbanism approach is preferable to the others for it acknowledges the agency of transnational actors and social groups. Likewise he is keen to underscore the agency of the state, for instance, in policing national borders, in addition to recognizing the political importance of nationalism and national identity. Discussing the question of spatial scale, cities, globalization and the European Union, Brenner (1999: 432) argues that despite globalization, both cities and states are still significant in the organization of contemporary global capitalism. We need therefore to be aware of the significance of the agency of the city as well as the state in global capitalism. Nigel Thrift (2000) argues that urban theory must broaden its horizons beyond a narrow focus on a few key cities, which then become emblematic for a particular brand of theory. Los Angeles becomes emblematic of postmodernism, Paris and Berlin emblematic of the modern city. Thrift argues that this narrow focus of theoretical work can sometimes blind researchers to the empirical realities, which could generate different lines of inquiry and theory generation. We should bear Thrift's argument in mind when we come to consider attempts such as Smith's to understand the relationship between globalization and the city. Smith critiques three major ways in which the relationships between globalization and the city have come to be understood, which he calls the 'time-space compression', 'global cities' and 'postmodern urbanism' approaches. He argues that his own lens for viewing these relations, what he calls 'transnational urbanism', is superior to these other approaches. Smith argues that this approach is preferable as it foregrounds agency in its analytical framework: 'it is an agency-oriented perspective that enables us to see how "globalization" is socially constructed by the historically specific social practices that constitute transnational networks' (2001: 182–3). Smith's perspective contrasts with Engin Isin (1999) who appears to buy more into the notion of the global city, although he does criticize the reductionist tendencies of this literature and in particular, the way in which class is discussed and theorized. Isin like Smith is critical of the global cities approach for its economic reductionism. He is also critical of the way in which class is treated within the global cities framework, arguing that it sets up a simplistic dichotomy of class relations based on conflict between an empowered global elite and a disenfranchised underclass. Isin (1999) like Smith is critical of the global cities literature, specifically in terms of its alleged failure to address new theoretical work on class and identity.

In this section I have argued that the relationship between globalization and the nation-state has dominated debates on the dreams and nightmares associated with globalization. However, cities are also deeply implicated within this politics of scale. I discussed the work of Neil Brenner who argued that cities are deeply implicated within global transformations. One of the major discourses that has been deployed to narrate these shifts has been cosmopolitanism, and it is to this that I turn in the next section.

Queer Cosmopolitanism

One of the major bones of contention that Engin Isin picks up on in his discussion of class, citizenship and the global city is namely that of cosmopolitanism. Isin objects to the application of the label 'cosmopolitan' exclusively to managerial and professional groups. Isin's (and Werbner's) interventions are significant in challenging the way class is framed in discussions of the global city and cosmopolitanism. For cosmopolitanism tends to get associated with a transnational elite, represented as 'sophisticated' taste-makers who make distinctions between themselves and Others. Cosmopolitanism tends to be treated as a disposition, which brings us to the focus on consumption. There are a number of ways that cosmopolitanism has been studied, but consumption is a key focus (though we must not lose sight of labour and the production of cosmopolitanism).

Before I go any further in discussing cosmopolitanism I should discuss definitions. Perhaps one of the most succinct definitions of this notoriously slippery concept is provided by Ulf Hannerz, who claims that cosmopolitanism should be primarily conceived in terms of 'first of all of an orientation, a willingness to engage with the Other' (1996: 103). Hannerz's definition of the cosmopolitan puts the emphasis on possessing knowledge about diverse cultural experiences, in order to become comfortable navigating between and within different cultural formations, contexts and spaces. In their discussion of citizenship and the politics of transnationalism, Isin and Wood (1999) examine the rise of a new cosmopolitan class of professionals and managers, who may identify more with their occupation and profession than the nation-state. Their prime loyalty may be to their professional body or career rather than to the nation-state of origin. Isin and Wood argue that in so doing they embrace the principles of cosmopolitanism. This statement must be treated with caution for cosmopolitanism is routinely associated with a professional elite. It is commonly seen as a class-based disposition. However, we also have to take on board the notion that cosmopolitanism comes from below as well as above, hence the use of the term 'working-class cosmopolitans' by Pnina Werbner (1999). Likewise Bruce Robbins calls for recognition of the multiplicity of ways in which cosmopolitanism is framed in order to take account of cosmopolitan experiences that are less a result of consumption choices, but instead framed by constraints:

> Understood as a fundamental devotion to the interests of humanity as a whole, cosmopolitanism has often seemed to claim universality by virtue of its independence, its detachment from the bonds, commitments, and affiliations that constrain ordinary nation-bound lives. It has seemed to be a luxuriously free-floating view from above. But many voices now insist ... that the term should be extended to transnational experiences that are particular rather than universal and that are unprivileged – indeed, often coerced. (1998: 1)

Robbins argues that cosmopolitanism cannot be seen in a singular manner as synonymous with an educated professional global elite. For the less privileged cosmopolitanism is not a matter of choice but shaped by coercive forces. From Beck's (2002) formulation of 'cosmopolitan society and its enemies' it is clear that cosmopolitan identity is contested and not available to all. In order to be a cosmopolitan it is necessary that others be excluded. Is cosmopolitanism the way forward here, in terms of thinking through the relationships between globalization (queer) desire and the production of (urban) space? It offers much promise, for it acknowledges the question of desire. I think we need to unpack the term 'cosmopolitan' further for it foregrounds and crystallizes many of the issues I examine in this chapter (and the book more generally for that matter). Those attending events such as the Gay Games are the people driving the globalizing processes. However for the rest, there is still the 'allure' of the glamour of such events as a form of cosmopolitan consumption, experienced vicariously from afar by reading through the international gay media, even though most people will never travel or get to experience such events in the raw (Schein, 1999; Boellstorf, 1999). They are a form of what Louisa Schein (after Benedict Anderson) has termed an 'imagined cosmopolitanism'. They are highly significant in helping to construct, frame and reproduce a global gay imaginary. Schein, writing on China, (see notes) argues that global media play a significant role in making products desirable to those who are not able to buy these goods. An imagined cosmopolitanism rests in the longing to be part of this global consumer culture. But is this consumption practice unique to China? One could make a very similar case for the consumption practices of working-class whites in urban Manchester or Lancashire. How is that different from the 'imagined cosmopolitanism' of owning brands such as Lacoste in Liverpool? Ownership of such brands in Liverpool or Manchester denotes that one has made it, is rich enough to be able to dress with class. Thus class distinction is central to the 'imagined cosmopolitanism' of street fashion in the north west of England. Chris Haylett (2001) describes the white working class as the illegitimate subjects of contemporary British political discourse Schein sets up an opposition of the global and the local, with the local in China desiring global brands as a marker of their cosmopolitanism and sophistication. Engagement with these brands reflects a longing to overcome the confines of China. Schein argues that what makes this cosmopolitanism imagined is the consumption of the marketed images rather than the actual buying of the brands these images are promoting:

> When this engagement is independent of actual acquisition of goods, when it is effected instead through engagement with promotional media and transnational cultural meanings, I refer to is as 'imagined cosmopolitanism'. (1999: 360)

So cosmopolitanism is about worldliness and knowledge (i.e. knowing about which brands are available), and 'imagined cosmopolitanism' for Schein means that even if you do not purchase these brands you consume them though the adverts, derive the magic from them (hence the comparison with cargo cults):

> Those who imagine themselves as cosmopolitans in China make themselves part of the world precisely through browsing the store shelves and imbibing and becoming fluent in signs of foreignness, whether in films, music, print media or other forms of communication. It is a kind of subjectivity that refuses the politics of difference, of

> disparate communities, of the historical positioning of Chinese mainlanders in inferior ranked positions in a global order. (1999: 361–2)

Reading through this quote one wonders how we can make a connection between the notion of worldliness, sophistication and sex. For instance consider the notion that 'experienced' means sexually experienced and competent, knowledgeable. I have argued that cosmopolitanism has become a significant new brand, a distinctive way of theorizing the links between transnationalism and culture that circumvents some of the reductionist and totalizing tendencies of some writing on global culture. Cosmopolitanism is significant and essays such as Schein's provide a clear example of the discussion of everyday life and popular culture. But does cosmopolitanism run the risk of becoming another form of universalism?

In this section I have outlined some of the main tensions in thinking through the way sexuality is implicated in theoretical work on globalization, transnationalism and the city. Smith's notion of transnational urbanism promises sexual dissidents a more central place within these relationships compared to the postmodern urbanism or global cities schools of thought. This is because culture is not marginalized and treated in a reductionist manner. Also there is the way that the local/global relationship is framed within the global cities discourse. The local is seen as static whereas the global is constructed as mobile. Smith argues that is a false opposition. He pays considerable attention to transnational actors and agents. Smith's commitment to agency means that the transnational urbanism approach is more useful for queers as it gives us conceptual space in which to be active agents in shaping the city. Likewise Isin also acknowledges the role of queers in thinking through the link between citizenship and identity. In the conclusion to his essay on urban citizenship, Nikolas Rose argues that the state is no longer the safeguarder of citizenship (if it ever was in the first place): 'At its most general, in contemporary games of citizenship, citizenship is no longer primarily realized in a relation to the state' (2000: 108). So for Rose, citizenship is de-centred and functions at many levels and scales, and is rooted in practices of everyday life. Rose puts much emphasis on what he terms 'the games of citizenship', and argues that these have been transformed in contemporary society. T.H. Marshall's conceptualization of citizenship has been criticized for its passive view of the citizen. This is contrasted with Nikolas Rose's view of the active contemporary citizen. Rose (2000: 108) argues that current discourses on citizenship put a lot more emphasis on the active nature of contemporary citizenship practices:

> Games of citizenship today entail acts of free but responsible choice in a variety of private, corporate and quasi-public practices, from working to shopping. The citizen as consumer is to become an active agent in the regulation of professional expertise.

> The citizen as prudent is to become an active agent in the provision of security. The
> citizen as employee is to become an active agent in the regeneration of industry. The
> citizen as consumer is to become an active agent for innovation, quality and com-
> petitiveness. The citizen as inhabitant is to enhance economic development through
> his or her intimate knowledge of the economic environment, through networks of
> trust and reciprocity. The citizen is to enact his or her democratic obligations as a
> form of consumption through new techniques such as focus groups and attitude
> research. (2000: 108)

Cities are increasingly seen as places of consumption and spectacle, with
Las Vegas as the extreme example, as cities compete to become desirable
spaces for tourism. Rose's games of citizenship are clearly interlinked.
Economic development and the success of cities become a duty of the
active citizen who must play an active role in, for instance, place promotion
or maintaining public safety, or being active in forging networks.

Urbanizing Queer Globalization

How is sexuality implicated within the changing nature of active urban
citizenship? We see that increasingly sexual dissidents are duty bound to
become active citizens in demonstrating civic pride and promoting their
city to visitors. I am minded of my first visit to Amsterdam, when I was
taken aback by how the men I met demonstrated a real pride in their queer
city, and were very keen to promote it to me as a great place to be queer,
with an almost religious zeal. They saw their role as ambassadors for their
city. This works on a more institutionalized level in New York City with
volunteer city greeters who show tourists around as a public service. Of
course, not everyone has the capital to be an active citizen. The obverse of
the 'good' active citizen is the deviant, pathological Other – the white,
working-class men who threaten this vision of urban civic pride. These are
the abject, embarrassing Other who, in Chris Haylett's (2001) view have
increasingly become 'illegitimate subjects' within political discourse. What
is the class basis of the games of citizenship discussed by Rose? How do
these operate to reproduce new legitimate public political subjectivities
such as respectable gays versus illegitimate, abject Others? How does the
representation of homophobic violence fit into the equation? From one
perspective, it would be possible to argue that homophobic violence constituted a form of resistance against affluent gays (especially given the
dominant representation of gays being one of affluence, aspiration and
sophistication). This view would deny the reality of homophobic attacks
against working-class and poor gays. Policy responses to, for instance, make
gay villages safer, must also be seen in terms of the economic advantages to

the businesses operating in the area. So campaigns to combat homophobic hate crime in these areas must be seen in the context of making these areas safer for investment.

The discussion in the earlier part of this chapter about entrepreneurialism leads me to think about the locational advantages for queer commerce and capital. The transnational professional and capitalist class is in a position to ascertain these locational advantages. In August 2002, Manchester's Mardi Gras event was threatened with cancellation because of conflicts between the city council, the police and the organisers – an association of local businesses in the village. Greater Manchester Police attempted to limit the area of the village where public drinking could be permitted in order to reduce disorder associated with drink. In response the organizers initially cancelled the event less than a week before it was due to take place, amid widespread recriminations and misguided accusations of police homophobia. Public events to discuss the situation attracted hundreds of people, and there was a real threat of Stonewall-style demonstrations and a march on Manchester Town Hall. In the end the organizers, council and police met and a somewhat scaled-down Mardi Gras went ahead. Listening to the public debates, political wrangles and the various conspiracy theories that abounded around Mardi Gras, I was struck with a profound sense that this was bad publicity for the gay village and for Manchester more generally. There was considerable awareness of how Manchester must compete with other queer cities to attract major events such as Europride. Thus any organizational and political problems with the event are seen as potentially damaging in terms of Manchester's image among the global queer community.

In *The Sexual Citizen*, David Bell and I argued that Iris Marion Young's discussion of the democracy of urban life was somewhat problematic. She claimed that the coming together of strangers is core to urban life. For Young, eroticism lies in the consumption of difference: 'we walk through sections of the city that we experience as having unique characters which are not ours, where people from diverse places mingle and then go home' (1990: 239). Straights may wish to consume (queer) difference and then go home. However not all differences can be consumed in this way – only the least threatening, least different aspects of queer culture can be commodified in this way. Conversely, such spaces may also provide a respite from the straight worlds for visiting queers. For street people then this is perhaps not possible. They cannot go home because they can't afford the fare. While Young argues that 'city life also instantiates difference as the erotic, in the wide sense of an attraction to the other' (1990: 239), Samuel Delany argues for the importance of contact between strangers as the basis of urban life. What Delany means by contact are the spontaneous encounters with strangers, which he argues can also take on an erotic form:

> contact is also the intercourse – physical and conversational – that blooms in and as 'casual sex' in public rest rooms, sex movies, public parks, singles bars, and sex clubs, on street corners with heavy hustling traffic, and in the adjoining motels or the apartments of one or another participant, from which nonsexual friendships and/or acquaintances lasting for decades or a lifetime may spring. (1999:123)

It is this contact that is spontaneous and cannot be promoted or produced by capital or the state. Cities can brings us into contact with strangers. Venues such as bath houses, but more particularly public cruising areas, have a particular significance as spaces where different worlds collide. As Delany notes there is something democratic about such spaces and such encounters, in the sense that they are public. However, they are obviously highly gendered spaces and are only public in the sense that women are excluded. In his essay on Delany's book, Eric Rofes (2001) maintains that contact enables identification and opportunities for communication and friendship across class and racial boundaries.

Delany's focus on contact makes me think about which forms of contact are seen as authentic. Michael Peter Smith is critical of the way authenticity is configured within some Marxist thinking on the postmodern city. Authentic contact between individuals within local communities is often contrasted with the inauthenticity of the spectacle promoted by global capitalism. The relationship of authenticity to queer is itself highly problematic. Queer culture as an entity has never been able to fit within authenticity, as discourses on authenticity are based on familiality, tradition, history. Markers of queer cultural and material production have been commonly derided as insignificant cultural forms – as trash. The question of what gets to be thought of as worthy and authentic of course rests on some notion of cultural authority[1]. One has to be ever attuned to problematic use of terms such as 'spectacle', for they do imply a certain value judgement about which forms of cultural production and practice are authentic, and which are not. Marxist writers on the postmodern city imply that urban spectacles are inauthentic cultural expressions. How then to locate the production of lesbian and gay pride festivals? How do these fit into the discussion of authenticity and spectacle? Spectacles are derided because they produce an inauthentic commodified encounter with difference, yet this is far too simplistic a value-judgement to apply to such events. Nikolas Rose writes well about the relationship between pleasure and the city:

> But pleasure has not evaded the networks of capture that filiate the advanced liberal city; transgression is itself to be brought back into line and offered up as a package of commodified contentment. The city of pleasure celebrated in poetry, novels, films and systematized in social theory has itself been fed into the programmatic imagination, in an alliance between city politics and commercial imperatives. A multitude of projects, in almost all major cities, seek to reshape the real

city according to this image of pleasure, not least in order to enter into the competitive market for urban tourism. (2000: 106)

Contrast this rather downbeat account of contemporary urban public cultural practice with Delany's quote at the start of the chapter. When I think about queer urban consumption practices, I am very tempted to say that in many respects Rose is correct. The commodified image of pleasure within urban queer spaces has been accompanied with the eradication of non-commercial spaces for public sex – the contact zones much discussed by Delany. It is also significant that debates on improving public safety that accompany schemes such as that in Times Square (which are promoted by big capital) tend to stress the commercial nature of venues for sex to be replaced by the 'spectacle'. Delany and Rofes argue that the commercial nature of sex venues is overstated. Delany assets that there were rich possibilities for encounters with strangers that were not commodified by capital. Some forms of encounters with difference are seen as authentic, others are not. For instance (queer) activist spaces can be a lot more elitist and exclusive than gay bars. I am also minded of the notion of authenticity as applied to Delany's account of Times Square, and Rofes' discussion of them. I think this enters the realm of memory and perhaps nostalgia. While Delany's account is far from romantic about the street and the sexual culture attracted to it, it is hard not to feel a certain legislated nostalgia for a lost world. Eric Rofes makes some interesting points about the gentrification: 'Delany shows that before the current regime of yuppification, sex was one of the primary modes of interclass contact, especially between men' (2001: 104). So while Delany and Rofes both bemoan yuppification, where do they fit into the shifting demography and economic geography of this neighbourhood? It is a commonplace to bemoan other settlers as yuppies, but does not the presence of professional, educated people such as Delany and Rofes already hint at gentrification?

That we do not get more embodied, autobiographic, less safe accounts of urban public sex is unsurprising given the risks of putting yourself on the line. Delany has himself been taken to task for the way he uses his own experience by Joan Scott (1993) in her essay 'The evidence of experience'. Rofes readily acknowledges his own privileged background and notes that class, race and gender differences mean he participates in these spaces on different terms. In an earlier essay I argued that gay men play a significant role in the gentrification process. They are attracted to these areas because they promise the forms of contact so lovingly depicted by Delany. So there is a balance between recognizing the power inequalities at work in such contact zones, while also celebrating the possibilities for queer self-transformation.

There are two main tendencies in the transformation of queer cities, and the notion of what is represented as an authentic queer encounter and what is seen as spectacle is central to my discussion of them. The first is the growth of the international lesbian and gay tourist industry infrastructure, plus national and city tourist agencies' promotion of these cities as spaces for lesbian and gay consumption and tourism. The second there is the purification of space associated with the eradication of difference and danger. Contacts between strangers celebrated by Delany – the chances for contact with difference – have been replaced with a commodified production of themed spaces. There are of course clear overlaps and connections between these two tendencies, for the promotion of safe spaces enables the promotion of lesbian and gay tourism to these areas. Such spaces see themselves in competition with one another and thus safety for visitors is a prime concern. As I have already argued this must be seen in a much broader context of global competition between cities to attract investment as Neil Brenner argues: 'on sub-national spatial scales, interspatial competition has intensified among urban regions struggling to attract both capital investment and state subsidies' (1999: 433).

In concluding this discussion I consider whether queer spaces have become spectacles. Lesbian, gay and queer claims on urban space are tentative. To some extent 'event cities' (after Tschumi's [1994] book of the same name) are highly volatile, ephemeral, transient interventions into urban space, though these events may play a significant role in reinforcing the place of queer cultures within the urban cultures and narratives about a particular city, as for instance in the case of Mardi Gras in Manchester or Mardi Gras in Sydney. Such events, while transitory, have an important symbolic value, not just for the queer communities, but also for the cities in reinforcing their image as cosmopolitan. Cosmopolitanism is a key term in the marketing of cities. It is useful for hinting at cultural diversity, while at the same time sanitizing these differences. We see that commercial lesbian and gay events such as Mardi Gras are gaining official recognition and state support, at the same time as authorities crack down on public sex and cruising grounds. In her essay on queer counterpublics in Taipei, Fran Martin argues that the increasingly tolerant position of the Taiwanese state towards lesbians and gay men (tongzhi) has been part of a state discourse in which 'Taiwan's government seeks actively to reposition the island, culturally as well as economically, in relation to an explicitly transnational imaginary' (2000:82). She cites the Taiwanese state's financial support and official recognition of the international success of Ang Lee's film *The Wedding Banquet* which had as its main focus the relationship between a Taiwanese and an American man. This contrasts quite markedly with other states in the region such as Singapore, which have been repressive in their treatment of sexual dissidence. However Martin argues that this new tongzhi-friendly policy stance has been accompanied by a police crackdown on public sex between men in New Park – an important queer counterpublic space. The attempt by the Taipei authorities to produce new public citizenship spaces to reflect Taipei's ambition to be a global city has led to attempts to displace tongzhi from New Park. Discussing statements made by the head of the Taipei Department of Urban Development, Martin argues that plans for the redevelopment of New Park reflected not so much a simple repressive position, but rather an attempt to construct a distinction between desirable, respectable working gays and those who used the park for cruising, who were categorized by Zhang as mainly 'students, the unemployed, and a small number of foreign nationals' (Zhang, quoted in Martin, 2000: 85). In forging this classed and racially-based distinction between desirable and undesirable homosexuals, Martin argues that the ability to participate in consumption is crucial to the state's recognition and validation of tongzhi:

> The proper citizen of the imagined modern, democratic city of Taipei is not necessarily a 'heterosexual' one, but is defined by certain indicatively middle-class leisure and consumption practices. In this sense, the rhetoric of the City Government effectively produced two kinds of homosexuality. One is characterized by class-bound practices of consumption (attendance at commercial gay venues), and constitutes the imagined subject of US-inflected minority rights discourses cited by the administration in order to project an image of Taipei as a 'modern democratic city' (2000: 85–6).

The class-based distinction between respectable gays who participate in consumption spaces and those Others who use queer counterpublic spaces such as New Park, is one that is significant elsewhere in framing inclusion and exclusion from city marketing and promotional campaigns.

Queer Place Promotion and City Marketing

I begin my discussion of queer place promotion and marketing by reflecting on the question of the relationship between gay pride and civic pride. In her essay 'Sporting bodies', Elspeth Probyn provides a fascinating reflection on the role of pride and shame within lesbian and gay sport in general, and the 1998 Gay Games in Amsterdam in particular. She argues that the celebration of Pride overlooks shame: 'Pride operates as a necessity, an ontology of gay life that cannot admit its Other' (2000: 19). There is a certain 'shame' about not possessing the requisite social, economic, cultural and body capital to participate in events such as the Gay Games, as Probyn continues: 'as an exemplar of queer pride, the Gay Games project erases shame, and as Gert Hekma argues, the Games combined asexuality with commercialization, and a total lack of connection with questions of human rights and politics' (2000: 14). While the Gay Games, it is argued, may be apolitical and asexual, such events clearly are not outside of politics, and they are powerful symbolic statements of queer visibility in urban space. However, we have to examine the pros and cons of this, particularly in asking what is implied by the term 'queer inclusion'. Is this term not something of an oxymoron, if one is true to the spirit of queer politics? Dereka Rushbrook argues that: 'Gay urban spectacles attract tourists and investment; sexually deviant, dangerous rather than risque, landscapes do not' (2002: 195). There is a question that immediately arises from Rushbrook's statement – for whom are gay urban spectacles organized and arranged? The debates about Manchester's Mardi Gras crystallized a whole series of issues around the claiming of queer space within Manchester's so-called Gay Village, which is threatened by gentrification. Ever aware of the dangers of using one city as emblematic of all cities, Manchester nevertheless provides a useful example for thinking through these issues and debates. What was fascinating about the chain of events was the way in which people reacted with a real sense of ownership over the village that was being threatened. While it may be easy to become blasé and complacent about such spaces given the proliferation of venues targeting the lesbian and gay market, it is apparent that many people care passionately about these spaces and feel a deep sense of personal investment in them. When the Mardi Gras was initially cancelled there was a great deal of anger from those who saw it as an attack on the community. Such events are marketed for the whole city, and in the past deliberately so in order to promote integration and inclusivity. Like the village itself, they are used to sell and market Manchester as a cosmopolitan city to the rest of the world:

> Manchester's stature as a European gay Mecca continues to thrive as visitors flock from all over to sample its unique spirit. At the heart of this fast-growing, post-industrial city sits the eclectic care society of the Lesbian and Gay Village – a cosmopolitan showcase bursting with pride, and one of the queerest pieces of real estate Europe has to offer ('Healthy Gay Manchester's Guide to Lesbian and Gay Greater Manchester', Healthy Gay Manchester, 1998).

However, such a claim for cosmopolitan inclusivity has brought its own series of problems and issues around the dilution of the queerness of the village (Bell, 2001; Binnie and Skeggs, 1999). So for whom are such events organized? On the one hand there are those such as Iris Marion Young who want to get a bit of difference, gain a frisson from their encounters with the Other, and also bolster their own sense of cosmopolitanism and distinction between themselves and others who are less knowing. On the other hand there are queer visitors for whom the experience of such spaces bolsters their gay identity. For homos in the heartland such spaces represent a break from heteroland. I wonder though whether such spaces have lost a lot of their symbolic power and meaning, now that more and more cities have developed their own gay villages. For instance, in the early 1990s Manchester's Gay Village was pretty remarkable and definitely something new in the UK. Now with the creation of other spaces within cities such as Birmingham and even Newcastle there has been a certain waning of this symbolic power. Here I think we need to bear in mind the discussion of the pink economy in Chapter 4. I argued that there are very real dangers of over-exaggerating the power of the pink economy, specifically in the way Michael Luongo (2000), for instance, claims that gays vacation on average four to five more times than straights. I argued that we have to pay attention to the detail of these statistics in the same way that Badgett un-picks data on the pink economy more generally. Second, we have to pay more attention to the politics behind the discursive construction of the pink economy. We have to also recognize the relationship between production and consumption: lesbians and gay men are workers, not simply consumers, and any discussion of queer place promotion and the marketing of cities must remember this. Luongo argues that the 1994 Gay Games and Stonewall 25 celebrations combined produced greater tourist revenue for New York City than the staging of the football World Cup, claiming that the lesbian and gay travel and tourism market is worth an estimated US$10 billion (2000: 111). Such figures must be treated with extreme care, as it is in the interest of all those concerned with the marketing of lesbian and gay tourism (as with other aspects of queer consumption) to exaggerate the consumer power of queers. There are also tensions between place promotion strategies adopted by cities and strategies to promote lesbian and gay tourism. For instance, in my discussion of the city of Amsterdam's marketing campaign in the early 1990s to attract American gay and lesbian tourists, I noted that the campaign was abandoned because of fears about how the city of Amsterdam was being represented abroad (Binnie, 1995). This also points towards distinction-making practices, through place-making practices. The distinctions here are between queers. White middle class gays don't want sleaze on their doorstep. One could also argue that even those who advocate sleaze and diversity may not actually like it on their doorstep. In the following section I deal with the social–spatial politics of sleaze. In addressing lesbian and gay tourism it is imperative to note the difference between the hype and the reality, specifically the dangers of over-stating the power of the pink economy.

The Social-Spatial Politics of Sleaze

Queer spaces have been notable for their transience and their ephemerality. Queer claims on urban space have always been tentative, though some patterns have become established and certain urban mythologies recycled to reproduce queer space. In Chapter 6 I argued that we have to pay attention to the notion of allure – why do people aspire to move in the first place? I argued that it was much more than the absence of homophobia, for many cities that attract such visitors and migrants (such as London) are actually located within national polities that have unfavourable policies towards lesbians and gay men. Writing about New York City, Sally Munt (1995) argues that it has a powerful symbolic meaning suggesting an almost mythic status among lesbians and gay men. Similar symbolic meaning is attached to major global cities such as Sydney and San Francisco. This is highly significant, as is the role of the media. As Mark Johnson has suggested in his essay on sexual dissident identities in the Philippines, for men who identified as gay, the imagining of the United States as a queer nirvana was significant in shaping their identity (1998: 696). This chimes with Louisa Schein's examination of cosmopolitan consumption and desire in China, which I discussed earlier. While symbolism and imaginary cosmopolitanism is highly important, what about concerted attempts to market cities as queer friendly destinations for lesbian and gay travellers and tourists? How do queer place marketing strategies mobilize queer connotations of place to promote tourism? What I am concerned with here is the changing role of the local state, for instance, in city promotion. If we accept that the changing nature of the local state lies in promoting entrepreneurialism and making cities funkier places to invest in, what about the role of lesbians and gay men as entrepreneurs? Who therefore are the entrepreneurs that are much sought after? Who are seen as creative agents to be welcomed and promoted by the (local) state? Among accounts of urban regeneration, Richard Florida's *The Rise of the Creative Class* has had a massive impact in the media and academia. Florida argues that gays and what he terms 'bohemians' play a major and hitherto unrecognized role in urban regeneration. He argues that US cities that have large numbers of these groups are among the most economically dynamic in the United States. However, Florida makes some simplistic and strange assertions about gays and place-making. For example, he argues that: 'to some extent, homosexuality represents the last frontier of diversity in our society, and thus a place that welcomes the gay community welcomes all kinds of people' (2002: 256). The implication here is that tolerance towards dissident sexualities can be equated with tolerance of entrepreneurialism. It is perhaps unsurprising therefore that Florida makes assumptions about what a homosexual looks like. He develops a 'Gay Index', in which he plots other indices of identity such as class with telling results:

> The Gay Index was positively associated with the Creative Class ... but it was negatively associated with the Working Class. There is also a strong relationship between the concentration of gays in a metropolitan area and other measures of diversity, notably the percent of foreign-born residents. (2002: 258)

Thus gays are seen as the obverse of class: being gay and working class appears to be a contradiction in terms for Florida. Compare this with the work of Delany and Rofes, who argue that lower-class queer folk are being increasingly pushed out of so-called 'desirable' inner-city gentrifying neighbourhoods. We have to bear in mind the key role of gays in gentrification, specifically in terms of aesthetics and desire. For instance, Rofes admits his ambivalence in relation to cross-class (and cross-racial) desire – the flip side of the contact with Others is the power imbalances implied within these contacts and relationships. Rofes admits that such contacts can have colonial tendencies, though what I appreciated about his discussion was his openness to the queering potentialities of such exchanges and contacts. Here we have to be attuned to messiness: such contacts may enable class and social advancement and to a certain extent ameliorate inequalities, or may reproduce and exacerbate the very real material inequalities and power relations.

Gay global events such as pride festivals and gay games have assumed a greater profile within lesbian and gay communities and have received increased attention from the wider media. In an essay on the Amsterdam Gay Games of 1998 focusing on the links between sport, sexuality, shame and pride, Elspeth Probyn notes that: 'the key tenets of the Games movement are "inclusion", "participation", "the achievement of one's personal best"' (2000: 18). She goes on to describe the opening ceremony and the endless speeches on themes of inclusivity. Yet the Games are far from inclusive in the sense of the cost involved. Clearly there is a great cost in being proud. As Probyn's discussion of the gay Australian rugby league player Ian Roberts' athletic, sporting body demonstrates, there is pride if you have the right body to be able to share in this global pride. The turn to sport within queer communities has to be seen in the context of the AIDS pandemic. The assertion of health and pride at such events is obvious, though. I am just a bit concerned that queer sport, like contemporary sport in general, promotes asexuality for commercial gain. But commercial events such as Sydney Mardi Gras and the Gay Games fit within a much broader agenda of how cities are being transformed – specifically in relation to one another in global competition for inward investment as part of the international queer tourist market. Nikolas Rose argues that, under contemporary global capitalism and citizenship:

The city becomes not so much a complex of dangerous and compelling spaces of promises and gratifications, but a series of packaged zones of enjoyment, managed by an alliance of urban planners, entrepreneurs, local politicians and quasi-governmental 'regeneration' agencies. But here, once more, urban inhabitants are required to play their part in these games of heritage, not only exploiting them commercially through all sorts of tourist-dependent enterprises, but also promoting their own micro-cultures of bohemian, gay or alternative lifestyles, and making their own demands for the rerouting of traffic, the refurbishment of buildings, the mitigation of taxes and much more in the name of the unique qualities of pleasure offered by their particular habitat. (2000: 107)

On an individual level, queer inhabitants play an active role in selling their city, for instance, as a form of enlightened self-interest. How does this relate to the queer city? This statement points towards the need for a much tighter and clearer conceptual framework for engaging with the pink economy and queer consumption. There are conflicts between the upbeat excitement of the hype associated with queer city promotion – which, as a practice of citizenship can clearly be seen as a form of inclusion – and the rather more pessimistic accounts of the disappearance of differences, and the increasing corporatization and blandness of such spaces. Who is excluded from this mirage of queer economic citizenship? I shall discuss this in the next section.

The Production of the Healthy City and the Purification of Space

The flip side of the production of supposedly safe spaces of queer consumption is that certain forms of queer cultural practice tend to get pushed out. Class is a clear factor, for the 'dangerous' working-class Other has to be excluded in order to produce a sanitized space for middle-class consumption. The paradox is that in some cases, the greater use of such spaces by a much broader range of the population, and specifically the more straights who are attracted in by the supposedly improved urban fabric and queer aesthetic, bring their own problems and may make the areas much less safe for queers. I will discuss this below by referring to the South of Market district within San Francisco. Nikolas Rose has made some telling observations about the relationships between urban governance and health. He argues that in the urban governance of health, responsibility for the management of health has been shifted to promote consumer citizens to be active in their everyday lives. Rose argues that because of this shift:

We no longer have the sick on the one side of a division, the healthy on the other – we are all, actually or potentially, sick, and health is not a state to be striven for only when one falls ill, it is something to be maintained by what we do at every movement of our everyday lives. (Rose, 2000: 101)

Rose focuses on the development of urban health spaces such as stress clinics and gyms. He argues that these are significant spaces where consumer citizens are encouraged to exercize control and discipline over their bodies as part of civic duty and being a responsible citizen: 'the imperative of health thus becomes a signifier of a wider – civic, governmental – obligation of citizenship in a responsible community' (2000: 101). However I maintain that class distinction is reproduced through practices to produce the healthy body and the diseased one. We become obligated to control and regulate our bodies as part of contemporary capitalism, to consume, to desire. It becomes our duty as active citizens to produce self-disciplined bodies. The promotion of a healthy body as a form of urban governance is mirrored through the purification of space. Gays are often perceived as model citizens of the urban renaissance contributing towards the gentrification and the production of desirable (hence commodifiable) cosmopolitan residential and commercial areas. Gays are attracted to neighbourhoods as pioneers, then others are attracted in because of the cachet and cultural capital. Both gays and straights, though, have been behind moves to push out the sleaze. For many conservative gays, gay male sex zones are seen as an embarrassment that must be cleaned up. Eric Rofes (2001) argues that conservative gay health officials and community leaders have often been among the fiercest critics of down-at-heel sex zones including areas commonly frequented by men in search for sex with men. Rofes argues that these spaces are seen as symbolic of the least easily assimilated elements of gay male sexual culture. Such spaces are seen as an embarrassment in the drive for political inclusion and assimilation, while gentrifying gay consumption spaces are seen as respectable reflections of straight society. Yet I would argue that both gay male sex areas and the asexualised gentrifying gay districts are both highly vulnerable and ephemeral phenomena. As the gay districts become gentrified and asexual, they become more desirable for wider gentrification and colonalization by trendy and less trendy straights. These new residents of the area will not tolerate noise and disturbances from nightclubs and late opening café bars and act to limit commercial venues. In this way the area becomes more respectable and gay commercial venues are forced out. However, as Lauren Berlant and Michael Warner (1998) suggest, gay male sex areas are also ephemeral as they are vulnerable to moralizing crusades such as that undertaken by Mayor Giuliani. Giuliani's zoning law constituted a concerted attack on public sex through making it impossible for these businesses to operate profitably, as Berlant and Warner argue: 'The law aims to restrict any counterpublic sexual culture by regulating its economic conditions' (1998: 562).

In the previous section I showed how transnational capital is involved in the production of queer spaces. I now go on to consider the opposite – i.e.

how globalization is leading to the destruction, sanitization and purification of queer space. How accurate is it to claim that 'globalization' is destroying gay men's sex areas and sleazy spaces more generally? It is the discourse of globalization by which cities have to be seen as nice, bland, safe and secure, attractive for inward investment, as they are cast into competition with one another. The discourse of globalization creates a set of 'truths' to justify certain political actions including the attack on sleaze. Often the sleaze factor is a ruse for an attack on sexual, racial and class diversity in the production of a safe, middle-class, heterosexual whiteness. The right to the city is becoming increasingly commodified and framed in terms of ability to pay. Who has the right to take up space in the city? In the 1980s campaigns against the spread of HIV and AIDS led to the bath houses being closed across urban United States. However Gayle Rubin argues that in fact other forces were significant, such as gentrification and globalization. In her work on the SOMA (South of Market) district of San Francisco, Rubin argues that gentrification has made the streets less safe for sexual dissidents. She argues this is ironic because the leather/SM culture has often been demonized and misrepresented as dangerous, when in fact consent and safety and the focus on trust are to the fore within the culture. On the other hand the growth of heterosexuals on the streets has made the streets less safe. Again the question of spatial scale is significant and the links between global and local. The global threat of communism was used in Cold War America to legitimize police operations against gay venues in San Francisco, hence Rubin writes: 'police action against gay haunts in the 1950s was typically expressed in political and moral terms, such as the crusades against communism or the need to protect women and children from the putative dangers of sexual psychopaths' (1998:251). Thus police action against gay bars was a response to threats about the sanctity of national borders. Such campaigns could therefore be seen as part of the reproduction of a respectable middle-class American national identity. One wonders what little has changed given what Rofes terms the Disneyfication of Times Square, and the claim that the space is made safer for capital. Interestingly Rubin argues that, by the late 1980s: 'South of Market had become a case study in urban succession' (1998:259). She suggests that these changes predated the onset of AIDS. She points to gentrification and the appearance of more mainstream, upmarket venues in South of Market. As a result of this process leather venues are being pushed out of the city altogether. There is a paradox in that gentrification destroys the sacred cow. The initial attraction to the contact zones means that they are destroyed, and differences are annihilated. The Other is pushed out and displaced. In the end, the people who made the area liveable in and desirable for a certain type of consumer are pushed out by higher rents and the rising price of property.

Conclusion

Earlier in the chapter I discussed Nigel Thrift's (2000) caution against using one city to exemplify all cities. In a similar vein here, we have to pose the question: does one queer city fit all? Can we make generalizations about the relationships between queer globalization, the city and the state? Are there general tendencies that are occurring with cities as different as Budapest, Cape Town, Rio de Janeiro, Taipei and Sydney compared with New York, London, Los Angeles or San Francisco? Moreover, what would it mean to be a citizen of a global queer society? Especially given what Martin Manalansan (1995) has said about the elitism of international lesbian and gay rights organizations such as ILGA? Writing about the ILGA conference associated with the Stonewall celebrations in 1994, he asserts that a number of delegates including 20 from the Philippines were prevented from attending the conference because either they could not afford the $300 registration fee, or they encountered difficulties in obtaining visas. It is clear therefore that not everyone can participate in the queer event city. Such mega-events tend by their nature to be exclusive – for instance the cost of admission to Sydney Mardi Gras circuit parties. They are by their very nature exclusive and fundamental to the production of a global queer elite. However, this does not mean that such events should necessarily be seen as cosmopolitan, for Manalansan's respondents are in many senses producing a more genuine cosmopolitanism, negotiating the very real dangers of a racist 'host' society. What Manalansan's statement demonstrates is that international activist spaces can be as undemocratic and exclusive as commercial ones.

In concluding this chapter I wish to tease out three final points. First, I have argued that contemporary urban transformations are reproducing forms of queer inclusion and exclusion. The forms of inclusion are highly selective in the sense that they depend on the ability to pay and, as I have hinted above, the ability to produce an accepted notion of what a disciplined queer body looks like. Questions of authenticity are fundamental to discussions of these processes of inclusion and exclusion. Who has the authority to legislate what is an authentic form of queer cultural practice, especially given that the discourse of authenticity has so routinely been used to trash queer cultural practices? If one accepts Rose's view of the changing nature of citizenship – that citizenship practices have become decentred from the state and that they operate at multiple sites and locations – what are the impediments and constraints to the rights of queers moving through the city? Likewise, what are the responsibilities of the queer citizen especially in terms of health and bodily discipline? There are clearly other impediments and constraints on the ability of queers to move through the city (such as disability), which I will discuss in the concluding chapter.

Note

1. As I have hinted earlier in this discussion, Schein's work raises issues of representation, for who is the arbiter of cosmopolitanism? Who gets to judge who or what is cosmopolitan?

9

Conclusion

In this book I have been critical of reductionist tendencies within political economic thinking on queer globalization. I argued that work on cyberqueer spaces demonstrates that it is possible to offer a more nuanced discussion that treads a careful line between affirmation of the utopian possibilities of queer globalization and attention to the questions of the material inequalities in terms of access to technology. In my discussion of queer globalization I have attempted to address material inequalities while maintaining an awareness of agency. While the literature on queer globalization has rightly provided a powerful critique on the ethnocentricity of lesbian and gay studies, I maintain that this needs to be supplemented by an awareness of the class basis of queer globalization. In Chapter 4 I argued that lesbians and gay men are not simply passive consumers of globalized commercial cultures but are also active as producers. There are myriad ways in which globalization is impacting on sexual dissident cultures and politics. In examining the material basis of sexual dissident politics I argued that we should be aware of the Europeanization of sexual politics. The development of the European Union as a global economic and political actor is having consequences in terms of the internal national sexual politics of countries such as Romania, which has been forced to reform its punitive laws on sexual dissidence. In addition I argued that in the UK, the processes of Europeanization and globalization of politics have a class basis in terms of New Labour discourses on social exclusion that frame poor whites as abject, nationalist, racist and homophobic compared to the would-be cosmopolitan middle classes.

An important theme in the book has been the notion of authenticity and I return to it here. We cannot avoid authenticity as so many claims for recognition are based on authentic membership of queer communities. It is therefore important to state the role of nostalgia and memory in the making of queer communities. In Chapter 8 I argued that globalization is helping to produce new forms of queer inclusion and exclusion within urban space. I argue that authenticity and the 'ability to pay' are key to queer claims on urban space. At the same time we witness the development of an increasingly homogenizing queer café and bar culture, which is more respectable and acceptable to mainstream society. Disadvantaged queers who are unable to make a claim on the city are excluded and are pushed out of cities. At the same time we witness the greater visibility of such spaces to mainstream tourism so that tourist guides recommend straights visit gay bars and commercial districts in San Francisco, Cape Town and Manchester in order to get a bit of cosmopolitan difference. Queer place promotion strategies also demonstrate an awareness of global competition. The everyday practices of queer citizens embody the queer city and sell it – they buy into the narrative about their city being a queer metropolis. Authenticity is also important within activist communities. Activist communities, like all communities, appear to be exclusive in terms of their membership and the class politics of ACT UP in New York have been well documented (Cohen, 1997). In my discussion of queer urbanism I noted a tendency towards nostalgia in recent writing on the subject. In addition I note a sense of nostalgia within, for instance, discussions of global AIDS activism. In *Globalizing AIDS* Cindy Patton admits nostalgia for the certainties of 1990s AIDS activism:

> If I sound nostalgic – as I have sometimes been accused – it is because I can only stutter the unspeakable memory of a time with no history. The fragment I write here, anamnesis, is my only possible homage to a time, like the times of revolutionaries struggling under martial law or other more obvious forms of state oppression, in which the lessons of only a year or two are lost because the people who committed their bodies to those politics are dead. Even if I cannot describe the scope of what they felt and did, I can remind us to stop forgetting – for a moment. But I am not longing for a return to some idyllic time of pure politics that never was; rather, I hope to call forth a future, or rather, to stop us from foreclosing a next moment that only scientific positivism and blind politics believe can be known in advance. (2002: 9)

The nostalgia is also mourning for lives lost in the pandemic. There is also a notion that many of the articles about AIDS activism and globalization in *From ACT UP to The WTO* (edited by Benjamin Shepard and Ronald Hayduk) read more like a nostalgic (if angry) story about the nature of activism in the Lower East Side of Manhattan. While I certainly empathize with the attempts to link queer and AIDS politics to the wider questions of inequalities under global capitalism, the geographical scope of the essays does appear somewhat limited. In Chapter 7 I argued that while AIDS is a threat to the sovereignty of many nation-states, in many respects it makes the state more significant. The very different national responses to AIDS in

Brazil and the Netherlands demonstrate the extent to which policies towards AIDS are themselves projects of nation building. The crisis to the legitimation of the state presented by AIDS offers the possibility for the reproduction of a national identity. AIDS has been described as a cosmopolitan virus able to make itself at home anywhere in the world.

In Chapter 2 I noted that sexual dissidents have tended to be constituted as a threat to nationalism. In nationalism the primacy of the nation over all forms of other identities and loyalty has meant that queers are a threat. However, while the main tendency of nationalism has been to exclude queers, many queers have also been attracted to nationalism and nationalist political projects. This has taken many forms from participation in nationalist liberation struggles against imperialism, to the nationalist politics of the Far Right such as fascist political movements in Russia. But beyond these extreme cases we also witness the more 'respectable' nationalism, which is implicit within the politics of assimilation of lesbian and gay political movements. Claims for sexual citizenship based on membership of the armed forces are routinely expressed in terms of lesbians and gay men being as loyal to the nation as heterosexuals.

This leads me on to another key theme of the book, namely the invisibility of national identity and questions within work on lesbian and gay studies and queer globalization. In particular I have been rather critical of the American bias of work in this area. Jyoti Puri argues against a simple internationalization of lesbian and gay studies arguing that this may reproduce a Western bias and dominance within theoretical models of gender and sexual identity, claiming that: 'such a move would reinforce the collusion of a mainstream Western-oriented lesbian/gay studies with the dominance of an US/Western style of sexual politics' (2002: 439). Instead, Puri calls for a radical re-thinking of sexual categories and basic building blocks of theoretical work about gender and sexuality: 'what might be useful is to re-examine the meanings of categories of sexual identity, their meanings and ramifications, and their possibilities and limitations across disparate settings' (2002: 439). Puri is right to draw attention to the predominance of 'queers of colour', in putting questions of nationalism and the transnational on the agenda of lesbian and gay studies. However, as my discussion of nationalism, and specifically the predominance of America within lesbian and gay studies in Chapter 2 shows, it is clear that this is also a problematic assertion. First the term 'queers of colour' like the term 'queer' more generally, has its roots in the United States' political system and political culture. It is also problematic in its ignoring of work outside the United States, for instance comparative analyses of sexual politics within European states such as the work of political scientists like Jan Willem Duyvendak. Moreover, writers such as Terry Goldie have expressed bemusement about the

American-centrism of lesbian and gay studies. It is both ironic and unfortunate that the promotion of awareness of questions of the nationalism and transnationalism within lesbian, gay and queer communities merely serves to reproduce an American-centric worldview. I examined the intersections of queer and postcolonial thinking in Chapter 5. I argued that while significant in challenging the ethnocentricity of lesbian and gay studies, postcolonialism is in danger of producing a theoretical purity and universalism where alternative ways of conceptualizing the relationships between sexual dissidence, globalization and national identity are squeezed out. The universalizing tendencies of postcolonial theory combined with the elitist tendencies of queer theory mean that bringing them together is dangerous. I have been critical of the evolutionary approaches to lesbian and gay identities and cultures. The chapter also argued that the focus on diaspora was problematic in that it reproduces the view that the state is less significant in global society.

Writing about moves to provide legal recognition of queer migration across national borders, Carl Stychin argues that in the deployment of rights in universal terms: 'the lesbian and gay subject, who claims citizenship rights in part on the basis of freedom of movement, becomes the quintessential cosmopolitan citizen' (2000b: 623). Such agendas are thereby often complicit with the neoliberal agenda that promotes the transnational flow of commodities and professional workers. As New Labour law reform on same-sex migration and residency in the UK demonstrate, the ability to claim this right will depend upon the ability to pay. This then reinforces the social and economic distinctions between sexual dissidents. In this context it is important to be aware of the relationship between affluence, poverty and homophobia. Peter Drucker argues that: 'for the majority of lesbians and gay men in the Third World, successful opposition to capitalism probably offers the best hope for the near future of loosening the constraints on their sexuality' (1996: 100).

I now wish to draw attention to some of the limitations of the book. There are a number of omissions that I wish to highlight. I also provide a number of pointers to further study on this area. For instance the I have not referred to questions of sustainability, for instance the environmental and ecological aspects of globalization. Essays in Benjamin Shepard and Ronald Hayduk's (2002) edited volume on urban protest and globalization demonstrate the forging of commonalities and alliances between the anti-globalization movement and queer activism. Despite these tentative alliances it is still very much the case, as the editors of the WTO volume argue that environmental questions and queer activism often appear poles apart. Anti-globalization activists have a strong anti-consumption, anti-pleasure ethic which appears hostile and rather opposite to a queer ethic of hedonism. Attempts to bring attention to the environmental consequences of queer consumption practices such as tourism do tend to reproduce a highly moralistic agenda. However, there are some attempts to consider, for example, the environmental damage done by queer tourism (like other tourism) to ecosystems and the pollution associated with mass air travel. Another issue related to eco-feminism is the question of the rural and the global queer. Environmental politics and the harmful impacts of tourism on the environment scarcely register within queer politics and theory. What the solutions to the problems of tourism are are somewhat problematic in my view. For instance there is the suggestion that tourists should only come to Hawai'i I if invited by queer community groups there (AFSC Hawaii I Gay Liberation Program, 2002). This presumes a level of knowledge is needed for such contacts to exist in the first place. Does this suggestion merely serve to promote a cosmopolitan knowledge of another culture, which inevitably is constructed against mass tourism? Could not an ethical tourism (no matter how well-intentioned) serve to reproduce elitism? This reinforces the point made earlier about authenticity in the sense that one form of cultural exchange and consumption of difference is being promoted here as authentic, as opposed to the inauthenticity of mass tourism.

In Chapter 6 my discussion focused on queer mobility and specifically on tourism and migration policies. This discussion demonstrated that the (often exaggerated) consumer power of lesbians and gay male tourists should not blind us to the obvious fact that lesbians and gay men face considerable obstacles in moving across national borders. In this context we must celebrate the increasing number of mainly Western states that are now willing to recognize persecution on the basis of sexual orientation as grounds for granting asylum. At the same time we must not lose sight of the fact that the prevalence of homophobic violence is one reason why people leave their country of origin in the first place. There are, however, less innocent interpretations of these legal changes, such as the notion that they reflect a new racism where attitudes towards homosexuality are a marker of a country's level of development. The course of world events since 11 September 2001 has reinforced the distinction between the civilized and the barbaric. As I have pointed out earlier in this book, lesbian and gay rights have become symbolically significant as a marker or reflection of a country's level of development and sophistication. The rise to prominence, then assassination of the gay Dutch far-right politician Pim Fortuyn attests to the extent to which support for lesbian and gay rights is used to legitimize Islamophobia. In his essay on the political debate in the Netherlands that was spurred by the homophobic public statements of an imam based in Rotterdam, Gert Hekma (2002) focuses on the intersections of homophobia in Islamophobia in contemporary Dutch society. Writing before

Fortuyn's assassination, Hekma forcefully argues that Dutch politicians who had previously been reluctant to associate themselves publicly with positive statements supporting the lesbian and gay communities in the Netherlands were quick to condemn the homophobic statements of the imam. He points to the fluidity of constructions of racism and homophobia arguing that:

> White people often came with the argument that 'we' should not surrender 'our' liberties to barbaric Muslims, playing once again the theme of Islamophobia, of enlightenment and rationalism versus tradition and supersitution. A century ago, the pederasty of the Muslims was a sign of their ferocity, nowadays their anti-gay attitudes are a sign of unenlightened prejudices. (2002:244)

Hekma is somewhat scathing in his criticism of the hypocrisy and cynicism lying at the heart of Dutch tolerance of sexual and cultural diversity, which is revealed in this debate.

In the introduction to this book I said that I did not intend the book to be a definitive statement about queer globalization. I did not want to produce a globalizing discourse about sexual dissidence. Any claims for knowledge in this book can only be tentative and partial. Some significant issues have been omitted; for instance, focusing on queer transnational urbanism in Chapter 8 has been at the cost of neglecting the rural dimensions of queer globalization. This reflects the neglect of the rural in writing on globalization more generally. There must be more research in this area, specifically research that does justice to the multiplicity of standpoints and contexts of queer globalization. I have attempted to challenge the invisibility of the nation and nationalism within discussions of sexual dissident politics and communities. I have sought to balance a critique of American and Euro-centrism while remaining aware of the dangers of reproducing an Anglocentric view of sexual cultures and identities. I have also noted that while written from the perspective of a human geographer, I have sought to embrace inter-disciplinarity and acknowledge the work of authors writing on this subject from a wider range of disciplinary contexts and backgrounds. Greater dialogue across disciplinary boundaries is imperative if we are to broaden our understandings of queer globalization.

References

Adkins, L. (2000) 'Mobile desire: aesthetics, sexuality and the "lesbian" at work', Sexualities, 3(2): 201–18.

Adkins, L. and Lury, C. (1999) 'The labour of identity: performing identities, performing economies', Economy and Society, 28(4): 598–614.

Alexander, M.J. (1998) 'Imperial desire/sexual utopias: white gay capital and transnational tourism', in E. Shohat (ed.) Talking Visions: Multicultural Feminism in a Transnational Age. Cambridge, MA: MIT Press. pp. 281–305.

Allen, J. (1996) Growing Up Gay: New Zealand Men Tell Their Stories. Auckland: Godwit Publishing.

Altman, D. (1982) The Homosexualization of America: The Americanization of the Homosexual. New York: St. Martin's Press.

Altman, D. (1996a) 'On global queering', Australian Humanities Review (electronic journal: www.lib.latrobe.edu.au/AHR/archive/Issue-July-1996/altman.html).

Altman, D. (1996b) 'Rupture or continuity: the internationalization of gay identities', Social Text, 14(3): 77–94.

Altman, D. (1997) 'Global gaze/global gays', GLQ: A Journal of Lesbian and Gay Studies, 3: 417–36.

Altman, D. (1999) 'Globalization, political economy, and HIV/AIDS', Theory and Society, 28: 559–84.

Altman, D. (2001) Global Sex. Chicago: University of Chicago Press.

American Friends Service Committee (2002) 'AFSC Hawai'i Gay Liberation Program: activist materials addressing tourism', GLQ: A Journal of Lesbian and Gay Studies, 8(1–2): 207–21.

Andeweg, R.B. and Irwin, G.A. (1993) Dutch Government and Politics. London: Macmillan.

Ashman, P. (1993) 'Introduction', in K. Waaldijk and A. Clapham (eds) Homosexuality as a European Community Issue. Dordrecht: Martinus Nijhoff.

Bacchetta, P. (1999) 'When the (Hindu) nation exiles its queers', Social Text, 17(4): 141–66.

Badgett, M.V.L. (2001) Money, Myths and Change: The Economic Lives of Lesbians and Gay Men. Chicago: University of Chicago Press.

Bancroft, A. (2001) 'Globalisation and HIV/AIDS: inequality and the boundaries of a symbolic epidemic', Health, Risk and Society, 3(1): 89–98.

Bauman, Z. (1987) Legislators and Interpreters: On Modernity, Post-modernity and Intellectuals. Cambridge: Polity Press.

Bech, H. (1992) 'Report from a rotten state: "marriage" and "homosexuality" in Denmark', in K. Plummer (ed.) Modern Homosexualities: Fragments of Lesbian and Gay Experience. London: Routledge. pp. 134–47.

Bech, H. (1999) 'After the closet', Sexualities, 2(3): 343–49.

Beck, U. (2002) 'The cosmopolitan society and its enemies', Theory, Culture and Society 19(1–2): 17–44.

Bell, D. (1994) 'Bisexuality – a place on the margins', in S. Whittle (ed.) The Margins of the City: Gay Men's Urban Lives. Aldershot: Ashgate. pp.129–41.

Bell, D. (1995a) 'Perverse dynamics: sexual citizenship and the transformation of intimacy', in D. Bell and G. Valentine (eds) *Mapping Desire: Geographies of Sexualities*. London: Routledge. pp. 304–17.

Bell, D. (1995b) 'Pleasure and danger: the paradoxical spaces of sexual citizenship', *Political Geography*, 14(2): 139–53.

Bell, D. (2001) 'Fragments for a queer city', in D. Bell, J. Binnie, R. Holliday, R. Longhurst and R. Peace, *Pleasure Zones: Bodies, Cities, Spaces*. Syracuse, NY: Syracuse University Press. pp. 84–102.

Bell, D. and Binnie, J. (2000) *The Sexual Citizen: Queer Politics and Beyond*. Cambridge: Polity Press.

Bell, D. and Binnie, J. (2002) 'Sexual citizenship: marriage, the market and the military', D. Richardson and S. Seidman (eds) *The Handbook of Lesbian and Gay Studies*. London: Sage. pp. 443–57.

Bell, D., Binnie, J., Holliday, R., Longhurst, R. and Peace, R. (2001) *Pleasure Zones: Bodies, Cities, Spaces*. Syracuse, NY: Syracuse University Press.

Bell, D. and Valentine, G. (1995) 'Queer country: rural lesbian and gay lives', *Journal of Rural Studies*, 11: 113–22.

Berg, L. and Kearns, R. (1998) 'American unlimited', *Environment and Planning D: Society and Space*, 16(2): 128–32.

Berlant, L. and Warner, M. (1998) 'Sex in public', *Critical Inquiry*, 24: 547–66.

Bérubé, A. (1996) 'Intellectual desire', *GLQ*, 3(1): 139–57.

Bhabha, J. (1996) 'Embodied rights: gender persecution, state sovereignty, and refugees', *Public Culture*, 9: 3–32.

Billig, M. (1995) *Banal Nationalism*. London: Sage.

Binnie, J. (1995) 'Trading places: consumption, sexuality and the production of queer space', in D. Bell and G. Valentine (eds), *Mapping Desire: Geographies of Sexualities*. London: Routledge. pp. 182–99.

Binnie, J. (1997a) 'Invisible Europeans; sexual citizenship in the new Europe', *Environment and Planning A*, 29(2): 237–48.

Binnie, J. (1997b) 'Coming out of geography: towards a queer epistemology', *Environment and Planning D: Society and Space*, 15(2): 223–37.

Binnie, J. (2000) 'Cosmopolitanism and the sexed city', in D. Bell and A. Haddour (eds) *City Visions*. London: Pearson. pp. 166–78.

Binnie, J., Longhurst, R. and Peace, R. (2001) 'Upstairs/downstairs: place matters, bodies matter', in D. Bell, J. Binnie, R. Holliday, R. Longhurst and R. Peace, *Pleasure Zones: Bodies, Cities, Spaces*. Syracuse, NY: Syracuse University Press. pp. vii–xiv.

Binnie, J. and Skeggs, B. (1999) 'Cosmopolitan sexualities: disrupting the logic of late capitalism?' Paper presented at the Fourth International Metropolis Conference, 8–11 December, Washington, DC.

Binnie, J. and Valentine, G. (1999) 'Geographies of sexualities: a review of progress', *Progress in Human Geography*, 23(2): 175–87.

Boellstorff, T. (1999) 'The perfect path: gay men, marriage, Indonesia', *GLQ: A Journal of Lesbian and Gay Studies*, 5(4): 475–510.

Brennan, T. (1997) *At Home in the World: Cosmopolitanism Now*. Cambridge, MA: Harvard University Press.

Brenner, N. (1999) 'Globalization as Reterritorialization: the re-scaling of urban governance in the European Union', *Urban Studies*, 36(3): 431–51.

Bretherton, C. and Vogler, J. (1999) *The European Union as a Global Actor*. London: Routledge.

Brown, M. (1995) 'Sex, scale and the "new urban politics": HIV prevention strategies from Yaletown, Vancouver', in D. Bell and G. Valentine (eds), *Mapping Desire: Geographies of Sexualities*. London: Routledge. pp. 245–63.

Brown, M. (1997) *RePlacing Citizenship: AIDS Activism and Radical Democracy*. New York: Guilford Press.

Brown, M. (2000) *Closet Space: Geographies of Metaphor from the Body to the Globe*. London: Routledge.

Butler, J. (1990) *Gender Trouble: Feminism and the Subversion of Identity*. London: Routledge.

Butler, J. (1997) 'Merely cultural', *Social Text*, 15(3–4): 265–77.

Cant, B. (1997) *Invented Identities? Lesbians and Gays Talk About Migration*. London: Cassell.

Champagne, J. (1999) 'Transnationally queer?', *Socialist Review*, 27(1–2): 143–64.

Chapin, J. (1998) 'Closing America's "back door"', *GLQ: A Journal of Lesbian and Gay Studies*, 4(3): 403–22.

Chauncey, G. (1994) *Gay New York: Gender, Urban Culture and the Making of the Gay Male World, 1890–1940*. New York: Basic Books.

Cheah, P. (1997) 'Posit(ion)ing human rights in the current global conjuncture', *Public Culture*, 9(2): 233–66.

Cheah, P. (1998) 'Introduction - part II', in P. Cheah, and B. Robbins (eds) *Cosmopolitics: Thinking and Feeling Beyond the Nation*. Minneapolis, MN: University of Minnesota Press.

Cheah, P. and Robbins, B. (eds) (1998) *Cosmopolitics: Thinking and Feeling Beyond the Nation*. Minneapolis, MN: University of Minnesota Press.

Child, R. (1993) 'The economic situation in member states', in K. Waaldijk and A. Clapham (eds) *Homosexuality, A European Community Issue: Essays on Lesbian and Gay Rights in European Law and Policy*. Dordrecht: Martinus Nijhoff. pp. 163–78.

Clark, D. (1993) 'Commodity lesbianism', H. Abelove, M.A. Barale and D.M. Halperin (eds) *The Lesbian and Gay Studies Reader*. London: Routledge. pp.186–201.

Clarke, E.O. (2000) *Virtuous Vice: Homoeroticism and the Public Sphere*. Durham, NC: Duke University Press.

Cohen P, (1997) '"All they needed": AIDS, consumption, and the politics of class', *Journal of the History of Sexuality*, 8: 86–115.

Cohen, R. (1997) *Global Diasporas: An Introduction*. London: UCL Press.

Conrad, K. (2001) 'Queer treasons: homosexuality and Irish national identity', *Cultural Studies*, 15(1): 124–37.

Crang, P. (1994) It's showtime: on the workplace geographies of display in a restaurant in South East England. *Environment and Planning D: Society and Space* 12(6): 675–704.

Cruz-Malave, A. and Manalansan IV, M.F. (2002) 'Introduction: dissident sexualities/alternative globalisms', in A. Cruz-Malave and M.F. Manalansan IV (eds) *Queer Globalizations: Citizenship and the Afterlife of Colonialism*. New York: New York University Press. pp. 1–10.

Dangerous Bedfellows (eds) (1996) *Policing Public Sex: Queer Politics and the Future of AIDS Activism*. Boston, MA: South End Press.

Delany, S. (1999) *Times Square Red, Times Square Blue*. New York: New York University Press.

Drucker, P. (1996) '"In the tropics there is no sin": sexuality and gay-lesbian movements in the Third World', *New Left Review*, 218: 75–101.

Drucker, P. (2000) 'Introduction: remapping sexualities', in P. Drucker (ed.) *Different Rainbows*. London: Gay Men's Press. pp. 9–41.

Duggan, L. (1995a) 'Queering the state', in L. Duggan and N. Hunter *Sex Wars: Sexual Dissent and Political Culture*. New York: Routledge. pp. 178–93.

Duggan, L. (1995b) 'The discipline problem: queer theory meets lesbian and gay history', *GLQ: A Journal of Lesbian and Gay Studies*, 2(3): 179–91.

Duncan, N. (ed.) (1996) *BodySpace: Destabilising Geographies of Gender and Sexuality*. London: Routledge.

Duyvendak, J.W. (1994) *De Verzuiling van de Homobeweging*. Amsterdam: SUA.

Duyvendak, J.W. (1996) 'The depoliticisation of Dutch gay identity, or why Dutch gays aren't queer', in S. Seidman (ed.), *Queer Theory/Sociology*. Oxford: Blackwell. pp. 421–38.

Edelman, L. (1992) 'Tearooms and sympathy, or, the epistemology of the water closet', in A. Parker, M. Russo, D. Sommer and P. Yaeger (eds), *Nationalisms and Sexualities*. London: Routledge. pp. 263–84.

Edensor, T. (2002) *National Identity, Popular Culture and Everyday Life*. Oxford: Berg.

Elman, R. A. (2000) 'The limits of citizenship: migration, sex discrimination and the same-sex partners in EU Law', *Journal of Common Market Studies* 38(5): 729–49.

Eng, D.L. (1997) 'Out here and over there: queerness and diaspora in Asian American Studies', *Social Text* 15(3–4): 31–52.

Enloe, C. (1990) *Bananas, Bases and Beaches: Making Feminist Sense of International Politics*. Berkeley, CA: University of California Press.

Escoffier, J. (1997) 'The political economy of the closet: notes toward an economic history of gay and lesbian life before Stonewall', in A. Gluckman and B. Reed (eds) *Homo Economics: Capitalism, Community, and Lesbian and Gay Life*. London: Routledge. pp. 123–134.

Espin, O. (1999) *Women Crossing Boundaries: A Psychology of Immigration and Transformations of Sexuality*. London: Routledge.

Essig, L. (1999) *Queer in Russia: A Story of Sex, Self, and the Other*. Durham, NC: Duke University Press.

Evans, D.T. (1993) *Sexual Citizenship: The Material Construction of Sexualities*. London: Routledge.

Fassin, E. (2001) 'Same sex, different politics: "gay marriage" debates in France and the United States', *Public Culture*, 13(2): 215–32.

Florida, R. (2002) *The Rise of the Creative Class*. New York: Basic Books.

Flinn, C. (1995) 'The deaths of camp', *Camera Obscura*, 35: 53–84.

Flynn, L. (1996) 'The internal market and the European Union: some feminist notes', in A. Bottomley (ed.), *Feminist Perspectives on the Foundational Subjects of Law*. London: Cavendish. pp. 279–97.

Flynn, L. (1997) '"Cherishing all her children equally": the law and politics of Irish lesbian and gay citizenship', *Social and Legal Studies*, 6(4): 493–512.

Fortier, A.M. (2001) '"Coming home": intersections of queer memories and diasporic spaces', *The European Journal of Cultural Studies*, 4(4): 405–24.

Fortier, A.M. (2002) 'Queer diaspora', in D. Richardson and S. Seidman (eds) *The Handbook of Lesbian and Gay Studies*. London: SAGE. pp. 183–97.

Franklin, S., Lury, C., and Stacey, J. (2000) *Global Nature, Global Culture*. London: SAGE.

Fraser, N. (1995) 'From redistribution to recognition? Dilemmas of justice in a "postsocialist" age?', *New Left Review*, 212: 68–93.

Fraser, N. (1997) 'Heterosexism, misrecognition, and capitalism – a response to Judith Butler', *Social Text*, 15(3–4): 279–89.

Gauntlett, D. (1999) 'Digital sexualities: A guide to internet resources', *Sexualities*, 2(3): 327–32.

Gibson-Graham, J.K. (2001) 'Querying globalization', in J.C. Hawley (ed.) *Post-colonial, Queer: Theoretical Interventions*. Albany, NY: State University of New York Press. pp. 239–75.

Giddens, A. (1992) *The Transformation of Intimacy: Sexuality, Love and Eroticism in Modern Societies*. Cambridge: Polity Press.

Goldie, T. (1999) 'Introduction: queerly postcolonial', *ARIEL: A Review of International English Literature*, 30(2): 9–26.

Gopinath, G. (1996) 'Funny boys and girls: notes on a queer South Asian planet', in R. Leong (ed.) *Asian American Sexualities: Dimensions of the Gay and Lesbian Experience*. London: Routledge. pp. 119–27.

Grace, F. (1999) 'Risky business: heterosexual credit and lending practice', *Sexualities*, 2(4): 433–49.

Gurney, P. (1997) '"Intersex" and "dirty girls": mass-observation and working-class sexuality in England in the 1930s', *Journal of the History of Sexuality*, 8(2): 256–90.

Halperin, D. (1996) 'A response from David Halperin to Dennis Altman', *Australian Humanities Review* (www.lib.latrobe.edu.au/AHR/emuse/ Globalqueering/halperin.html).

Hannerz, U. (1996) *Transnational Connections: Culture, People, Places*. London: Routledge.

Hanson, E. (1995) 'The telephone and its queerness', in S. Case, P. Brett and S.L. Foster (eds) *Cruising the Performative: Interventions into the Representation of Ethnicity, Nationality and Sexuality*. Bloomington: University of Indiana Press. pp. 33–58.

Harper, P.B. (1993) 'Eloquence and epitaph: black nationalism and the homophobic impulse in responses to the death of Max Robinson', in T.F. Murphy and S. Poirier (eds) *Writing AIDS: Gay Literature, Language, and Analysis*. New York: Columbia University Press.

Harper, P.B. (1997) 'Gay male identities, personal privacy, and relations of public exchange: notes on directions for queer critique', *Social Text* 34: 5–29.

Harris, R. (1993) 'The "Child of the Barbarian": rape, race and nationalism in France during the First World War', *Past and Present*, 141: 170–206.

Haver, W. (1996) *The Body of this Death: Historicity and Sociality in the Time of AIDS*. Stanford, CA: Stanford University Press.

Hayes, J. (2000) *Queer Nations: Marginal Sexualities in the Maghreb*. Chicago: University of Chicago Press.

Hayes, J. (2001) 'Queer resistance to (neo-)colonialism in Algeria', in J.C. Hawley (ed.) *Postcolonial, Queer: Theoretical Interventions*. Albany, NY: State University of New York Press. pp. 79–97.

Hawley, J.C. (ed.) (2001) *Postcolonial, Queer: Theoretical Intersections*. Albany: State University of New York Press.

Haylett, C. (2001) 'Illegitimate subjects? Abject whites, neoliberal modernisation, and middle-class multiculturalism', *Environment and Planning D: Society and Space*, 19(3): 351–70.

Healthy Gay Manchester (1998) 'Healthy Gay Manchester's Guide to Lesbian and Gay Greater Manchester'. Manchester: Healthy Gay Manchester.

Hekma, G. (2002) 'Imams and homosexuality: a post-gay debate in the Netherlands', *Sexualities*, 5(2): 237–48.

Hennessy, R. (2000) *Profit and Pleasure: Sexual Identities in Late Capitalism*. London: Routledge.

Herdt, G. (1997) *Same Sex, Different Cultures: Exploring Gay and Lesbian Lives*. Boulder, CO.: Westview Press.

Hewitt, A. (1996) *Political Inversions: Homosexuality, Fascism, and the Modernist Imaginary*. Stanford, CA: Stanford University Press.

Hindle, P. (2000) 'The influence of the gay village on migration to central Manchester', *The North West Geographer*, 3: 21–28.

Hirst, P. and Thompson, G. (1996) *Globalization in Question: The International Economy and the Possibilities of Governance*. Cambridge: Polity Press.

Hoad, N. (1999) 'Between the white man's burden and the white man's disease: tracking lesbian and gay human rights in Southern Africa', *GLQ: A Journal of Lesbian and Gay Studies* 5(4): 559–84.

Hoad, N. (2000) 'Arrested development or the queerness of savages: resisting evolutionary narratives of difference', *Postcolonial Studies*, 3(2): 133–58.

Holliday, R. (1999) 'The comfort of identity', *Sexualities*, 2(4): 475–91.

Holliday, R. (2001) 'Discomforting identities', in D. Bell, J. Binnie, R. Holliday, R. Longhurst and R. Peace, *Pleasure Zones*. Syracuse, NY: Syracuse University Press. pp. 55–83.

Holliday, R. and Thompson, G. (2001) 'A body of work', in R. Holliday and J. Hassard (eds) *Contested Bodies*. London: Routledge. pp. 117–33.

Holton, R.J. (1998) *Globalization and the Nation-State*. London: Macmillan.

Hull, I.V. (1982) 'The bourgeoisie and its discontents: reflections on "Nationalism and Respectability"', *Journal of Contemporary History*, 17: 247–68.

Ingram, B.G., Bouthillette, A.M. and Retter, Y. (eds) (1997) *Queers in Space: Communities, Public Places, Sites of Resistance*. Seattle, WA: Bay Press.

Isin, E. (1999) 'Citizenship, class and the global city', *Citizenship Studies*, 3(2): 267–83.

155

Isin, E. and Wood, P. (1999) *Citizenship and Identity*. London: Sage.

Jameson, F. and Miyoshi, M. (eds) (1998) *The Cultures of Globalization*. Durham, NC: Duke University Press.

Johnson, M. (1998) 'Global desirings and translocal loves: transgendering and same-sex sexualities in the southern Philippines', *American Ethnologist* 25(4): 695–711.

Joseph, M. (1998) 'The performance of production and consumption', *Social Text*, 16(1): 25–61.

Katyal, S. (2002) 'Exporting identity', *Yale Journal of Law and Feminism*, 14(1): 97–176.

Kelley, P., Pebody, R. and Scott, P. (1996) *How Far Will You Go? A Survey of London Gay Men's Migration and Mobility*. London: GMFA.

King, K. (1993) 'Local and global: AIDS activism and feminist theory', *Camera Obscura* 28: 79–98.

Kitchin, R. (1998) 'Towards geographies of cyberspace', *Progress in Human Geography*, 22(3), 385–406.

Knopp, L. (1990) 'Some theoretical implications of gay involvement in an urban land market', *Political Geography Quarterly*, 9: 337–52.

Kurzer, P. (2001) *Markets and Moral Regulation*. Cambridge: Cambridge University Press.

Lambevski, S. (1999) 'Suck my nation – masculinity, ethnicity and the politics of (homo)sex', *Sexualities*, 2(4): 397–419.

Lancaster, R. (1997) 'On homosexualities in Latin America (and other places)' *American Ethnologist*, 24(1): 193–202.

Lane, C. (1996) 'Christopher Lane responds to Dennis Altman', *Australian Humanities Review* www.lib.latrobe.edu.au/AHR/emuse/Globalqueering/ lane.html.

Larvie, S.P. (1999) 'Queerness and the specter of Brazilian national ruin', *GLQ*, 5(4): 527–57.

Lauria, M. and Knopp, L. (1985) 'Toward an analysis of the role of gay communities in the urban renaissance', *Urban Geography*, 6(2): 152–69.

Long, S. (1999) 'Gay and lesbian movements in Eastern Europe: Romania, Hungary, and the Czech Republic', in B.D. Adam, J.W. Duyvendak and A. Krouwel (eds) *The Global Emergence of Gay and Lesbian Politics*. Philadelphia: Temple University Press. pp. 242–65.

Lowe, D.M. (1995) *The Body in Late Capitalist USA*. Durham, NC: Duke University Press.

Luibheid, E. (1998) '"Looking like a lesbian": the organization of sexual monitoring at the United States-Mexico border', *Journal of the History of Sexuality*, 8(3): 477–506.

Luibheid, E. (2002) *Entry Denied: Controlling Sexuality at the Border*. Minneapolis, MN: University of Minnesota Press.

Luongo, M. (2000) 'The use of commercial sex venues and male escorts by gay tourists in New York City', in S. Clift and S. Carter (eds) *Tourism and Sex: Culture, Commerce and Coercion*. London: Pinter. pp.109–30.

McDowell, L. (1995) 'Body work: heterosexual gender performances in city workplaces', in D. Bell and G. Valentine (eds) *Mapping Desire: Geographies of Sexualities*. London: Routledge. pp. 75–95.

McDowell, L. and Court, G. (1994) 'Performing work: bodily representations in merchant banks', *Environment and Planning D: Society and Space*, 12(6): 727–50.

McGhee, D. (2000) 'Assessing homosexuality: truth, evidence and the legal practices for determining refugee status – the case of Ioan Vraciu', *Body and Society* 6(1): 29–50.

McGhee, D. (2001) 'Persecution and social group status: homosexual refugees in the 1990s', *Journal of Refugee Studies*, 14(1): 20–42.

McKee, A. (1999) 'Australian gay porn videos: the national identity of despised cultural objects', *International Journal of Cultural Studies* 2(2): 178–98.

Manalansan IV, M.F. (1995) 'In the shadows of Stonewall: examining gay transnational politics and the diasporic dilemma', *GLQ: A Journal of Lesbian and Gay Studies*, 2(4): 425–38.

Manalansan IV, M.F. (1996) 'Searching for community: Filipino gay men in New York City', in R. Leong (ed.), *Asian American Sexualities: Dimensions of the Gay and Lesbian Experience*. London: Routledge. pp. 51–64.

Manalansan IV, M.F. (2000) 'Diasporic deviants/divas: how Filipino gay transmigrants "play with the world"', in C. Patton and B. Sanchez-Eppler (eds) *Queer Diasporas*. Durham, NC: Duke University Press. pp. 183–203.

Manderson, L. and Jolly, M. (1997) 'Introduction: sites of desire/economies of pleasure in Asia and the Pacific', in L. Manderson and M. Jolly *Sites of Desire/Economies of Pleasure: Sexualities in Asia and the Pacific*. Chicago: University of Chicago Press. pp. 1–26.

Marcuse, P. and van Kempen, R. (eds) (2000) *Globalizing Cities: A New Spatial Order*. Oxford: Blackwell.

Markwell, K. (2002) 'Mardi Gras tourism and the construction of Sydney as an international gay and lesbian city', *GLQ: A Journal of Lesbian and Gay Studies*, 8(1–2): 81–99.

Martin, F. (2000) 'From citizenship to queer counterpublic: reading Taipei's New Park', *Communal/Plural*, 8(1): 81–94.

Massey, D.B. (1993) 'Power-geometry and a progressive sense of place', in J. Bird, B. Curtis, T. Putnam, G. Robertson and L. Tickner (eds) *Mapping The Futures: Local Cultures, Global Change*. London: Routledge. pp. 59–69.

Moore, L. (2000) 'Acts of union: sexuality and nationalism, romance and realism in the Irish national tale', *Cultural Critique* 44: 113–44.

Moran, L. (1999) 'Law made flesh: homosexual acts', *Body and Society*, 5(1): 39–55.

Mosse, G.L. (1982) 'Friendship and nationhood: about the promise and failure of German nationalism', *Journal of Contemporary History*, 17: 351–67.

Mosse, G.L. (1985) *Nationalism and Sexuality: Middle-Class Morality and Sexual Norms in Modern Europe*. Madison, WI: University of Wisconsin Press.

Munoz, J.E. (1999) *Disidentifications*. Durham, NC: Duke University Press.

Munt, S. (1995) 'The lesbian flaneur', in D. Bell and G. Valentine (eds). *Mapping Desire: Geographies of Sexualities*. London: Routledge. pp. 114–25.

Munt, S. (1998) 'Sisters in exile: the lesbian nation', in R. Ainley (ed.), *New Frontiers of Space, Bodies and Gender*. London: Routledge. pp. 3–19.

Nagel, J. (1998) 'Masculinity and nationalism: gender and sexuality in the making of nations', *Ethnic and Racial Studies*, 21(3): 242–69.

Nardi, P. (1998) 'The globalization of the gay and lesbian socio-political movement: some observations about Europe with a focus on Italy', *Sociological Perspectives*, 41(3): 567–86.

Negron-Muntaner (1999) 'When I was a Puerto Rican lesbian: meditations on "Brincandoel charco: portrait of a Puerto Rican"', *GLQ: A Journal of Feminist Geography*, 5(4): 511–26.

O'Neill, J. (1990) 'AIDS as a globalizing panic', in M. Featherstone (ed.) *Global Culture*. London: SAGE. pp. 329–42.

O'Neill, J. (2001) 'Horror autotoxicus: the dual economy of AIDS', in R. Holliday and J. Hassard (eds) *Contested Bodies*. London: Routledge. pp. 179–185.

Ong, A. (1999) *Flexible Citizenship: The Cultural Politics of Transnationality*. Durham, NC: Duke University Press.

Otalvaro-Hormillosa, S. (1999) The homeless diaspora of queer Asian Americans, *Social Justice*, 26(3): 103–22.

Parker, A., Russo, M., Sommer, D. and Yaeger, P. (1992) 'Introduction', in Andrew Parker, M. Russo, D. Sommer, and P. Yaeger (eds), *Nationalisms and Sexualities*. London: Routledge. pp. 1–18.

Patton, C. (1999) '"On me, not in me': locating affect in nationalism after AIDS"', in M. Featherstone (ed.) *Love and Eroticism*. London: SAGE. pp. 355–73.

Patton, C. (2000) 'Migratory vices', in C. Patton and B. Sanchez-Eppler (eds) *Queer Diasporas*. Durham, NC: Duke University Press. pp.15–37.

Patton, C. (2002) *Globalizing AIDS*. Minneapolis, MN: University of Minnesota Press.

Pettman, J.J. (1996) *Worlding Women: A Feminist International Politics*. London: Routledge.

Phelan, S. (2001) *Sexual Strangers: Gays, Lesbians and Dilemmas of Citizenship*. Temple University Press: Philadelphia, PA.

Phillips, A. (1999) *Which Equalities Matter?* Cambridge: Polity Press.

Phillips, O. (1997) 'Zimbabwean law and the production of a white man's disease', *Social and Legal Studies*, 6: 471–92.

Phillips, O. (2000) 'Constituting the global gay', in C. Stychin and D. Herman (eds) *Sexuality in the Legal Arena*. London: The Athlone Press. pp. 17–34.

Phillips, R. and Watt, D. (2000) 'Introduction', in R. Phillips, D. Watt and D. Shuttleton (eds) *De-centring Sexualities: Politics and Representations Beyond the Metropolis*. London: Routledge.

Plummer, K. (2001) 'The square of intimate citizenship: some preliminary proposals', *Citizenship Studies*, 5(2): 237–53.

Porter, D. (1997) 'A plague on the borders: HIV, development, and traveling identities in the golden triangle', in L. Manderson and M. Jolly (eds) *Sites of Desire/Economies of Pleasure: Sexualities in Asia and the Pacific*. Chicago: University of Chicago Press. pp. 212–32.

Probyn, E. (1996) *Outside Belongings*. London: Routledge.

Probyn, E. (2000) 'Sporting bodies: dynamics of shame and pride', *Body & Society*, 6(1): 13–28.

Pryke, S. (1998) 'Nationalism and sexuality, what are the issues?', *Nations and Nationalism*, 4(4): 529–46.

Puar, J. (2002) 'Circuits of queer mobility: tourism, travel, and globalization', *GLQ: A Journal of Lesbian and Gay Studies*, 8(1–2): 101–37.

Puri, J. (2002) 'Nationalism has a lot to do with it! Unravelling questions of nationalism and transnationalism in lesbian/gay studies', in D. Richardson and S. Seidman (eds) *The Handbook of Lesbian and Gay Studies*. London: SAGE 427–42.

Quinn, V. (2000) 'On the borders of allegiance: identity politics in Ulster', in R. Phillips, D. Watt and D. Shuttleton (eds), *De-centring Sexualities: Politics and Representations Beyond the Metropolis*. London: Routledge. pp. 258–77.

Rahman, M. (2000) *Sexuality and Democracy: Identities and Strategies in Lesbian and Gay Politics*. Edinburgh: Edinburgh University Press.

Raimondo, M. (2001) '"Corralling the virus": migratory sexualities and the "spread of AIDS" in the US', paper presented at the Sexuality and Space: Queering Geographies of Globalization conference, New York City, February.

Richardson, D. (1998) 'Sexuality and citizenship', *Sociology*, 32(1): 83–100.

Richardson, D. (2000) *Rethinking Sexuality*. London: SAGE.

Robertson, R. (1992) *Globalization: Social Theory and Global Culture*. London: Sage.

Robbins, B. (1998) 'Introduction part I: actually existing cosmopolitanism', in B. Robbins and P. Cheah (eds) *Cosmopolitics: Thinking and Feeling Beyond the Nation* Minneapolis, MN: University of Minnesota Press. pp. 1–19.

Rofel, L. (1999) 'Qualities of desire: imagining gay identities in China', *GLQ: A Journal of Lesbian and Gay Studies* 5(4): 451–74.

Rofes, E. (2001) 'Imperial New York: Destruction and disneyfication under Emperor Giuliani', *GLQ: A Journal of Lesbian and Gay Studies* 7(1): 101–09.

Rosamond, B. (1999) 'Discourses of globalization and the social construction of European identities', *Journal of European Public Policy*, 6(4): 652–68.

Rose, K. (1994) *Diverse Communities: The Evolution of Lesbian and Gay Politics in Ireland*. Cork: Cork University Press.

Rose, N. (2000) 'Governing cities, governing citizens', in E. Isin (ed.) *Democracy, Citizenship and the Global City*. London: Routledge. pp. 95–109.

Rostow, W.W. (1994) *The Stages of Economic Growth: A Non-Communist Manifesto*. Cambridge: Cambridge University Press.

Rubin, G.S. (1993) 'Thinking sex: notes for a radical theory of the politics of sexuality', in H. Abelove, M.A. Barale and D.M. Halperin (eds) *The Lesbian and Gay Studies Reader*. London: Routledge. pp. 3–44.

Rubin, G.S. (1998) 'The miracle mile: South of Market and gay male leather, 1962–1997', in
J. Brook, C. Carlsson and N.J. Peters (eds), *Reclaiming San Francisco: History, Politics, Culture*.
San Francisco: City Lights Books. pp. 247–272.

Rushbrook, D. (2002) 'Cities, queer space, and the cosmopolitan tourist', *GLQ*, 8(1–2):
183–206.

Salecl, R. (1994) *The Spoils of Freedom: Psychoanalysis and Feminism After the Fall of Socialism*.
London: Routledge.

Sánchez Eppler, B. and Patton C. (eds) (2000) *Queer Diasporas*. Durham, NC: Duke
University Press.

Sandfort, T., Schuyf, J., Duyvendak, J.W. and Weeks, J. (eds) (2000) *Lesbian and Gay Studies:
An Introductory, Interdisciplinary Approach*. London: SAGE.

Schein, L. (1999) 'Of cargo and satellites: imagined cosmopolitanism', *Postcolonial Studies*, 2:
345–75.

Scholte, J.A. (2000) *Globalization: A Critical Introduction*. London: Macmillan.

Schoppmann, C. (1995) 'The position of lesbian women in the Nazi period', in G. Grau (ed.)
Hidden Holocaust? Gay and Lesbian Persecution in Germany 1933–45. London: Cassell.
pp. 8–15.

Scott, J.W. (1993) 'The evidence of experience', in H. Abelove, M.A. Barale and DM. Halperin
(eds) *The Lesbian and Gay Studies Reader*. London: Routledge. pp. 3–44.

Sedgwick E. (1985) *Between Men: English Literature and Male Homosocial Desire*. New York:
Columbia University Press.

Seidman, S. (1998) 'Are we all in the closet? Notes towards a sociological and cultural turn in
queer theory', *European Journal of Cultural Studies*, 1(2): 177–92.

Seidman, S., Meeks, C. and Traschen, F. (1999) 'Beyond the closet? The changing social meaning of homosexuality in the United States', *Sexualities*, 2(1): 9–34.

Shepard, B. and Hayduk, R. (eds) (2002) *From ACT UP to the WTO: Urban Protest and
Community Building in the Era of Globalization*. London: Verso.

Sieg, K. (1995) 'Deviance and dissidence: sexual subjects of the Cold War', in S. Case, P. Brett
and S.L. Foster (eds) *Cruising the Performative: Interventions into the Representation of
Ethnicity, Nationality and Sexuality*. Bloomington: University of Indiana Press. pp. 93–111.

Sinfield, A. (1996) 'Diaspora and hybridity: queer identities and the ethnicity model', *Textual
Practice*, 10(2): 271–93.

Skeggs, B. (2002) 'Techniques for telling the reflexive self', in T. May (ed.) *Qualitative Research
in Action*. London: SAGE.

Skelton, T. (1995) '"Boom, bye, bye": Jamaican ragga and gay resistance', D. Bell and
G. Valentine (eds) *Mapping Desire: Geographies of Sexualities*. London: Routledge. pp. 264–83.

Sklair, L. (2001) *The Transnational Capitalist Class*. Oxford: Blackwell.

Smiegel, F. (1995) 'Shop-talk: exchanging narrative, sex, and value', *Modern Fiction Studies*,
41(3–4): 635–55.

Smith, A.M. (1991) '"Which one's the pretender?" Section 28 and lesbian representation', in
T. Boffin and J. Fraser (eds) *Stolen Glances: Lesbians Take Photographs*. London: Pandora
Press. pp. 128–39.

Smith, A.M. (1994) *New Right Discourse on Race and Sexuality: Britain, 1968–1990*.
Cambridge: Cambridge University Press.

Smith, M.P. (2001) *Transnational Urbanism: Locating Globalization*. Oxford: Blackwell.

Smith, N. (1993) 'Homeless/global: scaling places', in J. Bird, B. Curtis, T. Putnam and
L. Tickner (eds) *Mapping the Futures: Local Cultures, Global Change*. London: Routledge.
pp. 87–119.

Smith, N. (1997) 'The satanic geographies of globalization: uneven development in the 1990s',
Public Culture, 10(1): 169–89.

Smyth, A. (1995) 'The state of lesbian and gay studies in Ireland', paper presented at The
Future of Gay and Lesbian Studies conference, Utrecht, July.

Smyth, C. (1995) 'Keeping it close: experiencing emigration in England', in Ide O'Carroll and Eoin Collins (eds), *Lesbian and Gay Visions of Ireland: Towards the Twenty-First Century*. London: Cassell. pp. 221–33.

Sontag, S. (1989) *AIDS and its Metaphors*. Harmondsworth: Penguin.

Stychin, C. (1998) *A Nation By Rights: National Cultures, Sexual Identity Politics and the Discourse of Rights*. Philadelphia, PA: Temple University Press.

Stychin, C. (2000a) '*Grant*-ing rights: the politics of rights, sexuality and European Union', *Northern Ireland Legal Quarterly*, 51(4): 281–302.

Stychin, C. (2000b) 'A stranger to its laws': sovereign bodies, global sexualities, and transnational citizens', *Journal of Law and Society* 27(4): 601–25.

Stychin, C. (2001) 'Civil solidarity or fragmented identities? The politics of sexuality and citizenship in France', *Social and Legal Studies*, 10(3): 347–75.

Stychin, C. (2002) 'From integration to civilisation: reflections on sexual citizenship in a European legal order', paper presented at the Gender, Sexuality and Law II conference, Keele University, June.

Tan, C.K. (2001) 'Transcending sexual nationalism and colonialism: cultural hybridization as process of sexual politics in '90s Taiwan', in J.C. Hawley (ed.) *Post-colonial, Queer: Theoretical Interventions*. Albany, NY: State University of New York Press. pp. 123–37.

Tan, M. (1996) 'A response to Dennis Altman from Michael Tan in the Phillippines', *Australian Humanities Review* (www.lib.latrobe.edu.au/AHR/emuse/Globalqueering/tan.html).

Thrift, N. (2000) '"Not a straight line but a curve", or, "Cities are not mirrors of modernity"', in D. Bell and A. Haddour (eds) *City Visions*. Harlow: Pearson. pp. 233–63.

Tinkcom, M. (2002) *Working Like a Homosexual: Camp, Capital, Cinema*. Durham, NC: Duke University Press.

Tolentino, R.B. (1996) 'Bodies, letters, catalogs: Filipinas in transnational space', *Social Text*, 48 14(3): 49–76.

Tomlinson, J. (1999) *Globalization and Culture*. Chicago: University of Chicago Press.

Tsang, D.C. (1996) 'Notes on queer 'n' Asian virtual sex', in R. Leong (ed.) *Asian American Sexualities: Dimensions of the Gay and Lesbian Experience*. London: Routledge. pp. 153–62.

Tschumi, B. (1994) *Event-Cities*. Cambridge, MA: MIT Press.

Urry, J. (1990) *The Tourist Gaze*. London: Sage.

Urry, J. (1995) *Consuming Places*. London: Routledge.

Urry, J. (2000a) 'Mobile sociology', *British Journal of Sociology*, 51(1): 185–03.

Urry, J. (2000b) 'Global flows and global citizenship', in E. Isin (ed.) *Democracy, Citizenship and the Global City*. London: Routledge. pp. 62–78.

Valentine, G. (1993) 'Negotiating and managing multiple sexual identities: lesbian time-space strategies', *Transactions of the Institute of British Geographers*, 18: 237–48.

Von Moltke, J. (1994) 'Camping in the art closet: the politics of camp and nation in German film', *New German Critique*, 63: 76–106.

Waaldijk, K. and Clapham, A. (eds) (1993) *Homosexuality as a European Community Issue: Essays on Lesbian and Gay Rights in European Law and Policy*, Dordrecht: Martinus Nijhoff.

Wakeford, N. (2000) 'Cyberqueer', in D. Bell and B. Kennedy (eds) *The Cybercultures Reader*. London: Routledge. pp. 403–31.

Wakeford, N. (2002) 'New technologies and "cyber-queer" research', in D. Richardson and S. Seidman (eds) *Handbook of Lesbian and Gay Studies*. London: Sage. pp. 115–44.

Warner, M. (1993) 'Introduction', in M. Warner (ed.) *Fear of a Queer Planet: Queer Politics and Social Theory*. Minneapolis, MN: University of Minnesota Press. pp. vii–xxxi.

Watney, S. (1995) 'AIDS and the politics of queer diaspora', in M. Dorenkamp and R. Henke (eds), *Negotiating Lesbian and Gay Subjects*. London: Routledge. pp. 53–70.

Weeks, J. (1999) 'The sexual citizen', in M. Featherstone (ed.) *Love and Eroticism*. London: SAGE. pp. 35–52.

Wells, P. (1995) *The Duration of a Kiss*. London: Minerva.

Werbner, P. (1999) 'Global pathways: working class cosmopolitans and the creation of transnational ethnic worlds', *Social Anthropology*, 7(1): 17–35.

Weston, K. (1995) 'Get thee to a big city: sexual imaginary and the great gay migration', *GLQ*, 2(3): 253–77.

Yar, M. (2001) 'Beyond Nancy Fraser's "perspectival dualism"', *Economy and Society*, 30(3): 288–303.

Young, I.M. (1990) *Justice and the Politics of Difference*. Princeton, NJ: Princeton University Press.

Young, I.M. (1997) 'Unruly categories: a critique of Nancy Fraser's dual systems theory', *New Left Review*, 222: 147–60.

Žižek, S. (1997) 'Multiculturalism, or, the cultural logic of multinational capitalism', *New Left Review* 225: 28–51.

Index

The Globalization of Sexuality